A New Dictionary of Political Analysis

Geoffrey Roberts
Reader in Government, University of Manchester
and
Alistair Edwards
Lecturer, Department of Government, University of Manchester

Edward Arnold
A division of Hodder & Stoughton
LONDON NEW YORK MELBOURNE AUCKLAND

© 1991 Geoffrey Roberts and Alistair Edwards

First published in Great Britain 1991

Distributed in the USA by Routledge, Chapman and Hall, Inc.
29 West 35rd Street, New York, NY 10001

British Library Cataloguing in Publication Data

A new dictionary of political analysis.
  I. Roberts, Geoffrey   II. Edwards, Alistair
  320.03
ISBN 0-340-52860-5

Typeset in 10/11 Times by Saxon Ltd
Printed and bound in Great Britain for Edward Arnold, a division of
Hodder and Stoughton Limited, Mill Road, Dunton Green,
Sevenoaks, Kent TW13 2YA by
Biddles Ltd, Guildford & King's Lynn

Preface

Like other areas of enquiry, political analysis generates its own special vocabulary. New words are coined, existing words are appropriated and given technical definition. This process of coinage and refinement is necessary for the development of clear and precise investigation, expression and understanding. But clarity and precision are not universally apparent. Some political science texts, even some of those encountered by students at an early stage of their studies, seem to require the reader to make frequent forays into more specialised literature, simply to decipher some of the terms used. Of course, when acted upon, these interruptions are a valuable part of learning. In the end, a proper understanding is only gained piecemeal, through wide reading. But such a process occurs all too rarely. Few students have the time to pursue it thoroughly, many do not have immediate access to sufficient library resources, and it is a habit of study which may only develop slowly. Although this dictionary offers a partial solution to these problems, it is not an encyclopaedia: entries do not provide comprehensive information on their topics. They try to give concise definitions, draw important distinctions between similar terms, indicate different usages, and point out the problems of definition in particular cases. The aim is to provide immediate assistance to the reader whose comprehension of a text is impeded by unfamiliar or imperfectly understood expressions.

Perhaps the most difficult task in preparing a work of this type is the selection of terms. The process of politics is influenced by every issue affecting human interests. Moreover, political science is an area of enquiry which is especially eclectic in its use of terms, techniques and theories drawn from the other social sciences, the natural sciences, and from the study of history, philosophy and law. No clear lines mark the boundaries of political science or its terminology. In order to clarify the aim of the dictionary, and the particular needs it tries to satisfy, we have provided a brief outline of the main principles governing the inclusion and exclusion of terms.

Criteria used for the selection of entries

The terms defined are those likely to be encountered in a political science text. Generally these comprise: the terms of empirical investigation (e.g. 'coalition'); the principal analytical approaches and empirical theories (e.g. 'coalition theory'; 'systems analysis'); the basic terms of such approaches and theories (e.g. 'minimum-winning coalition'; 'gatekeepers'); terms used in discussing the central questions of philosophy and methods of enquiry (e.g. 'determinism'; 'survey research').

More particularly, we have concentrated on terms that are neologisms, or which have meanings or applications in political science distinct from their meanings in everyday usage (e.g. 'satisfice'; 'exit'; 'paradigm'), and on central political science concepts, the basic meaning of which may be clear in ordinary language, but where in political science extra precision is needed, special connotations exist, or vigorous dispute arises concerning the value of different formulations (e.g. 'power'; 'bureaucracy'). The application of these criteria involves the exclusion of a number of specific categories: there are no entries for individual political actors or writers. Named individuals are only mentioned where their names have become labels for some set of ideas (e.g. 'Marx' for Marxism), or where their work has originated or strongly influenced the use of a term (e.g. 'Michels's iron law of oligarchy'; 'Weber's ideal types of authority'), or for exemplification (e.g. 'Stalin's Russia' as an example of totalitarianism). There are no entries for localized political institutions and phenomena (e.g. *'politburo'*, *'perestroika'* and *'glasnost'*) except where such institutions have been adopted in a number of different countries (e.g. 'ombudsman'). Some common and important non-English terms, used to denote more general phenomena are included (e.g. *'dirigisme'* and *'putsch'*). We have not tried to include terms which relate primarily to normative political theory or the history of political thought. However some of these terms are, for a variety of reasons, also encountered in modern political science and are therefore included. Thus, 'authority' and 'utilitarianism' are included, but 'justice' and 'antinomianism' are not. Terms which relate to specific policies and issues are omitted (e.g. 'monetarism' and 'mutual assured destruction'). We have also excluded terms which are adequately defined in good English dictionaries and for which no detailed outline of political usage appears necessary (e.g. 'competition'; 'crisis').

Finally, there are many terms which may be encountered in political science that are drawn from other disciplines, or are a part of the terminology of some particular approach or technique. Such terms are generally used without proper explanation only in the more specialised and advanced texts. We have therefore excluded all but the most basic concepts of, for instance, philosophy, Marxism, and statistical analysis. Some of the works which deal with these excluded categories are recommended below.

Composition

We have chosen not to cross-reference terms in the main body of text for each entry. Instead, a set of related terms appears at the end of most of the entries. These should be consulted in order more fully to understand an expression, and its place in political analysis. This should be of assistance even where the entry itself may appear to offer a satisfactory and self-sufficient definition. The cross-referenced terms include: expressions used in the entry which are of special importance to its understanding; terms relating to or contrasting with the defined term; terms similar in appearance but which, in fact, refer to quite different ideas. Where a term is used in two or more quite distinct senses, and these cannot be indicated briefly, separate entries are provided (e.g. *convention (a): the institution; convention (b): procedural convention*).

Works for further reference

Especially recommended are:
Vernon Bogdanor (ed.), *The Blackwell Encyclopaedia of Political Institutions*, Oxford, Basil Blackwell, 1987.

J. Eatwell, M. Milgate and P. Newman (eds), *The New Palgrave Dictionary of Economics*, London, Macmillan, 1987.

Paul Edwards (eds), *The Encyclopedia of Philosophy*, New York, Collier MacMillan, 1973.

David L. Sills (ed.), *The International Encyclopedia of the Social Sciences*, New York, Collier MacMillan, 1979.

Geoffrey K. Roberts
Alistair Edwards

Acknowledgements

We take this opportunity to thank our families, friends, colleagues and students, whose support and suggestions have been invaluable. Special thanks are due to Martin Burch, Michael Evans, David Farrell, Norman Geras, Ian Gough, David Howell, Peter Humphreys, Michael Moran, Geraint Parry, Terry Peach, Hillel Steiner, Ursula Vogel, Michael Waller, and Bruce Wood, each of whom provided some of the clearest and most constructive comments that one could wish for; and to Shahnaz Holder who painstakingly merged our separate contributions into the final typescript. The responsibility for errors, shortcomings and omissions remains, of course, our own.

A

Absentee voting Provision for certain categories of electors to cast votes in elections without attending the official polling station in person. Such categories may include the infirm, the disabled, and those likely to be absent from their constituency on the day of the election because of, for example, business commitments. Votes can then be cast by post or by a proxy voting in the absentee voter's stead, depending on the rules of the electoral system of the country concerned. See also: *proxy*.

Absolute majority See: *majority*.

Absolutism A doctrine and form of government within which no constitutional limits are imposed on the powers of the sovereign institution. The absolutist sovereign claims the right to rule unconstrained by legal precedent, custom or the rival claims of other political or social institutions. Such a right may be claimed and yet not fully exercised, in the sense that many social and economic activities may remain free from central direction. In such cases, absolutism is distinct from totalitarianism. See also: *autarchy; autocracy; judicial review; rule of law; sovereignty; totalitarianism.*

Additional member system (AMS) An electoral system which combines representation of single- or multi-member constituencies by candidates elected by means of majoritarian or preferential voting methods with 'supplementation' – either from party lists (national or regional) or from unelected candidates with the best results –' to produce an overall proportional distribution of seats among parties. The German electoral system uses such an arrangement, for instance. It should be noted that the larger the percentage of members of a legislature or other body elected directly in constituencies, and the smaller the area to which party lists (or supplementation from unelected candidates) apply, the less proportional the overall result will be. See also: *electoral system; proportional representation.*

Administrative law Law regulating the activity of the executive branch of government in the carrying out of its duties through subordinate departments and agencies, including those of local government. Although there is considerable overlap between administrative and constitutional law, some distinctions may be drawn. Constitutional law is concerned primarily with the basic rights and duties of government and citizen, and with the relationship between branches of government. Administrative law cannot be wholly detached from such matters but is primarily concerned with whether agencies of the executive branch have acted within their powers, through the due processes, exercising reasonable care and according to the requirements of natural justice.

The process of administrative law may be carried out by special administrative courts (as in most continental European countries) or through the ordinary courts of law (as in the UK and USA). In the latter instance, cases may be equivalent to ordinary civil matters of tort, contract or criminal law, although the executive often enjoys protection from legal action not extended to private individuals or bodies.

In member countries of the European Community, on matters covered by Community Law, the question of the validity of a decision taken by a national court may be taken before the Court of Justice of the European Communities, where there is no judicial remedy under national law. See also: *administrative tribunal; constitutional law; due process; executive; ombudsman.*

Administrative tribunal Administrative tribunals are bodies with both judicial and administrative characteristics, created by governments to determine disputes arising from the administration of statutes passed by the legislature. These disputes may be between citizen and state, arising directly from the administrative decision of a government department, or between citizens, arising from regulatory legislation intended to protect one of the parties. Membership of tribunals is not limited to legally qualified persons; lay members and various types of expert are frequently included. Tribunals are intended to provide a speedier, cheaper and less formal method for the settlement of disputes than could be provided through the courts. The flexibility of their proceedings is particularly useful in dealing with technical questions, e.g. of planning and land use. Widely divergent procedures are adopted by tribunals dealing with different areas of administration and kinds of dispute.

Examples include tribunals concerned with disputes over taxation assessments, welfare payments, the granting of licences, industrial safety, and discrimination in employment. Further special appellate tribunals also operate in some areas, and appeal to the courts on matters of law is usually possible. In England, the constitution and practice of tribunals is monitored by the Council on Tribunals, an advisory body established in 1958. See also: *executive; ombudsman.*

Adversary politics Some political scientists draw an important distinction between consensual political processes, in which participants share a common purpose in terms of seeking to reach mutually satisfactory goals, and adversarial politics, based on the resolution of conflicting aims and purposes on the part of groups of participants, parallel to the adversarial process of prosecution and defence found in British court proceedings. Adversary politics is a perspective on the British political process which found particular expression in S. E. Finer's edited collection of essays: *Adversary Politics and Electoral Reform* (London, Antony Wigram, 1975). The central thesis was that British party politics had developed as an adversarial form of relationship because of the simple-majority electoral system, and that the style of adversary politics resulted in inconsistent and damaging policies produced by single-party governments which enjoyed the support of only a minority of electors. This was contrasted with the more consensual style of politics in countries such as the German Federal Republic, based upon coalition governments supported by majorities of the electorate through proportional representation systems of election, and in which successive governments usually include a centre party, whose participation moderates the more extreme positions of its governing partners. The idea of adversary politics was thus utilised as a major argument by proponents of reform of the British electoral system. Their argument is that adversary politics is encouraged by the simple-majority electoral system. Under this system, parties are influenced or controlled by their activists, and these tend to be more ideologically extreme than the party's memberships or electorates. Such activists play a leading role in the selection of candidates, especially in safe seats, and they tend to select the more ideologically committed applicants rather than moderates. Once in office, a single-party government, supported by its parliamentary party composed largely of such ideologically committed MPs, is unconstrained by any need to bargain and compromise with coalition partners, and can reverse legislation introduced by the previous government. State control of the steel industry and industrial relations legislation are two very obvious examples of such reversals in British politics since the second world war. Critics of adversary politics therefore maintain that, because of its production of more extremist policy programmes, and because of the insecurity and disorganization which reversals of policy involve, adversary politics is harmful for the economic and social situation of the country. See also: *consensus*.

Agenda setting The ability or the duty to construct an agenda for a political organization: a committee, a party meeting or conference, a local government council, a cabinet, etc. Such agenda setting influences or even determines three things: the inclusion or exclusion of issues, the priority afforded to issues and the timetabling of issues (which might be of tactical significance, for example by leaving important issues to the end of an agenda, when prospective opponents may have left the meeting). Agenda setting is therefore seen as an important political resource.

According to some theorists of political power, agenda-setting can be used to indicate the range of issues regarded as worthy of discussion in a political community, as affected by prevailing ideologies and political routines. See also: *non-decision*.

Aggregation of interests See: *interests*.

Alienation A condition of separation from part of the self or from the political and social order.

For Marx, the principal form of alienation in capitalist production involved the relation of the labourer to the product of labour. The product embodies labour and in that sense is a part of the labourer's own self. Yet the product is removed from the labourer and forms part of the external power exercised over the labourer. This relation, and the more general relations of production with which it is associated, stifle creative potential in the alienated labourer.

Other senses of alienation focus on the lack of any deep attachment to social and political roles, even where superficial or mechanical conformity is present. Alienation is here associated with a lack of political integration, a failure of political socialization, apathy, and fragility of support for the political system. See also: *anomie; Marxism; political integration; political socialization*.

Alignment See: *dealignment; realignment*.

Alternative vote system A system for the election of candidates using preferential voting, employed in single-member constituencies or to select a single office-holder. Voters number candidates in order of preference. A candidate who obtains in excess of 50% of first preferences is elected. If no candidate meets this requirement, the candidate with the fewest first preferences is eliminated, and that candidate's ballot papers are redistributed to other candidates according to the second preferences shown on them. This process is repeated as often as necessary to produce a candidate with more than fifty per cent of total votes. The system is used to elect the lower house of the Australian legislature and in some elections in organizations such as student unions. It was proposed in 1917 by the Speaker's Conference on Electoral Reform for parliamentary elections in Britain, and was again put forward as a bill in 1930, but in neither case did the proposal become law. The system does eliminate the possibility of candidates being elected with only a minority of votes (as happens frequently in British parliamentary elections), but is not, and is not designed to be, a system of proportional representation of parties. See also: *electoral system; preferential voting; proportional representation; single transferable vote system.*

Analogy A resemblance between aspects of two or more otherwise dissimilar things. Analogies have been drawn between electoral systems and economic markets; political systems and biological organisms; political and computer systems; election campaigns and battles; policy making and games. The initial assertion of analogy may be used in a number of ways: as an imaginative device for suggesting hypotheses and lines of investigation; as a preliminary explanatory sketch suggesting the rough shape of some of the processes involved; as the first step in an attempt to show that the underlying processes are basically the same, i.e. that there is 'more than mere analogy' between two systems. These uses proceed from a conjecture that is provisional in the extreme. Since an analogy does not, in itself, provide a grounded explanation of the processes under enquiry it must be treated with caution. Similarities may turn out to be superficial, irrelevant and misleading. See also: *explanation; hypothesis; model.*

Anarchism The view that government and authority are artificially imposed, morally wrong and dispensable; society should rather be ordered through free agreements between groups formed for the satisfaction of the full range of human needs and aims. This spontaneous order of freely cooperating individuals should replace the coercive and exploitative arrangements comprised by law and the state. Within this position disagreements exist on a number of central issues: the degree to which violence is necessary and justified in overthrowing the state; whether private property is necessary for individual freedom or is a means of coercion; the degree to which collective organization is legitimate. Differences on such basic matters allow broadly anarchist sentiments to appear across the political spectrum, in both left and right-wing thought, and lead to divisions within anarchism itself. See also: *anarcho-syndicalism; authority; ideology; Marxism; new right; power; society; state.*

Anarcho-syndicalism An important element within European and American socialist and trade union politics in the early twentieth century. The movement, broadly anarchist in that it is opposed to the concept of the state, emphasized the role of trade-union (French: *syndicat*) organization in political action and social transformation. Unions comprise the organizational means to replace state power with rule through workers' associations. The term is now applied to tendencies (particularly in French and Latin American trade unions) rather than to any recognizable movement and is sometimes used to describe trade union action that aims directly to challenge the authority of the state.

In the early years of the twentieth century a comparable movement, known as 'guild socialism', existed in Britain. Guild socialists held that industrial organizations should be collectively governed by those concerned in production, including managerial and administrative staff; each industry should direct its production, for the common good, through democratic national guilds (resembling medieval guilds) standing between the individual and the state; consumer interests should also be represented through a number of institutions; and the state should play a largely coordinating and non-coercive role. See also: *anarchism; corporatism (a): ideology; socialism*.

Anomie An absence of laws, rules or norms. The term is used to describe the condition of individuals who are unable to internalize social constraints, or the condition of societies with conflicting or disintegrating norms.

Anomie has been used in political analysis to explain deviant political behaviour, extremist politics etc. Its occurrence is regarded as more likely in periods of change such as industrialisation, rapid political development, revolution and civil war. See also: *alienation; norm*.

Apportionment The process of devising geographic boundaries for constituencies, and allocating constituencies among administrative areas (countries, provinces, states in the USA, etc.). Under majoritarian systems of election, the precise geographic boundaries of a constituency, the relative distribution of population among constituencies, and the socio-economic characteristics of electorates in constituencies may all affect seriously the probable outcomes of elections in ways that would not generally apply in proportional representation systems of election. Hence some non-partisan method of apportionment is often sought, and that method is also used to reapportion constituencies from time to time to take account of the relative increases and decreases in population in different constituencies. Since broad equality of size of electorates is often a principal consideration in majoritarian electoral systems, periodic reapportionments need to occur. In the USA, congressional districts are reapportioned following each decennial census, and this is usually a task for the state legislatures. In the United Kingdom, non-partisan Boundary Commissions for England, Wales, Scotland and Northern Ireland reapportion constituencies every 10–15 years or so. Natural boundaries (e.g. the Isle of Wight), existing county boundaries, and the desirability of maintaining the integrity of local communities are additional criteria affecting the apportionment of seats in the United Kingdom.

Apportionment may also refer to the allocation of delegates among branches, areas, groups, etc., to representative institutions, e.g. trade unions and political parties. See also: *gerrymandering*.

Aristocracy Originally meaning 'rule by the best', by an elite selected (perhaps self-selected) according to supposed possession of a monopoly of certain qualities or attributes deemed desirable in a group of rulers, and usually considered to be acquired through birth, such as wisdom (Plato's *Republic*), racial purity (the Nazis in occupied territories of eastern Europe), noble birth often associated with landed property (feudal and post-feudal Britain), or caste (parts of India at various periods). Today the term is more usually employed as a description of a ruling class or group whose right to rule derives from birth into a hereditary nobility, in contrast to an oligarchy, whose right to rule lacks such legitimacy. See also: *elite; oligarchy; technocracy*.

Arrow's theorem See: *social choice theory*.

Articulation of interests See: *interests*.

Attitudes An individual's orientations to situations or objects, expressive of that person's preferences or evaluation. Attitudes are mental states and, not being directly observable, are inferred from behaviour (including verbal behaviour). Attitudes may be distinguished from other mental categories, being more persistent than motivations, more specifically related to named situations and objects than are ideologies, inherently concerned with evaluation (contrast beliefs, which may relate to the truth of empirical hypotheses), and arising from but not being identical to basic values.

Attitude measurement, or attitude scaling, involves the observation, classification and analysis of behaviour held to be expressive of particular attitudes. Measurement is concerned with, for example, the intensity, content and consistency of attitudes. Methods adopted often include the use of questionnaires containing statements about particular situations or objects and eliciting responses in terms of the degree of favourable or unfavourable reaction.

Attitude study has been used in many areas of political analysis, e.g. voting behaviour, legislative and judicial behaviour, political socialization and integration, regime support. A typical attitude study might attempt to explain the presence of a particular type of political system by reference to the character of attitudes within the society. Studies of the 'authoritarian personality', for instance, have tried to show that support for authoritarian political ideologies is associated with authoritarian attitudes underlying a much wider range of social behaviour, attitudes which may be rooted in experience of parental attitudes to status.

The use of attitudes in analysis has been criticized on a number of counts: the process of enquiry may alter or generate attitudes rather than observe them; there is nothing inherently measurable in an attitude and measurement is therefore arbitrarily imposed; attitudes offer only a crude and simplistic picture of the complex reasons underlying actions; many of the attempts to explain political phenomena by citing attitudes appear tautological. See also: *behaviouralism; ideology; values*.

Attitude scaling See: *attitudes*.

Autarchy Literally self-rule. Used to characterize an independent sovereign state or an absolute government. See also: *absolutism; autarky; autocracy; autonomy; sovereignty*.

Autarky Literally self-sufficiency. Used to denote a nation-state's ability to supply its material needs from within its own borders. Sometimes confusingly (and mistakenly) spelled 'autarchy'. See also: *autarchy*.

Authoritarianism Any doctrine of rule by command with little or no attention to public opinion, individual rights, government by consent or the idea of legitimate opposition. See also: *absolutism; democracy; dictatorship; liberalism; opposition; public opinion; totalitarianism*.

Authority Like the related concepts of power, influence and leadership, authority is a basis for securing assent or compliance concerning a decision or course of action. It is, however, usually given a distinctive meaning resting on the nature of the grounds of such assent or compliance. With power, it is ultimately the contingent operation of coercive sanctions; with influence, it is some persuasive reason or attitude; with leadership, it is reliance on some form of accepted superiority. However, for many analysts, the distinctive basis of authority is the ability to secure assent or compliance on the grounds of basic values or rules, generally recognized as legitimate. These, embodied in an authoritative person, institution, decision or action, provide the linkage between legitimacy and authority, and to the otherwise unhelpful definition of authority as the exercise of legitimate power.

Weber's classification of types of authority remains influential. Traditional authority rests on the long-standing customs and habits of a society; rational-legal authority on clear legal norms; charismatic authority on the personal qualities of an individual (thus blurring the distinction, drawn above, between authority and leadership). Another distinction is sometimes drawn: between *de jure* and *de facto* authority. In so far as authority rests on rules, it confers the right to demand compliance but not necessarily the ability to secure it. A government may constitutionally possess *de jure* authority but, if it lacks the ability to enforce its commands, it is without *de facto* authority. To talk of authority in these terms is to blur the distinction between authority and power. See also: *leadership; legitimacy; power*.

Autocracy A form of absolutism marked by two typical features: the exercise of power by a single leader; political power exercised through the arbitrary will of the leader rather than through known laws, without responsibility to an electorate or any other political body. Examples include Stalin, Hitler, Idi Amin of Uganda, and President Francois Duvalier ('Papa Doc') of Haiti. See also: *absolutism; autarchy; dictatorship; totalitarianism*.

Autonomy The condition of self-government. Sovereign states are autonomous with regard to other states; regional governments may possess autonomy in certain areas of law-making, granted by central government; social institutions may also be granted autonomy in the making of rules governing their area of activity.

The term is commonly used in political analysis in a different and non-constitutional sense. Here 'the autonomy of the state' refers to the ability of the state to pursue its own distinct interests, rather than simply reflecting or acting as agent for the interests of social groups, typically the dominant class or classes. See also: *autarchy; federation; Marxism; sovereignty; state*.

Axiom A proposition in scientific or social scientific analysis which is to be taken as self-evident, requiring itself no further proof. Axioms are thus basic statements which constitute the fundamentals of a scientific discipline, and from which hypotheses, laws and theories may be developed.

B

Balkanization A process of breakdown or division into mutually hostile states or factions. A process so described has usually been brought about by an external body seeking to fragment its neighbours or competitors. The term was first applied to the policy pursued by Russia towards the states of the Balkan peninsula in the late nineteenth century.

Bandwagon effect An increase in support for a candidate or party in an election, supposedly due to communication of a prediction of the likely outcome of that election in favour of the candidate or party (e.g. by publication of opinion poll findings), and which would not have occurred, or would have been smaller, had such a prediction not been communicated. See also: *underdog effect*.

Bargaining theory The study of negotiation (including political negotiation) by means of various approaches, formal models, theories, etc. Among the methods used are game theory, small group experimentation, formal analysis derived from economic science, conflict studies and psychological approaches.   Among the topics of major interest in the study of political bargaining are the institutional context within which bargaining occurs; the values of the actors involved; the methods of communication of bargaining moves; the possibilities of salient solutions being accepted; methods of completion of the bargaining process; etc. Areas of political behaviour to which bargaining theory is relevant include coalition formation; bilateral and multilateral international negotiation; legislative behaviour, especially where party discipline is relaxed; negotiations in committees; elections where votes are open rather than by secret ballot. See also: *conflict approach; game theory*.

Behaviouralism A term applied, often critically, to analysis displaying most or all of the following commitments: political science cannot be autonomous but can only be an aspect of more general theories of individual behaviour; the basic unit for political analysis is the individual behaving within the political environment; verifiable scientific explanations should be developed, couching hypotheses in strictly operational terms and using available quantitative techniques; prescriptive statements should be avoided and the personal values of the investigator should not be allowed to interfere with research. In stressing these aims behaviouralists attempt to avoid what they see as the main shortcomings of other approaches: a tendency towards untheoretical description; a concentration on the legal and constitutional aspects of the state; a readiness to mix normative questions with questions of fact.

Behaviouralism should be distinguished from behaviourism, a position in some respects similar, but more narrow and essentially an approach to the study of psychology. Behaviourism holds that psychological theory should refer only to phenomena that can be directly observed and objectively measured. Since the mental states of agents do not satisfy these criteria any reference to consciousness should be avoided and psychology should comprise only the identification of associated stimuli and responses; the intervening mind of the agent is treated as a black box.

Behaviouralism is often criticized: for its excessive reluctance to go beyond what is directly observable; for a consequent theoretical superficiality; for the selection of areas for investigation most susceptible to techniques of measurement rather than for their interest or importance; and for its sometimes naive claims to value-freedom (ie. normative neutrality).

An explicit commitment to the behavioural approach is particularly apparent in American political science of the 1950s, though a similar orientation is present in much work throughout this century. See also: *black box technique; empiricism; normative theory; operationalization; political behaviour; political science; positivism.*

Bicameral Describes a legislature with two chambers, as found in the large majority of democratic states, all federal states, and all but one of the 50 states of the USA. In bicameral legislatures, it is usual for the lower house to be directly elected, but the membership of the upper house can be the product of one, or a combination of several, methods: hereditary succession (the House of Lords in the United Kingdom parliament); nomination (the Canadian Senate); delegation by provincial governments (the Bundesrat in Germany); or election (the US Senate). The functions and relative importance of the second chamber vary considerably from country to country. Many have a revising function for legislative proposals and some have a – usually restricted – right of legislative veto. In federal states, it is usual for the upper house to have a primary function of representing and defending the rights and interests of constituent provinces. See also: *federation; unicameral.*

Bipolarity The tendency for elements to cluster around two extreme positions on some scale, hence used in politics especially in two contexts. In international relations the term indicates a tendency for states to group into two opposed blocs or alliances, especially since 1945 in the 'cold war' confrontation between the USA and its allies, and the Soviet bloc. In electoral studies, it refers to the situation where voters tend to choose one of two opposed parties or party blocs, sometimes referred to less precisely as a situation of polarization. See also: *polarization.*

Black box technique Any analytic technique employing the concept of a 'black box' to refer to some complex set of interactions. This 'black box' is then characterized in the analysis only by its inputs and outputs, ignoring, for the purposes of the analysis, any detailed conversion processes occurring within the 'black box'.

The technique has been used in, for example, psychological and behavourial analysis, organizational analysis, systems-based approaches in political analysis, etc. An example in the analysis of a political system would be in the study of policy-making, where inputs from parties and interest groups were investigated, as were outputs in the form of policy decisions, but the legislature or other policy-making body was designated as a 'black box', ignoring procedures by which inputs were converted into outputs. Such utilization of the concept of a 'black box' may be on grounds that such processes of transformation are excessively complex, or are irrelevant for the purposes of that particular analysis.

Block vote A system of voting in which delegates vote on behalf of a group which they represent, by casting an undifferentiated vote, weighted according to the relative size of the membership of the group which the delegates represent. Affiliated trade unions at the conferences of the Labour party and the Trades Union Congress vote in this way, for instance. The votes of states in the electoral college to elect the president and vice-president of the United States also are given as block votes. See also: *voting*.

Bolshevism A doctrine comprising Lenin's analysis of capitalist development and, linked to this, a programme for revolutionary party organization and activity. The main tenets include the view that capitalism had, by the late nineteenth century, entered its final, imperialist phase; the division of the world among the major capitalist powers would prevent full and indigenous capitalist development in countries such as Russia; the Russian proletariat, weak in itself, must seize the earliest opportunity for revolution, in alliance with other groups, notably the peasantry; a highly disciplined party must lead the revolutionary struggle, using whatever clandestine and violent tactics that may be necessary; the party's role and structure must be maintained after it has gained state power, to establish a new form of the state, to act as the one true representative of workers and peasants, and to crush counter-revolutionary activity. (For most of his political career, Lenin rejected the possibility of an imminent socialist revolution in Russia, aiming instead for a radical bourgeois-democratic revolution in order to create a better basis for an open struggle for socialism. However, in 1917 he changed his view to allow for the more direct revolutionary pursuit of socialism.)

Disagreement over these matters led to a split in the Russian Social Democratic Labour party (renamed the Communist party of the Soviet Union in 1918), at its Second Congress in 1903. Lenin and his supporters were the larger faction, becoming known as 'Bolsheviks' (members of the majority), as opposed to 'Mensheviks' (members of the minority). The term continued to be applied to the CPSU and so 'bolshevism' is now sometimes extended to cover all aspects of the ideology and practice of Soviet communism.

Lenin's successor, Joseph Stalin, pursued the goal of 'socialism in one country' in a particularly brutal, dictatorial and dogmatic fashion. Communist parties and policies displaying similar tendencies are often referred to as 'Stalinist'. 'Trotskyism' denotes the views associated with Leon Trotsky, originally a Menshevik, then a Bolshevik, later one of Stalin's chief opponents. Trotskyism principally comprises: internationalism and a commitment to world revolution, together with the view that early successes are more likely in underdeveloped countries; a belief in the need for a sustained and widespread reconstruction of societies from below ('permanent revolution'); and a strategy of 'entrism' (sometimes 'entryism'), infiltration and subversion of other parties and movements. See also: *communism; imperialism; Marxism; social class; socialism*.

Bourgeoisie See: *social class*.

Bourgeoisification See: *embourgeoisement*.

Budget For political institutions, such as local government authorities, states, and the European Economic Community or the United Nations Organization, the budget is the periodic statement of expected revenues (in the form of taxes, levies and other income), generally related to proposed expenditures, usually for a twelve month period. Beyond its formal, 'balance-sheet' function, a budget is also necessarily a political document of great significance, as indicated by the status in governments accorded to finance ministers and by the jealousy with which legislatures protect their rights and privileges in relation to the budgetary process. Since most policies incur expenditures, or are concerned with the redistribution of wealth, control of the budget is, in a very real sense, control of the executive branch of government.

Since such control has come to be seen as a process necessarily extending over longer periods than a year, and since proposed expenditures on policy projects also often extend over multi-year periods, systems of longer-term budgeting and the explicit linkage of budgeting to the assessment of governmental goals, such as Planning-Programming-Budgeting Systems [PPBS], have been developed.

Buffer state A state located between the boundaries of two larger states, which by its existence reduces the likelihood of an attack by either of those states on its rival, both by its neutral status vis-á-vis the potential combatant states and by its interposed territory. Poland acted as a buffer state between the Soviet Union and Germany in the inter-war period, until the pact between the Soviet Union and Nazi Germany was signed in 1939.

Bureaucracy In its more common usage, the term refers to any set of governmental (or other administrative) officials, possessed of certain traits of excessive formality, use of verbiage or jargon in communication, inflexibility of procedure, and insistence on the powers – and limitations – of their office: in other words, 'red tape'. The prevalence and effects of such 'bureaucratic' structures and organization have been analyzed by social scientists such as M. Crozier.

In social science, the concept is both more specific and neutral. Its earlier sense of 'rule by officials' (rather than by elected politicians or hereditary rulers, for instance) has tended to be replaced by its employment as a term to describe a particular pattern of administrative behaviour, associated with certain types of social organization, and identifiable by reference to a constellation of objective criteria. Usually associated with political administration, it can also denote a form of religious, educational, industrial or other category of administrative organization.

The classic statement of bureaucracy as a social phenomenon is that of Max Weber, who classed it as one of three 'ideal types' of rule. He identified as criteria of bureaucratic organization: official jurisdictional areas laid down by laws or rules; the principle of office hierarchy, involving clear lines of supervision of lower offices by higher offices; work based on the preservation of written records ('files'); training and specialization of personnel in office management skills; devotion of full attention of officials to their official activity, at least during the stated hours of their employment; the existence of procedural rules, defined, generalized and able to be learned by all officials. Bureaucracy was thus the epitome of rational organization in politics and administration, as distinct from organization based on patronage, caste, ideological conformity, or other principles. It therefore involved a career-based, appointed administrative service of fixed status and tenure, with salary linked to rank and a known rank-order of advancement. It also presupposed certain features of society, such as the existence of a monetary economy, large-scale organization of tasks and resources, the availability of modern methods of communication, cultural acceptance of 'rationality' in administrative decision making (rather than, say, nepotism or bribery) and of legal authority as the basis of the legitimation of leadership, and a tendency to the centralization of power. In turn, bureaucracy has its own effects on social organization: a tendency towards its own perpetuation; consequential educational changes directed towards recruitment to the bureaucratic domain based on expertise; and a tendency towards the democratization of political life, probably on a 'mass party' basis, as a result of the establishment of the principle of rationality (rather than ideology, class-based patronage or other principles) in decision-making and open recruitment to administrative positions.

Theoretical and empirical studies of bureaucracy have focused, inter alia, upon the decision-making procedures within bureaucracies and the internal politics of bureaucratic organizations. See also: *authority; ideal type; public administration*.

C

Cabinet The committee of leading ministers of the government, for the purposes of confidentially discussing the business of the executive, taking the political decisions necessary to deal with pending business and, in those countries which have a system of 'cabinet government', formulating new policies. Generally the cabinet is presided over by the prime minister or, in some systems, by the head of state. Cabinets are found in most western democracies, and in many developing countries also. Membership is generally confined to ministers in charge of the major departments of state and thus usually is drawn exclusively from the governing party, or parties of a coalition government. A small number of leading politicians who do not run ministries, possibly holding sinecure appointments (such as in Britain the Lord President of the Council or the Chancellor of the Duchy of Lancaster, and, when a Conservative government is in power, the chairman of the party) may also be members.

Most cabinet-based systems devolve a lot of work and decision making to committees (notably the United Kingdom, France, Spain), though in some countries, such as Germany and Ireland, the development of committees has been marginal. The power – and thus the collective political responsibility – of the cabinet and, where appropriate, its committees, varies from country to country. It is particularly powerful in Britain, less so in Germany, and even less so in presidential or semi-presidential systems such as the USA and the French Fifth Republic.

In the context of French politics and the political system of the EC, the term must be distinguished from the *cabinet* of a minister or EC commissioner, which is the small group of personal staff appointed by the minister or commissioner to supply advice and assistance. See also: *executive*.

Capitalism A form of economic organization in which those who privately own and control the means of production (or 'capital') pay wages to workers, in return for the application of their labour power to the means of production, producing goods for profitable market exchange in order to accumulate further capital. 'Capitalist societies' are those in which this mode of production is predominant, but in which there will also be other elements: for instance, the vestiges of feudal relations.

Some of the features of capitalism start to appear in western Europe during the feudal period, principally through the development of trade and the commercialization of agricultural production, but the term is more usually associated with the subsequent process of industrialization. The form of capitalism developing during the nineteenth century in Britain and the United States provides the typical model, and has important implications for the political aspects of capitalism. In these countries, capitalism is ideologically associated with liberalism and *laisser faire*, limiting the functions of the state to the maintenance of external security, law and order, and the market framework. This view envisages state intervention in the economy only to remove hindrances to the free operation of market forces, e.g. by legislating against monopolies and restrictive practices. Thus capitalism is strongly associated with, though distinct from, the system of free market exchange.

Despite this model of the 'natural' development and political requirements of capitalism, capitalist production has elsewhere developed under quite different political conditions. Among the later industrializing countries, notably Germany and Japan, governments pursued much more interventionist policies, actively fostering capitalist production and more quickly creating large and powerful industrial enterprises. Other variations are arguably present in the course of the more general development of capitalism: the rise of joint-stock companies and the employment of managers have led to a separation of ownership from control in many enterprises; more recently, the pattern of ownership has shifted, with ownership increasingly vested in financial institutions; capital has become more concentrated, tending towards monopoly; the division of interest has sharpened between financial and industrial institutions. One of the most significant political developments has been the growth of state intervention in the form of regulation, nationalization, and the provision of welfare, a trend that has become less easily identifiable in the last decade. Whether such measures help or hinder the processes of capitalism is a matter of some dispute. See also: *corporatism (b): ideal type; exploitation; feudalism; free trade; imperialism; industrial society; interventionism; liberalism; Marxism; nationalization; social class; socialism; state capitalism; welfare state.*

Case-study method A systematic method of analysis which depends on the deliberate and detailed study of a single case (in political science, the study of, for instance, a political party organization, an election campaign, an international crisis, a specific policy decision, or an interest-group campaign), as an alternative to comparative analysis of several 'cases'. The chief purposes of the case-study method are: as a teaching device, to enable students to examine the fullest possible range of variables and data involved in an example of a particular type of political phenomenon; and as a research method, to derive and to test hypotheses and relationships by the thorough examination of detailed cases. Cases may be studied by any combination of methods and approaches, e.g. interviews, documentary evidence, simulation, or gaming. See also: *comparative analysis.*

Catch-all parties A concept developed by Otto Kirchheimer to apply to political parties, usually large in size, which seek electoral support across lines of class, ethnic, religious or other cleavages rather than focusing their appeal on one such sector of society (such as the working-class or Catholic voters), and which therefore also dilute their ideological basis by developing pragmatic, flexible policy programmes to appeal to a wide range of interests and interest groups. The German term: *Volkspartei* ('people's party') applied to the Christian Democrats and, after the 1959 Bad Godesberg congress, the Social Democrats in the Federal Republic of Germany bears very similar connotations. See also: *cleavage; interest; party.*

Caucus A gathering of members of a political party or other political organization to select candidates for electoral campaigns (especially at local level: the nomination caucus was a predecessor of the nominating convention in the USA, and caucuses selected constituency candidates in Britain and Germany, for example, in the nineteenth century), to discuss matters pending before a legislative body, to settle political strategies, etc. The term sometimes denotes an inner group of a party, where the power of the caucus within the party is strong and when its decisions can be enforced as binding on the members of the party in the context in which it operates (the national legislature, a city council, etc.). In some cases, decisions of a caucus may be binding on those in office (e.g. in a cabinet). Though associated with American and Australian politics especially, the term has been applied in British and other contexts, particularly at the level of local politics. In the USA the term may also be applied to a subgroup within the party legislative group, which, on the basis of a common interest, meets together on a regular basis to coordinate strategy or to discuss shared problems. See also: *faction; party.*

Cell A basic unit of organization within a political party or movement, usually of a clandestine nature, and often based on a neighbourhood or work place. Cells are typically small (3-20 members), active and tightly disciplined. A cell-structure consists of vertical rather than horizontal linkages between organizational units, facilitating centralized direction and minimizing the damage caused by defection or the discovery of subversive activities. The term is applied particularly to units of organization in various communist parties, although it was officially abandoned in the USSR in 1939. See also: *bolshevism; party*.

Cession The voluntary transfer of territory by its ruler or government to some other ruler or state. The territory ceded may be, for example, part of a peace settlement; an exchange of territories; a sale for monetary consideration; or, in historical times, an item in a royal marriage contract. Though circumstances may impel a ruler or government to cede territory, the act of cession itself is differentiated from conquest by the formal existence of voluntary choice.

Examples of cession: the transfer of Hong Kong from China to Britain under the Treaty of Nanking (1842); the return of Alsace-Lorraine to France by Germany under the Versailles Treaty (1919); the 'Louisiana Purchase' by the USA from France (1803); and the purchase of the Virgin Islands by the USA from Denmark (1917). See also: *treaty*.

Charisma Originally a theological term meaning 'a talent or gift given by God' or 'a gift of grace'. It now denotes the extraordinary personal qualities of an innovative or revolutionary leader whose followers believe to possess, for instance, religious or magical powers. More rarely, the term is extended to symbols and institutions associated with such leadership.

The duration of charismatic leadership may be limited. Failure to achieve goals may weaken the beliefs of followers, or the very success of the movement may produce leadership of a more routine and institutionalized character. Most social scientific usage follows Weber in distinguishing charismatic leadership from traditional and rational-legal forms. Talk of charismatic institutions, referred to above, seems to blur this distinction.

Hitler, Gandhi and Fidel Castro are among those usually cited as examples of charismatic leaders, though the term tends to be applied popularly to almost any public figure with some modicum of personal magnetism or charm. See also: *authority; leadership; legitimacy*.

Chauvinism Exaggerated patriotism and nationalistic pride, involving unrealistic assessments of the virtues of the chauvinist's own country and scorn for the qualities of other countries. It is probably derived from the French soldier, Chauvin, who was a character in a French play of the 1830s and who exhibited nationalist characteristics. It is similar to, but less obsessive than, xenophobia.

A derived term has come to be used also in feminist rhetoric, where 'male chauvinism' is an epithet directed at those males who are suspected of harbouring and expressing, consciously or subconsciously, beliefs that men are in some ways superior to women: in the workplace, intellectually, etc. See also: *feminism; nationalism; xenophobia*.

Christian democracy An ideological movement which provides the basic orientation for conservative parties in several European and some Latin American states where the Catholic faith is strong. Examples include the Christian Democratic parties of Italy and Germany, and the People's party of Austria. Historically, the movement had its origins in the Catholic political parties of the nineteenth and early twentieth centuries, and their protective attitudes to the church and its teachings in relation to political and social issues. It is primarily, though, a post-1945 phenomenon, arising from the wish in many European countries to associate political ideals with Christian ethics after the war, and in some countries (such as the Federal Republic of Germany) has become deliberately cross-denominational in orientation. Whilst in most countries Christian Democratic parties are on the right of the political spectrum, because of their conservative attitude to property rights, to the role of the state in society, and to the protection of the family, as well as because of their marked distrust of socialism and hostility toward communism, they are nevertheless often interventionist in relation to economic policy and social welfare. Christian democracy seeks to reconcile or supersede class differences, and many Christian Democratic parties receive considerable cross-class support in elections. See also: *Christian socialism*.

Christian socialism An ideological attitude that holds that necessary linkages exist between the ideals of Christianity and the goals of socialism, and which thus seeks to provide an alternative justification for socialism to that of Marx. Christian socialism, whether in the form of a separate party or as a tendency within other parties (including some Christian Democratic and Socialist parties), stresses the moral obligation of the state, on behalf of society, to provide for the welfare of its citizens, with such provision financed as necessary by redistributive taxation. It has been prominent in some states in pacifist or nuclear-disarmament movements.

It is important *not* to include the Christian Social Union (CSU) of Bavaria as a Christian Socialist party, despite its name. It is the Bavarian sister-party of the Christian Democratic Union in Germany. See also: *Christian democracy; socialism; welfare state*.

Citizen A member of a state entitled to such civil and political rights as exist in that state, and owing obligation in respect of those rights, as contrasted with others, including residents, who do not possess such rights or obligations. The extent to which citizenship is conferred depends on the state and its regime. In some states in the past, only those who were wealthy or of high birth qualified for citizenship; in other states, women were excluded from all or most of the rights and obligations of citizenship. Religion or ethnic origin have been other criteria of exclusion. Slaves were not regarded as citizens in, for instance, ancient Greece or the pre-civil war USA. Citizenship can be distinguished from nationality: not all citizens will also possess the rights of 'nationals' within a state. There usually exists a body of law which provides legal definitions of citizenship and non-citizenship in its codes and which can be used to decide on disputed cases of citizenship. See also: *civil rights*.

Civil rights Those freedoms and privileges within a society which belong to the citizen, and the denial of which is regarded as a denial of the status of citizen. Such denial may be on grounds of race, gender, class, religion or other social characteristic, or may be as a deliberate act of sanction for those convicted of particular offenses. The details of which rights and privileges fall into the category of civil rights vary from society to society and over time. They may include, for example, the right to vote and to stand for election, the right to the due process of law, and the right to freedom from political and social discrimination. Marshall, in his book *Citizenship and Social Class* (Cambridge, Cambridge University Press, 1950), developed the idea that civil rights have evolved from the traditional rights of the citizen – equality before the law and freedoms of speech and religion – into political rights, such as the franchise, and to social rights associated with the development of the welfare state in the twentieth century.

If civil rights are called into question, it is the duty of the courts to resolve disputes, often by reference to the constitution, or to precedent or common law (as in Britain). The civil rights movement in the USA has been concerned especially with the assertion of equal rights and the elimination of political and social discrimination on behalf of the negro population, for instance.

A distinction must be made between civil rights and human rights: those rights, irrespective of legal or constitutional provision, held to belong to every individual, regardless of gender, race, religion, nationality, etc. However, many constitutions contain provisions for the protection of both types of rights: the Declaration of the Rights of Man (in the preamble to the French constitution), the US constitution and its first amendments, and the German constitution, for example. The UN Declaration of Human Rights also enumerates rights, some of which fall into either category. See also: *citizen*.

Civil society See: *society*.

Civil war The occurrence of armed hostilities between two (or more) relatively large groups within a state, both possessed of political organization, usually contesting the right to rule in a society or the right of one of the belligerent groups to secede. A civil war may be distinguished from a rebellion because of the claims by the insurrectionary group to exercise political power, and is differentiated from a revolution by the approximate balance of forces on each side; though a revolution may precede, accompany or follow a civil war. Examples of civil wars include that in the USA (1861-65); the civil war following the Bolshevik revolution of 1917; the war in Nigeria following the attempted secession of Biafra in the nineteen-sixties, and the war in Ethiopia, involving the secessionists of Eritrea province, in the nineteen-eighties. See also: *insurrection; revolution; secession; war*.

Class See: *social class*.

Classification The process of grouping phenomena on the basis of some differentiating quality which they share, e.g. the classification of societies as capitalist or non-capitalist; of party systems as one, two or multi-party; of voters into social or age categories. Classification may follow an explicitly stated typology but is also implicitly involved in any designation of political phenomena.

Research is sometimes described pejoratively as 'mere classification', the implied criticism being that grouping similar items together and giving them a common name is a poor substitute for explanation. But classification may also be pre-emptive in highlighting some aspects of phenomena and obscuring others. Classificatory schemes should therefore be carefully scrutinized, not just for their consistency, clarity and ease of operation, but also for their ability to generate useful and accurate hypotheses and, most crucially, their relation to the theoretical purposes to which they are put. See also: *conceptual framework; hypothesis; ideal type; theory; typology*.

Cleavage A condition of fundamental and persistent division among members of a political group or political system, which has political relevance, such as social class, religion, national identity, ethnic origin or language. Cleavages may be the cause of civil war, policy disagreements, ideological conflicts, etc., and may become the basis of divisions between political parties and the cause of the foundation of interest groups or movements, as well as, in extreme cases (such as Northern Ireland, Belgium and Sri Lanka) be the basis of distinctive political subcultures in society. The purpose of political integration is to overcome cleavage divisions to an extent sufficient for the political system to persist and function. Where an individual is associated with two or more different divisions he or she may be subjected to the dilemma of 'cross-cutting cleavages' when faced with, for example, voting decisions. A working-class Catholic in Italy, for instance, may be torn between voting for a socialist or communist party because of class identity, or the Christian Democratic party because of religious affiliation. See also: *interests; interest group; movement; party; pluralism; political culture; political integration.*

Clientelism A set of relations between 'patrons' and 'clients' in which patrons, enjoying high status, wealth and influence, dispense patronage, in the form of protection, access to state- or party-provided benefits, material rewards, jobs, prestige, etc., to their clients in return for political support. Since such rewards are often in breach of law, particularly electoral law, clientelism is strongly associated with corruption. Even where the forms of patronage and support are legally sanctioned, clientelist relations effectively deny proper democratic participation and citizenship. Where clientelism dominates politics, effective opposition may be stifled by the governing party's monopoly control of patronage. Beside the appeal of the reciprocal inducements themselves, clientelist relations are maintained through traditional forms of authority or by coercion. Clientelism resembles, and in some cases emerges from, the feudal relation between lord and vassal. Some social anthropologists have claimed that clientelism is a necessary stage in the development of the modern centralized state.

Analysis of clientelism has developed mainly as a branch of exchange theory, concentrating on the reciprocity of its relations, and on its role as a source of political integration and modernization. Seen in this way, clientelism appears as a phenomenon which is independent of class, since it comprises political alignments which cut across class divisions. However, broader perspectives show that clientelism may be one way in which a state can survive while promoting the interests of a minority class, and through which members of a dominant class can maintain their position.

Clientelism is a significant factor in third world politics, particularly where landowners occupy powerful positions in rural communities; for instance, in Latin America; in communities where other social ties are weakened or dissolved (e.g. in urban areas where clientelist relations replace community relationships for rural incomers) and in societies undergoing the stresses of modernization. It is also identifiable in more modernized systems, for instance in Italy. The term is also used to describe aspects of party politics in the USA, but these are more commonly referred to as 'machine politics'. See also: *authority; corporatism (b): ideal type; exchange theory; faction; feudalism; machine politics; modernization; political development; political integration; populism; social class; state.*

Closed coalition A coalition in which all the participating parties are contiguous on some specified policy dimension (e.g. the 'left-right' scale) and no party is excluded which, on that dimension, lies between any two participating parties. A coalition may be 'closed' on one dimension (e.g. economic policy) but 'open' on another (e.g. foreign policy). See also: *coalition; open coalition.*

Coalition A combination of two or more political actors (who may be, for example, individuals, political parties, interest groups, or even states) formed to achieve by joint action some goal which is mutually advantageous, and which, generally, might not be attainable without such a combination. More particularly, it refers to a government composed of two or more parties, in order to secure a working majority in a legislature, to reduce partisan politics at a time of crisis, or for some other reason.

The study of coalition formation has been an important subarea of political science for some years. In particular, alongside case-studies and comparative empirical studies of coalition formation, theoretical approaches based on, for example, game theory, bargaining theory and other formal approaches have become influential. The works of W. Riker and A. de Swaan have been especially important in developing hypotheses concerning the size of coalitions. This is likely to be the smallest possible combination of actors which exceeds 50% of votes in a legislature or other institution, i.e. 'minimal winning', or the smallest possible combination of actors which exceeds 50% of votes taking into account the constraint that parties or other actors be adjacent to each other on some relevant policy dimension, i.e. 'minimal winning and closed'. Other studies, e.g. those of Pridham and Laver, emphasize the importance of complex sets of factors, such as the extent to which political parties in coalitions can be treated as unitary actors, and the time dimension in any series of coalitions. The study of the termination of coalitions has not yet received much theoretical attention.

Coalition government seems to be more usually associated with proportional systems of election, since these make it less likely than majority systems that one party will attain a governing majority alone. Coalitions may also exist within legislatures without relating to coalition government (e.g. in the UN General Assembly). Electoral coalitions, such as the Liberal-SDP alliance in Britain in the 1983 and 1987 elections, or those among various groups of parties in the Volkskammer elections in the German Democratic Republic in 1990, are more usually termed 'electoral alliances'. See also: *closed coalition; game theory; minimal-winning coalition; minimum-winning coalition; open coalition.*

Coat-tails effect The coat-tails effect refers to the increased probability that a candidate for some office will be elected because of the popularity of another candidate – usually for some higher office – who also appears on the ballot paper. The term originated in the USA, to refer to some popular presidential candidate (usually one seeking re-election, such as Eisenhower in 1956) assisting by his presence on the ballot the election 'on his coat-tails' of his party's candidates for Congress, state governor, etc., who would otherwise probably not have been elected. The term can thus only be applied to ballots, containing simultaneously candidates for at least two offices, or possibly to elections for multi-member constituencies..

Cohort analysis The division of a social group into subgroupings (cohorts) based on the chronological intervals at which the subgroupings were able to acquire certain specified characteristics or experiences. For example, an electorate might be divided according to the year in which the members of each cohort could first cast their votes in a general election.

Cohort analysis permits the examination of variations in attitudes and behaviour between different cohorts, the underlying hypothesis being that shared experience (e.g. of war, economic slump or boom, a particular style of political leadership) may exert lasting influence on political behaviour. See also: *cross-sectional analysis; longitudinal studies*

Collective action problem See: *public goods*.

Collective choice A term sometimes used to cover the areas of both public choice theory and social choice theory. See also: *public choice theory; social choice theory*

Collectivism The doctrine or practice – directly opposed to individualism – of social organization on the basis of collective control of economic production and political decisions. It is particularly associated with forms of socialism.

The term is used differently by different writers, particularly when drawing distinctions between varieties of socialist doctrine. Sometimes collectivism is distinguished from syndicalism, on the grounds that syndicalism involves decentralized producer democracy, and is identified with state socialism, on the grounds that state socialism consists of administration by the whole people. More usually, these usages are reversed, on the grounds that syndicalism involves real collective participation in decision making, while state socialism consists of administration on behalf of, not by, the people. These different usages reflect the possibility that control may be exercised collectively at one level of society, but not at another. See also: *anarcho-syndicalism; communism; individualism; nationalization; socialism; state socialism*.

Colonialism The practice of occupying undeveloped territory beyond the boundaries of the colonizing state. Such occupation may be by means of force or by peaceful settlement especially of unpopulated territory. The purposes which define colonial settlement are the exploitation of the economic resources of the colonized territory: land, labour or raw materials; the availability of the colony as a captive market for exports from the parent state; and the potential utility of the colony for political or strategic purposes. Colonialism is distinguished from imperialism: by the fact that a colony is usually either uninhabited before settlement, or occupied by inhabitants of a different ethnic group, whereas imperial territories may be inhabited by members of the same ethnic group as the imperial state, e.g. as in the Austro-Hungarian empire; by the emphasis in colonial settlement on economic exploitation, whereas, in some empires, territories may become politically, economically and culturally integrated with the parent state; and by the emphasis on settlement in colonization but not necessarily in imperial conquest.

The term 'internal colonialism' refers to the practice by a state of treating some – usually territorially peripheral – region of that state as though it were a colony, for economic exploitation. See also: *colonization; imperialism*.

Colonization The process of creating colonies by settlement on the part of inhabitants of the colonizing state in territories beyond the boundaries of the parent state. See also: *colonialism*.

Commonwealth In its most general sense, it refers to any independent political community. More particularly, historically it was the name given to the regime of Cromwell following the civil war in England (1649-60), and it is part of the formal title of Australia and some US states such as Massachusetts. Its more usual application is to refer to the organization of states, all formerly part of the British Empire, which remain in voluntary association, and which recognize the British monarch as 'Head of the Commonwealth'. There is a Commonwealth Secretariat based in London (created 1965), and regular meetings of heads of state, finance and education ministers, etc., which act as integrative mechanisms. See also: *colonialism; imperialism*.

Commune A group organizing its own work and social relations through some system of collective decision making and, usually, exercising common ownership and control of goods produced and other property.

Such arrangements have been recommended chiefly by writers regarded as utopians, particularly the utopian socialists. The Israeli *kibbutz* is a frequently cited modern example.

The term 'commune' is also used to denote a basic area of local administration, e.g. in France. In addition to this usage, the name '*Paris Commune*' (or just '*the Commune*') is used for an insurrectionary grouping prominent in the revolutionary power struggles between 1792 and 1794, but may alternatively refer to the 72 days of revolutionary communist administration in Paris in 1871, following the Franco-Prussian war, at which time less enduring *Communes* were proclaimed in other French cities. See also: *communism; local government; utopianism*.

Communism A doctrine which advocates, or a form of society which practises, the communal ownership of all property, or of the means of production and exchange. In its fully developed form, communist society would be classless, economic and political relations non-exploitative, and distribution governed by need. The sort of political organization envisaged by Marx comprised a system of mandated representation, based on the direct democratic decisions of local communes, allowing for extensive consultation with and reference to constituents. This system, towards which the Paris Commune of 1871 displayed tendencies, bears little resemblance to the generally centralist and authoritarian practices of ruling communist parties, in both state and party institutions.

Marx and Engels appear to have adopted the word, e.g. in the *Communist Manifesto* of 1848, to avoid the connotation of middle-class utopian schemes with which 'socialism' had become associated. Often the two words are used interchangeably but two principal distinctions may be encountered: communism may be treated as a form of socialism, differing from other forms primarily in its emphasis on fundamental social and economic change as a prerequisite for political change, rather than as a consequence of it; alternatively, 'socialism' may refer to the transitional condition of a society, in the course of its pursuit of communism, before the abolition of class division is achieved.

'Primitive communism' is used to denote a period of communal organization, preceding slavery, based on family groups and tribal ownership. It is also applied to the form of peasant agricultural production, based on the village community, found in parts of pre-revolutionary Russia and in many areas of Asia. The presence of these communal forms of organization has encouraged the view that a modern communist state could be developed without a prior period of capitalist industrialization.

'Eurocommunism' denotes the programme put forward by some western European communist parties (e.g. in Italy, France and Spain) in the 1970s and 1980s, advocating a gradual evolutionary path to a communist society, through the institutions of parliamentary democracy. See also: *bolshevism; collectivism; commune; democracy; exploitation; Marxism; social class; social democracy; socialism; utopianism.*

Community A term defined in a wide variety of ways, sometimes synonymously with 'society' or 'social group', but often denoting a group closely bound by status, kinship, a sense of common identity, etc., contrasted with the looser, more impersonal, and predominantly commercial relationships comprising modern societies. In this last sense, liberal society is sometimes described as lacking a sense of community and liberal social theory as failing to recognize the value of community.

In political science the term usually denotes some subgroup within the society, defined territorially (e.g. a town or village), ethnically (e.g. the Afro-Caribbean and Asian communities in European societies), or occupationally (e.g. the medical community). These criteria are sometimes combined, as in the expression 'mining community' which usually denotes some territorial area within which the occupation of miner plays a significant role. A political community is, in these terms, defined as a social group that shares a common political culture and within which the members exhibit a high degree of shared political activity. See also: *community studies; liberalism; political culture; society; status; subcommunity.*

Community studies The community, in the sense of a local territorial area containing a well-defined social system in which the bulk of the individual members' social transactions occur, has provided political science with a unit of manageable size for analysis, but of sufficient complexity to be of significance and interest. Thus 'community studies' has become an important branch of political science, and particularly of political sociology.

Most political studies of communities (rather than of local government) have been American and have concentrated on aspects of community power, its structures and its methods of making decisions. The works of Floyd Hunter, Robert Dahl, Matthew Crenson and John Gaventa have been among the most influential in these areas. Britain, continental Europe and modernizing post-colonial states have also been regions in which such studies have been undertaken.

The methods and conclusions of community studies are much debated. Use of the 'reputational approach' has been criticised for its tendency to portray elite domination of the community, whilst the 'decisional approach' has been accused of bias towards pluralist or polyarchal conclusions. The idea of agenda setting through 'non-decisions' has been branded either insufficiently behavioural, or too restricted to the behaviourial approach, depending on the position of the critic. Beyond these arguments about the best means to study the relative political power of individuals, the attention of some scholars has switched to power as an effect of structure. More generally, empirical studies have attempted to draw conclusions that are not limited to the particular community under investigation, attempts which have been criticized on the grounds that the political life of the chosen community was untypical of other communities, or of politics at the national level.

Community studies are not, of course, limited to the study of community power. Among other aspects of political life investigated are membership of community organizations; levels of political participation; ethnic differences in community politics; the structure and behaviour of political parties at the community level. See also: *behaviourialism; community; elite; local government; non-decisions; polyarchy; power; reputational approach; structuralism.*

Comparative analysis A method of analysis used in the social sciences, including political science, to describe, classify and explain data by making observations of similarities and differences to be found in the various items being analyzed: (e.g. agrarian pressure groups; constitutional courts; processes of political socialization; revolutionary ideologies), or in the same item over different time periods (e.g. the number of women candidates elected at British general elections in the twentieth century; veto decisions of US presidents). From such comparison it is possible that statements concerning the causes and effects of differences and similarities may be made, classifactory schemes designed, and new relationships discovered. To this extent comparison is fundamental to the scientific analysis of political phenomena. However, comparative analysis is also regarded as a specific and significant subarea of political science, with its own methods and problems.

Comparative analysis as a method in politics is at least as old as Aristotle, but its self-conscious growth as a specialized area in the discipline can be dated from after the second world war, when political scientists attempted to be more systematic and rigorous, more 'scientific', and to go beyond the limits of the institutional and legalistic description of western politics that had formed the staple of the discipline in the past. Works of deliberate comparison came to form the core of this subarea, whether concerned with comparing formal institutions of political systems (generally the concern of comparative government) or with informal institutions, political functions, ideologies, processes and political cultures (which, together with comparative government, may be said to comprise the field of comparative politics).

Several major methodological problems have been identified. Comparison itself presupposes an initial conceptual framework or classifactory scheme, according to which selection and rejection of items for comparison can be undertaken; yet one of the purposes of comparative analysis is to discover new relationships and classifications, so any such initial scheme has to be tentative and capable of modification. The level of comparison is another problem; too general a level may well lead to the omission of significant detail and the production of broad, but unilluminating, generalizations, but comparison conducted at too specific a level may be over-detailed and supply generalizations too narrow in scope to be useful as explanation. All comparison must involve similarities across two or more cases, but also sufficient differences to make comparison valuable; whether the similarities or the differences are the variables to be explained by comparative analysis is a decision concerning the strategy of comparative inquiry which has to be made on a case-by-case basis. Problems of language, of the validity of comparison of apparently similar components or processes from different cultures, of the availability of data and the intrusion of bias, also complicate comparative analysis. See also: *comparative government; comparative politics; ethnocentrism; political analysis.*

Comparative government Though often used interchangeably with the term 'comparative politics' (e.g. as the title of a textbook or of an academic course), comparative government may usefully be distinguished as the study of states and their governmental institutions and processes on a comparative basis. Such usage is defended by those political scientists who emphasize the special and distinctive status of the state as a political organization in contrast to non-state organizations. Thus the comparison of regimes (as conducted for example by Aristotle) and their stages of development, of legislatures, executives and judicial bodies together with their functions, of systems of local government and decentralization, of constitutions, and perhaps also of the political collectivities – parties and pressure groups – that seek to use or influence power within the state, as well as of systems of election, of leadership selection and succession, of revolutions and civil war, all would fall within the scope of comparative government. See also: *comparative analysis; comparative politics; government (b): the study area.*

Comparative politics Though often used interchangeably with the term 'comparative government' to describe comparative studies in political science, 'comparative politics' can usefully be distinguished as being a wider and more inclusive area of study and analysis. As well as being concerned with the comparative study of the state, its institutions and processes, it also includes in its scope the wider range of political structures, functions and values found in both state and non-state political contexts, such as leadership, political socialization, the resolution of political conflict, bargaining, decision-making in political institutions, and political communication. See also: *comparative analysis; comparative government.*

Concept The network of meaning conveyed by a term which represents an idea of some category of objects, phenomena, processes, relations, etc., e.g. the concepts of class, interest, political socialization, power. Concepts are the elements from which complex statements are constructed about relationships, and which form their explanation. Thus a theory or scientific law will consist of several interrelated concepts.

It should be stressed that words are merely labels for concepts and that the same word may, in different hands, designate a number of different concepts. See also: *conceptual framework; essentially contested concepts; law (a): scientific law; operationalization; theory.*

Conceptual framework The term is most often applied to a set of concepts providing the means of classifying phenomena for analysis, but not in itself constituting developed theory or explanation of those phenomena. No very sharp distinction may be apparent between the conceptual framework of, for instance, Marxism, and the more substantive theory that it has developed, but the framework might be regarded as the set of tools with which the basic components of the finished product (the theory) are selected and fashioned. Thus a theory can be revised or replaced without necessarily changing the conceptual framework within which it is expressed. See also: *classification; concept; explanation; model; theory.*

Condominium The government of a territory (such as a colony or a protectorate) where sovereignty is divided between at least two external powers, on a concurrent basis. Egypt and the United Kingdom governed the Sudan on this basis prior to its independence in 1956, and the New Hebrides territory was governed as a condominium by France and the United Kingdom. See also: *protectorate.*

Confederation A form of government in which several autonomous states have agreed to vest certain defined and limited powers (e.g. trade, defence) in a new collective authority, whilst still retaining their separate identities and – in all other respects – independent sovereignties. Territorial contiguity of component states is a usual, but not an essential, feature of a confederation. Confederations differ from federations in the retention of sovereignty by the component states of a confederation over all matters except the limited powers voluntarily ceded to the confederal authority. They also tend to be in practice less permanent than federations, usually disintegrating after a period, or transforming into federations. Examples of confederations are: the newly independent American states between the signing of the Articles of Confederation and the promulgation of the US constitution (1781-89), the Southern Confederacy in the US civil war, and various confederations of German states in the 19th century before the Second Empire was formed. See also: *federation; sovereignty.*

Conflict approach A conflict approach to political analysis focuses in particular on: (a) the political behaviour of individuals and groups in terms of the competition between them for the values which are distributed by political means; (b) the processes by which conflict – over policies, priorities, methods of attaining goals or of selecting leaders – are resolved; and (c) the effects of conflict on the structures of the political system. In the case of international politics, where conflict has been one of the principal concepts in study and research, relations between state political systems can be examined in large part in terms of conflict approaches. Such approaches include the use of formal models, such as game theory; various mathematical techniques where the variables of the conflict situation can be quantified; bargaining theory; the study of communication; and techniques such as gaming and simulation. See also: *bargaining theory; game theory; political system; politics; simulation*.

Consensus A condition of agreement within a political community (usually, but not necessarily, one sharing a common territory), relating to any or all of the following: the definition and composition of the political community (i.e. that the groups contained within it belong together); the goals or purposes of the community; the procedures to be used in arriving at authoritative decisions in and for the community; the policies to be adopted by the community. Whilst consensus cannot be precisely measured, indications of its decline or disappearance could include: the growth of separatist movements; increases in the incidence of direct action or other forms of political violence; decline in political participation; or the growth of support for anti-system parties or movements. In the systems analysis framework developed by David Easton, consensus is related to the input of support for the regime or the political community.

The term is sometimes used in the context of 'consensus politics', to indicate a basis for political debate and decision where outcomes are to be produced by agreement, as far as possible, in contrast to conflict models of politics, where outcomes are decided as a result of adversarial processes. See also: *conflict approach*.

Conservatism A belief in the value of existing institutions and practices, not in the sense of opposition to all change but rather as a concern to maintain what is valuable and to conduct politics as a process of pragmatic adjustment. This belief is rooted in a view of society as a seamless web of tradition, delicate in its structure and not adequately understood in terms of abstract or mechanistic theory. The individual is portrayed as naturally a creature of society, not as the bearer of individual rights out of which society is artificially constructed. The task of government is to protect, rather than direct, existing institutional groups and, as far as possible, to redress grievances and resolve problems through the established framework. Above all, conservatism stands against calls for the fundamental transformation of society and state, especially those programmes appealing to abstract and utopian ideas of social and political improvement. In developing its objections to abstract theorizing and radical change, conservatism often appears ideologically opposed to liberalism, particularly in its attitude to the individual. This apparent opposition between traditional conservative and liberal ideas produces tension within modern conservative parties which have, as in Britain, absorbed the influence of the new right. More generally, the pragmatic and anti-ideological elements of the conservative tradition appear to conflict with attempts to present conservatism as a systematic ideology with a coherent philosophical basis. Conservatism suggests an acceptance of inequality, class division and hierarchical organization. For this reason the term 'conservative' is rather loosely extended to describe entrenched hierarchies, resistant to all calls for change, of whatever political character. In this sense both right-wing dictators and hard-liners within communist regimes have been called conservative. See also: *contract theory; hierarchy; ideology; liberalism; new right; pragmatism; radicalism*.

Consociational democracy A form of democracy identifiable in certain societies which are characterized by their possession of well-defined sections or 'segments' of the community: e.g. different religious denominations, sizeable linguistic or ethnic groups, distinctive regional, class or cultural groups. Such pluralistic societies in some cases develop a style of democratic order which differs from majoritarian democracy by the institutionalization of power-sharing (e.g. through coalitions, sometimes – as in Austria for many years – grand coalitions). This power-sharing involves widespread proportional allocation of political and other offices within the state (not only ministries, but civil service posts, seats on public boards supervising broadcasting services, etc.). It also involves regard for the autonomy of the sections or segment where that can feasibly be exercised (e.g. by the allocation of air time to all major segments for public broadcasting services), and regard for the rights and interests of each segment, to the extent of recognizing their right to a veto on decisions which affect their vital interests (e.g. the linguistic regions of Belgium today, particularly with regard to cultural and educational policies). Consociational democracy is thus a mode of rule conducive to political integration in a society which otherwise might experience stresses stemming from the different interests of the segments. Multi-lingual and multi-confessional countries sometimes provide clear cases of consociational democracy: the Netherlands; Belgium; Austria; Switzerland; to an extent the Lebanon and Cyprus, before in each case religious or nationalist tensions resulted in civil war and destroyed the carefully crafted arrangements for consociational power-sharing. In some ways, the European Economic Community could be said to have exhibited many of the features of consociational democracy.

A detailed analysis of consociational democracy is to be found in Arendt Lijphart, *Democracy in Plural Societies*, (New Haven, USA, Yale University Press, 1977). See also: *cleavage; democracy; minority; political integration; veto*.

Conspiracy theories Belief systems which include the notion that certain social phenomena of importance, particularly those considered to be harmful or evil, are the result of a conspiracy among certain members of society, who sometimes are regarded as agents of a foreign power. People who subscribe to such a theory often claim to possess evidence, in which they believe uncritically, concerning the people and the strategies involved in the conspiracy, and often regard it as their obligation to expose and defeat the plot that they have uncovered. In other cases, the existence of some conspiracy is inferred from the general incidence of benefits and costs falling to certain groups or classes in society: those who suffer losses (whether of a material or non-material kind) blaming their situation on a – perhaps vague – conspiracy on the part of those who gain.

Many examples have existed in history of widespread conspiracy theories (e.g. anti-Catholicism; Populism in some of its forms), but anti-Semitism in its modern form (e.g as based on the *Protocols of the Elders of Zion*) and anti-Communism in the United States (e.g. the 'witch-hunts' of Senator

Joseph McCarthy) are two of the more important twentieth century examples in terms of their effects on society. See also: *populism*.

Constituency A group of voters (the constituents) entitled to elect a representative or a delegate. It is thus in public elections usually a territorially-defined set of inhabitants, ranging from a ward in local government elections to the massive constituencies in Great Britain for elections to the European parliament, the states in the USA for senatorial elections, and the national constituency in Israel for elections to the Knesset. In some political organizations the constituency may be a grouping defined by function or other criteria, e.g. a member union within a confederation of trade unions.

A secondary usage refers to the group or sector of society from which a politician derives influence, independent of formal electoral arrangements: e.g. a spokesman for the military in an autocratic government, a representative of a party's youth organization at an annual party conference, or a candidate from an ethnic minority elected to the national legislature. See also: *apportionment; gerrymandering*.

Constitution A fundamental statement of laws governing the functions and relationships of political institutions within a political community, a statement of the limits set to the powers of such institutions, and usually also containing a catalogue of the rights of citizens. In most cases the constitution will be a single, codified written document, but some states such as the United Kingdom have an 'unwritten' constitution, because no single codified statement of the constitution exists, and because the constitution is held to consist in part of unwritten conventions.

Constitutions may be created by many means, including the use of a constitutional convention, imposition by some external power, an Act of the legislature, or confirmation of a constitutional document by the people through a plebiscite. Constitutions may legitimately be amended, usually only by processes laid down in the constitution itself, and these processes are often deliberately made complicated and difficult in order to emphasize the superiority of constitutional provisions in relation to ordinary legislation, though in an unwritten constitution such amendment is much simpler. Where the constitutions are relatively easy to amend, they are termed 'flexible' constitutions. Some parts of a constitution may be declared to be unamendable. Most constitutions are preceded by a preamble, setting out such matters as the justification for the constitution, ideological premises upon which it is based, and claims to territory not yet incorporated into the area of application of the constitution (such as the preamble to the Basic law of the Federal Republic of Germany prior to reunification in 1990, with its claim that the Basic Law was temporary pending eventual reunification).

In many countries there exists a process of judicial review, generally involving a constitutional court or similar institution, which can void any law or action of the government, or of other groups or individuals, if these conflict with the judges' interpretation of the constitution. See also: *civil rights; constitutional law; constitutionalism; convention (a): the institution; convention (b): procedural conventions; government (a): the institution; judicial review*.

Constitutional law The rules and procedures, and judicial decisions concerning those rules and procedures, regarding the structures of government, their principal powers and functions, and the relationships among them. In political communities possessing a written constitution, the constitution itself will be a primary source of constitutional law, while in all states a major source will be the decisions of the courts of law which interpret such rules.

In Britain the study of constitutional law includes the general principles of constitutional doctrine such as the supremacy of parliament and the rule of law (Britain lacks a written codified constitution); the law, conventions and procedural rules relating to parliament, including its powers and elections to the House of Commons; the powers of the monarch and the executive government; the role of the judiciary in relation to constitutional matters; the rights and duties of the citizen in relation to government. In the USA the subject would include the study of the constitution and interpretations of its content by the judiciary; the federal relationship; the functions and powers of the president, his executive government, and the Congress. See also: *administrative law; constitution; judicial review; rule of law*.

Constitutionalism The term has two related meanings: one concerning constitutionalism as practice, the other as positive valuation of that practice.

Constitutionalism as practice is the ordering of political processes and institutions on the basis of a constitution, which lays down the pattern of formal political institutions and embodies the basic political norms of a society. The constitution not only regulates the relationships of organs of government to each other; it also limits the discretionary powers of government, and, in doing so, protects the citizen. Such regulation and limitation require arbitration by some judicial body (e.g. in the USA by the Supreme Court and in the Federal Republic of Germany by the Constitutional Court, which apply judicial review to government acts; in Britain by the ordinary system of courts and civil and criminal remedies), as well as enforcement. Thus while the USSR, for example, possesses a constitution, neither the specific machinery for its enforcement nor acceptance of its constraints by the political authorities is much in evidence. Though not found exclusively in democratic regimes, constitutionalism is a basic requirement of a democracy.

As a term of valuation, constitutionalism refers to the idea of those who wish to preserve, or introduce, the political supremacy of a constitution within a particular state, to act as protector of the citizen from arbitrary government and as a statement of political relationships, especially where such a statement and such protection do not already exist in satisfactory form. Stress is laid on the 'rule of law' as a fundamental concept from which constitutionalism derives. See also: *constitution; rule of law*.

Content analysis A technique employed in social science to measure and classify the characteristics in an item of communication, according to an objective set of pre-selected categories. The unit of measurement in text may be, for example, the word, the sentence, the theme, and in non-verbal communication the sign or the symbol. In political science, content analysis has been used to study variation in themes in the nomination acceptance speeches of US presidential candidates, the analysis of propaganda, and the comparison of party election manifestos in British elections. See also: *political communication*.

Contract theory An account of social and political relationships which presents society, or the state, or both, as a product of binding mutual undertakings between individuals or groups. The terms of this agreement or 'social contract' establish obligations to obedience on the part of the subjects and may impose limits on the powers of government, for instance that it should act only in the interests of the people, or that it should rule according to certain constitutional principles.

Contract theory occupies a central position in western European political thought from the late eleventh to the late eighteenth century. Its origins are sometimes traced to early Greek thought but may more plausibly be identified in medieval views of feudal relationships between monarch, lord and vassal. As contract theory develops, its focus shifts from the reciprocal duties of status groups to the transfer of natural rights through the voluntary consent given by rational individuals of equal status.

The precise status accorded to the social contract may vary considerably between different writers. For some the contract is an actual event, either historically identifiable (e.g. the coronation of a monarch) or one which must have taken place at the unrecorded inception of society or government. For others the contract is more obviously a fictional device, either hypothetical (it is *as if* a contract actually occurred), or ideal (the contract provides a normative ideal against which the legitimacy of government may be judged).

Contract theory has been revived during the last thirty years. Hypothetical and ideal contractarian models are now common in collective choice theory and in political and moral philosophy. See also: *convention (b): procedural convention; feudalism; law (c): natural law; state*.

Contradiction A relation of conflict between elements of a system (an individual's belief system, a political system, the totality of a social system) such that some essential aim or requirement of the system cannot be satisfied. For instance, it has been argued that the legitimacy of the state in advanced capitalist societies partly depends on the state's presentation of itself as separate from the private sphere of production. But a combination of external economic competition and internal political demands may force the state to intervene directly in production in order to sustain weak industrial sectors. Thus the legitimacy of the liberal system is threatened; a contradiction is manifested.

The term is often employed by Marxists in analyzing the forces generating changes within a system, particularly those forces inherent in capitalism itself which may constitute conflict threatening the very existence of the capitalist system, i.e. conditions favourable to revolution. Such analysis is open to the criticism that it underestimates the capacity of systems to absorb and accommodate pressure, using the strong term 'contradiction' where 'conflicting tendencies' might better serve. See also: *dialectic; legitimacy; liberalism; Marxism*.

Convention (a): the institution Meetings of political groups for various purposes are sometimes termed 'conventions' when they are formally 'convened' for a stated aim. Two major types of such conventions are: constitutional conventions, where delegates or representatives meet to formulate a new national or provincial constitution, e.g. in the USA in 1787, in Germany in 1919 (the Weimar Constitution) and in the German Federal Republic in 1948-49 (the Bonn Constitution); and nominating conventions, as held by the major political parties in the USA, to select nominees for, in the case of the national conventions, the presidential and vice-presidential elections, and to draft a platform for them to put forward as policy proposals. See also: *constitution; convention (b): procedural convention.*

Convention (b): procedural convention Rules which state norms or procedures regulating political relationships and imposing obligations on political actors, but which are not enshrined in law or backed by legal sanctions.

Conventions arise to give guidance to conduct where more formal rules are silent or ambiguous. They are usually unwritten and generally develop from precedent, but may be matters of agreement between political actors. They may be altered or reinterpreted as circumstances change, but, if breached, may well give rise to a political crisis, or to the need for a more specific legal rule to govern such cases in the future. Because conventions are often unwritten, and because there is no authoritative tribunal for their determination, their precise content is often a matter of interpretation, a feature which enhances flexibility in application but which may lead to dispute.

In the absence of a written constitution, the British parliamentary system is rich in conventions. Neither the office of prime minister nor the cabinet was established by law, and their powers and practices are accepted largely by convention. The power of the prime minister to choose the date of dissolution of parliament (subject to the five-year limit imposed by the Parliament Act 1911), the duty of a minister to abide by decisions of the cabinet or to resign, the so-called 'law and custom of parliament' set out in Erskine May's *Parliamentary Practice*, are all conventional. In the United States, the law confers the right to elect the president on the members of the electoral college but, by convention, these members are bound to cast their votes for the candidate who obtains a plurality of the popular vote in their state.

A similar meaning of convention may be found in political philosophy and rational choice analysis. 'Convention' denotes the mutual coordination of action by a number of individuals without the use of explicit agreement or binding undertaking. The recognition of a mutual interest may be sufficient to produce coordinated action even without the explicit communication of that recognition. Thus convention occupies a position somewhere between contract and custom and is used as an alternative to these in explaining social behaviour.

The term is also used to refer to agreements between states which have a treaty-like form, e.g. the European Convention on Human Rights, and the Geneva Conventions on the rules of warfare. See also: *contract theory; convention (a): the institution; custom; pact; protocol (a): ceremonial; protocol (b): agreement; rational choice analysis; treaty.*

Convergence thesis The idea that the imperatives of modern government will inexorably compel capitalist and socialist states and societies to become increasingly similar: to converge. These imperatives include the increased need for economic and social planning in capitalist societies, the inescapable use of market forces in socialist societies to produce economic rationality and growth, the growing importance of international factors vis-à-vis the economies and societies of all states, and the spread of problems such as AIDS, drug addiction and international crime across state boundaries. According to the thesis, these imperatives encourage the development of bureaucratic organizations, whether in capitalist or socialist societies, to design and implement rational policies to cope with these challenges, policies which will converge in spite of the ideological differences between types of society. The thesis was developed in the 1950s and 1960s, when planning became more fashionable and widespread in capitalist states, but recent events in the Soviet Union and eastern Europe suggest that convergence, if such exists, is towards the capitalist model rather than towards some 'mixed economy' version of state capitalism..

Corporatism (a): ideology An ideology sometimes thought to be closely associated with fascism, particularly with Italian fascism, but more broadly associated with Catholic social theory. Managers and workers should be organized into corporations (or 'syndicates') which regulate and represent each trade or branch of industry. Parliament should be replaced by a corporative chamber, representing the interests of the various corporations. The integrated management of economic interests is thus supposed to displace political conflict. In so far as such practices were instituted in Italy they remained under the control of fascist state officials. See also: *anarcho-syndicalism; Christian democracy; fascism.*

Corporatism (b): ideal type An ideal type model of state action, usually applied to western liberal democracies, particularly popular in the late 1960s and 1970s. Within the model, interests are represented through a limited number of hierarchical associations, expressly or tacitly acknowledged by government as the principal legitimate source of policy demand.

Variations exist between different models of corporatism. One model (sometimes called 'corporate pluralism') may treat the state as an instrument for the implementation of broad policies agreed by the relevant associations of interests. Another model (sometimes called 'statist corporatism') draws attention to the advantages accruing to state elites from corporatist integration. See also: *ideal type; pluralism; state*

Correspondence rules See: *operationalization.*

Corroboration See: *verification.*

Counter-revolution An attempt to restore by force the status quo ante which existed before the occurrence of a successful revolution. See also: *revolution.*

Coup d'état A change of regime brought about by illegal and unconstitutional action on the part of a holder, or group of holders, of some political or military office. A coup d'état often involves violence, though this may be limited in extent. It may be preceded by a conspiracy concerned with obtaining certain political or military offices for sympathizers, such as a key ministry, a strategic military command, or control of important communication facilities.

It is similar to a revolution in so far as its purpose involves a relatively sudden and illegal change of regime; it differs from a revolution in that it does not call on mass support to effect regime change (though initiators of a coup may seek legitimation of such change by a plebiscite or mass demonstration), and does not involve radical social change such as might be expected to accompany a revolution. A *putsch* is a form of coup d'état.

Examples of coups include: the initiation of imperial regimes by Napoleon Bonaparte and Louis Napoleon in France; Cromwell's seizure of power in England; the Nigerian military coup in 1966-67; the military coup in Chile in 1973. See also: *palace revolution; plebiscite; putsch; regime; revolution.*

Critical election An election at which party realignment or party dealignment occurs, signalling a radically revised pattern of relationships within the party system. It is difficult to identify critical elections when they occur; they are usually labelled as such in retrospect, when the longer-term pattern of changed party relationships can be observed. See also: *dealignment; realignment.*

Cross-cutting cleavages See: *cleavage.*

Cross-sectional analysis Analysis by means of the employment of comparisons at the same point in time of several areas or cases representing different stages of development or different subcategories of the factor under investigation: e.g. the political awareness of a child, adolescent, an adult of working age and a retired adult, or voting preferences of farmers in each of the member-states of the European Community. See also: *cohort analysis; longitudinal studies; panel study.*

Cube law A law which sets out a mathematical relationship between the share of the seats in the legislature which a party will obtain, and the proportion of the vote which it receives, provided (a) that a system of simple majority voting is in use, and (b) that only two parties are in contention. Where two parties, A and B, contest an election, the law predicts that if the votes are divided in the ratio $X:Y$ the seats won will be allocated in the ratio $X^3:Y^3$. Research into recent elections in Britain and other countries using majoritarian systems of election indicates that the law is at best only suggestive of an approximate effect, and that electoral outcomes are affected by complicating factors which often produce results which differ substantially from those predicted by the cube law. See also: *psephology.*

Cumulative vote A system of voting whereby electors are given more than one vote each, and they can allocate these votes either by giving several candidates one vote each, or by giving one or more candidates two or more votes. For example, if each elector has three votes, one vote each may be given to three candidates, or all three votes to one candidate, or one candidate may receive two votes and another one vote. The system has been used for elections e.g. to the Swiss and Luxembourg legislatures, the Illinois state legislature; and certain German city councils, such as Munich. See also: *electoral system; second ballot system.*

Custom The norms implicit in routinely performed actions, or the actions embodying elements of the culture or tradition of an institution.

So defined, 'custom' may be difficult to distinguish from 'habit' or 'convention'. No rigid distinctions should be drawn between these terms.

Dealignment

Usages differ and the precise meaning intended by a particular writer may only be apparent in the given context. However, within political analysis some broad, and frequently employed, distinctions may be discerned: habitual behaviour is typically unreflective and often unconsciously performed, while conventions are followed because they are seen to contribute to the effective working of an institution. Reasons can also be offered for customary behaviour but are more concerned with politeness, or the value of ceremony, than with the functional efficiency of a particular action. Thus, the different basic patterns of speech used by each individual member of parliament may be largely habitual; the required forms of words for ceremonial occasions in parliament are customary; speech within the established procedures for debate is conventional.

The term 'customary law' denotes traditional, usually unwritten, procedures for establishing rights and duties and settling disputes without the use of codified law or specific legislative process. In legal theory the role of custom (in the broad sense of common social practice) is an important point of dispute: between, for instance, those who argue that law simply *is* custom and that law-makers do not, strictly speaking, 'make' laws but 'find' them within the established traditions of the society, and those who see law as sovereign command, distinct and independent from custom. See also: *convention (b): procedural convention; law (b): stipulative law; legislature; norm; positivism; protocol (a): ceremonial.*

D

Dealignment

A process whereby some section of the electorate no longer votes for a party according to its identification with some fundamental social cleavage (e.g. social class, religious denomination, ethnic or linguistic grouping), but instead its members vote on more pragmatic grounds, thus affecting to a radical extent the relative strengths of parties at elections. See also: *electoral volatility; party identification; realignment.*

Decision An act of choice made by an individual, organization or institution, that puts an end to deliberation by selecting, from a range of perceived alternatives, some goal or means of attaining some goal.

The alternatives perceived will be circumscribed by various constraints, from the environment and from within the decision-making structure itself. The rules and procedures governing the process of decision making may also be important factors affecting the choice of a decision.

In politics, decisions are made in many forms and at various levels: policies; votes (for candidates for office and for substantive and procedural proposals); implementing or executive decisions; organizational decisions. See also: *decision-making analysis; incrementalism; non-decision; policy*.

Decision-making analysis The analysis of political systems, processes and behaviour, focusing on the political decisions that are made, the structures involved in decision making, the factors influencing the outcomes of the process, the political costs of decisions, and the selection of actors for decision-making roles. Though sometimes used synonymously with policy analysis, decision-making analysis is distinguished both by its concern with decisions that are not in themselves policies (e.g. with voting decisions), and by its concentration on the decision stage in policy-making, whereas policy analysis is concerned also with processes that precede and follow the decision (e.g. implementation).

To describe the outcome of a complex policy process as a decision may imply that the process resembles that of individual deliberation and choice. Some decision-making models, notably the 'rational actor' model, explicitly adopt this position, others avoid it and stress instead some aspect of the internal processes that may contribute to the outcome, for instance routines and procedures (in the 'organizational process' model), or strategies adopted by competing elements within the system (in the 'political bargaining' model).

Both within and beyond these basic models, many different approaches have been used in analysis: the formal techniques of game theory and rational choice; the identification of variables or stages in the decision-making process; case studies of decisions and decision-makers, some based on laboratory simulations; studies of the social and economic background, values and career ambitions of decision-makers; studies based on models of communications and information flows within systems; studies of the relationships between institutional structures and styles of decision making; and a wide range of studies on various types of voting decisions. Examples of each of these may be found in analyses of local, national and international decision-making. This range of approaches reflects the centrality of decision-making analysis in political science and the readiness of analysts to draw on contributions from other disciplines. See also: *bargaining theory; community studies; decision; decision theory; game theory; incrementalism; non-decision; policy; policy analysis; psephology; rational choice analysis; simulation*.

Decision theory An area of formal enquiry concerned to develop principles of rational choice for situations where intercomparable, quantitative costs and benefits, and probabilities, may be assigned to the various possible outcomes. See also: *game theory; rational choice analysis; utility*.

Delegated legislation Legislation, or rules and orders with the force of legislation, made by a subordinate officer (such as a minister) or institution under powers delegated by a superior institution (such as a legislature). Such legislation made under delegated powers is usually subject to scrutiny by the delegating institution, and is usually capable of being nullified by that institution. In the British parliament, for example, opportunities for scrutiny and nullification may be through a requirement that an affirmative resolution be passed before the delegated legislation can take effect, or a provision that it takes effect automatically after lapse of a stated period of time unless in the interim a negative resolution is passed nullifying the delegated legislation.

The purposes of delegated legislation are, in particular, to save the time and energy of members of the legislature, to enable specialized rules to be applied especially on technical matters (e.g. safety standards), and to provide flexibility, for example in situations of emergency such as a state of war. See also: *devolution*.

Democracy A form of rule in which the people (in Greek, the *demos*) exercise political power, either by acting as the policy-making authority (direct democracy), or through their choice of those making policy on their behalf (representative democracy).

Historically, the typical examples of direct democracy have been the fourth century BC Athenian, and seventeenth and eighteenth century New England 'town meeting' models. In these cases the citizenry met periodically to discuss issues, receive reports from executive officials, and take decisions. The growth in size of the populations of cities and states, the areas they cover, and the complexity and frequency of issues requiring consideration, plus the inability or unwillingness of a population to devote much time to political participation, set limits to the extension of direct democracy. Democratic participation is now chiefly through the election of representatives, sometimes supplemented by occasional referenda and plebiscites. It has been suggested that widespread access to modern information technology might provide the means for regular expressions of popular will, a process sometimes referred to as 'teledemocracy'.

Democracy is generally defined by reference to the procedural and substantive principles which appear necessary to its operation. Those in political office should act in the interests of the people. Government should operate through the rule of law. Those in political office should be accountable to, and removable by, the people, either directly or through their representatives. The opportunity to participate must be equal: all citizens should be able to vote, and the vote of every citizen should count equally. Policy disagreements should be resolved by the principle of majority decision, perhaps with the additional requirement of special majorities, e.g. for constitutional amendments (although there are models of democracy, often called 'unitary' or 'consensus' models, which require discussion to continue until some decision acceptable to all is reached, rather than discussion being terminated by an adversarial expression of will). The interests of minority groups should be afforded some protection: the idea of democracy should not include the tyranny of the majority. A range of basic civil liberties, e.g. of speech and assembly, must be maintained. The possible effects of improper influence on the voter should be minimized: this is usually taken to imply the secret ballot, limitations on electoral expenditure, and laws regulating mass media communications during the election period.

These criteria will be ranked differently in order of importance by different analysts. In addition, no actual political system will clearly and unarguably satisfy every one of the criteria: various intermediary organizations with varying degrees of power will, for instance, intervene between citizen and governmental decision. Because of these, the application of the term 'democracy' to any existing state will always be open to argument. Liberal conceptions of democracy stress the value of individual rights and liberties, usually within the context of a system of representation through party electoral competition. Western theorists generally stress those criteria associated with an equal opportunity to influence the decision-making procedures. Others, including some socialists and Marxists, may regard such procedural criteria as of little consequence, so long as exploitative class relationships and inequality of actual political power remain: the interests of the people (interpreted and acted upon by the ruling party), not their actual choices, are treated as paramount. These conceptual differences underlie the different terms, 'liberal democracy' and 'people's democracy', the former being used to characterize political systems like those of the western European states and the USA, the latter being used (usually by sympathizers) to denote the type of system practised until recently in the socialist states of eastern Europe.

Empirical investigations of democracies include: studies of voting behaviour and party competition; examinations of the impact of pressure group activity; and, usually comparative, studies of the factors thought likely to generate and sustain a stable democratic system. Theoretical work includes: the construction of ideal types of democracy and its various forms; normative analysis of the values associated with democracy; and rational choice models of electoral behaviour and democratic decision making. See also: *aristocracy; autocracy; consociational democracy; dictatorship; direct democracy; egalitarianism; majority; oligarchy; participation; polyarchy; populism; representation; rule of law; totalitarianism*.

Democratic socialism See: *social democracy*.

Demography The study of the statistical aspects of human population, especially the analysis of the numbers and distribution of population in a specific territorial area: the age and sex compositions of populations; their marital, occupational and other relevant social characteristics; size of family units; birth, death and migration rates; and changes in all these over time. From such studies demographers have observed the economic, social and political causes and effects of changes in the characteristics of populations, and have developed a range of special mathematical techniques for analyzing their data.

Dependency theory A blanket term used to denote a number of theories offering similar explanations for the continuing economic, political and social problems of the third world, particularly Latin America. Dependency is said to exist when the economic system of a country is internally fragmented and its key elements more connected with, and therefore more affected by, external factors such as the decisions of multinational companies, the needs of the developed capitalist countries, and changes in the international capitalist system. Dependent economic systems therefore lack the capacity for autonomous development and are unresponsive to state programmes for widespread and general modernization. Industrialization occurs only in certain specialized sectors and the benefits of economic growth are not widely shared. Divisions within the society are deepened and the prospects

prospects for stable democratic government are diminished. See also: *colonialism; political development*.

Determinism Generally, the belief that all events may be subsumed under a set of laws and are governed by the forces so described. In political analysis the term is used more narrowly to denote the belief that events can be sufficiently explained by reference to laws or causes in one particular sphere, other factors being irrelevant or secondary to the primary determining set. Thus some varieties of Marxism (and some readings of Marx) are described as 'economic determinism' or 'technological determinism', suggesting that the explanation offered for all political and social phenomena is reduced to the effects of economic forces or technological developments. Other forms of determinism have been based on race, religion, climate and family structure.

The principal difficulty for determinist accounts lies in establishing a clear distinction between the determining and the determined factors. For instance, Marx held that 'relations of production' determined legal and political structures, yet property relations arguably belong to both the determining and determined categories. See also: *explanation; law (a): scientific law; Marxism; reductionist theories*.

Devolution The delegation of specific powers to some subordinate unit of government, e.g. the control of certain functions of government by the Northern Irish government and legislature prior to the assertion of direct rule by the British government in 1972. It is thus a more limited and specific term than decentralization, and the fact that the central government retains a constitutional and legal right to withdraw or vary devolved powers differentiates it from the territorial distribution of powers within a federation. See also: *federation*.

d'Hondt method The d'Hondt method is a way of calculating how seats in a legislature, or other elective offices, should be distributed among candidates from party lists (or lists based on some other criterion) in a proportional representation system of election. It is named after its inventor, Viktor d'Hondt. The Federal Republic of Germany employed this method for elections to the Bundestag 1949-83, but has since used the Hare-Niemeyer method of allocation of list seats.

The total number of valid votes for each party list is divided successively by 1, 2, 3, 4, ... etc. The quotients so produced for all the parties are ranked in order, and the available seats are allocated to the parties in the order of these quotients. As an example, suppose ten seats are to be distributed among five party lists, and 120,000 valid votes have been cast:

Party A	Party B	Party C	Party D	Party E
48,000*	30,000*	24,000*	12,000*	6,000*

Dividing these by 2, 3, and 4 (there is no need to go further in this case) would produce the following quotients to add to those represented by the totals above:

24,000*	15,000*	12,000*	6,000	3,000
16,000*	10,000*	8,000	4,000	2,000
12,000*	7,500	6,000	3,000	1,500

The ten seats would therefore be allocated to those quotients marked by an asterisk (*) and would result in Party A receiving four seats, Party B three seats, Party C two seats, and Party D one seat. If only five seats had been available, Party A would have had three seats and Parties B and C one seat each.

This system of distribution may give different results at the margin which are more favourable to larger parties than other systems of allocating seats. See also: *proportional representation*.

Dialectic Originally meaning the art of criticism and argument, this term is now applied to a range of positions on the dynamic nature of consciousness and reality and on their mutual relation. Thought and therefore history (Hegel), or history and therefore thought (Marx), or all material processes (Engels), proceed and develop through the generation and resolution of contradictions. Some Marxists and a small number of other political analysts use the term to mean, more loosely, that all political phenomena should be conceptualized in terms of their relation to a complex and changing social totality. See also: *contradiction; Marxism*.

Dictatorship A form of political rule by one person, who governs unrestricted by legal, constitutional or conventional constraints. Dictatorship is thus a variety of autocracy. Dictators usually obtain power by unconstitutional, often violent means, and retain it by force. The rationale offered by the dictator for the assumption of power, its continuation and the violence necessary to preserve his rule is generally the supposed existence of internal dissension or external threat. The problem of legitimacy is often met by resort to plebiscites, the drafting of new constitutions, etc. Leadership succession is always a problem for dictators, since any designated successor may prove a threat to the power and rule of the dictator, and any introduction of a formal process of leadership succession could be employed to replace the dictator.

There is a special category of constitutional dictatorship, in which a dictator assumes emergency powers under legal and constitutional provisions in time of crisis, for limited periods. The original provision for dictatorship in the republican constitution of ancient Rome, and the powers contemplated under Article 48 of the Weimar Constitution in Germany after the first world war were examples of this.

Non-constitutional dictators have included: Julius Caesar, Oliver Cromwell, and General Franco. See also: *absolutism; autocracy; leadership; plebiscite; totalitarianism*.

Direct democracy Rule by the people of a state, town, or other political community or institution, by means of their direct, unmediated participation in decision making, rather than through the election of representatives. Direct democracy has been limited in the past to communities which have been small enough to permit citizens to meet together in one place. Thus it has been associated with some of the Greek city-states in ancient times, township meetings in some parts of New England, some of the smaller cantons in Switzerland, and parish meetings in small rural communities in Britain, as well as with institutions such as student unions in universities, and trade union branches in business enterprise. Modern interactive communication techniques would, were it desired, now allow for large numbers of citizens to vote directly on proposals in their own homes, by means of television, but this would be costly and time consuming, and would remain only a reactive form of decision making. Devices such as the recall, initiative and referendum have been used to modify representative democracy by an admixture of direct democracy in some states and substate organizations. See also: *democracy; initiative; recall (a): the institution; referendum.*

Dirigisme See: *interventionism.*

Disjointed incrementalism See: *incrementalism.*

'Dries' See: *'Wets and Dries'.*

Droop quota A method of calculating an electoral quota under a single transferable vote electoral system. The quota (Q) is derived by dividing the total number of valid votes (V) by the number of seats to be filled (S) plus one, and adding one to the result. As a formula:

$$Q = \frac{V}{S+1} + 1$$

This calculation produces a number representing the smallest whole number of votes which will elect, say, four members in a 4-member constituency, but will not elect five. For example, if 80,000 valid votes are cast in a constituency to elect four members, the quota is 80,000/5 plus 1 = 16,001. Only four candidates (and not five) arithmetically can obtain this quota. See also: *electoral quota; single transferable vote system.*

Due process A term adopted from the fifth amendment of the US constitution, but applicable in all states which respect the rule of law, signifying that no person should be subject to penalties or disadvantage through the operation of state power against that individual, except by strict adherence to constitutional and legal procedures. This includes in particular all the requirements associated with the notion of a 'fair trial', including the right to hear and challenge evidence, the right to provision of qualified legal aid in submitting a defence, etc.

E

Economic theories of politics A general term for deductive approaches that produce models of political action based on the assumption of the rational pursuit of goals by individuals. Theories so designated have the same general character as those labelled 'rational choice' but most work referred to as 'economic' explicitly draws on the formal techniques of analysis developed by economists. See also: *game theory; political economy; rational choice analysis.*

Egalitarianism Most simply, the belief that individuals are, or should be treated as, equals. The most common respect in which this belief is held relates to equality of political rights, including rights to participate in political activity, and equality of treatment by the law. The term is also used for beliefs in equality of a more extensive sort: equality of opportunity to pursue goals; equality of reward, including material welfare, status, power, etc. See also: *civil rights*.

Election A method for the selection of persons to fill certain offices through choices made by an electorate: those qualified to vote under the rules and procedures of the electoral system. Elections are *direct* when the votes of the electorate are given for candidates for the office concerned, but are *indirect* when the electorate first chooses representatives or delegates, who then choose from the candidates for office. Elections may also be *single* or *multiple*, depending upon whether the election is to fill a single office (such as electing a member to the House of Commons from a constituency) or to elect several candidates at once (the annual elections to the National Executive Committee at the Labour party conference in Britain, and certain local elections in the United Kingdom and the USA, for instance). See also: *electoral college; electoral system; indirect election; psephology; voting*.

Electoral college A body of electors charged with the responsibility of electing to some office, and themselves usually chosen by a wider electorate, though in some cases the members of an electoral college may be appointed or serve ex-officio (e.g. the College of Cardinals which meets to elect a new Pope). The president and vice-president of the USA are elected by an electoral college, whose members are themselves elected in each state by the voters. The president of Germany is elected by a special electoral college, consisting of members of the lower chamber of the national legislature (the Bundestag) together with an equivalent number of members of Länder parliaments. The president of France under the constitution of the Fifth Republic was elected in 1962 by an electoral college of local dignitaries and the members of the French parliament, but the constitution was then changed to allow direct elections. The leader and deputy-leader of the British Labour party are elected by a special electoral college representing Labour MPs, the local constituency party organizations, and the affiliated trades unions. The nominating conventions of the parties in the USA which select presidential and vice-presidential candidates could also be regarded as electoral colleges, since the delegates are elected by party members or sympathizers to fulfil that function. See also: *election; indirect election*.

Electoral quota Electoral systems involving multimember constituencies or party lists, based either on proportional representation or preferential voting, require a method of allocating seats among parties or candidates according to the votes cast for them. The method adopted for such allocation is the electoral quota, meaning the minimum number of votes required which a candidate must receive in order to be declared elected, whether in a constituency or as one of a party's list of candidates.

There are many different types of electoral quota. For proportional representation systems using party lists, the method of simple division of the number of votes cast by the number of seats available can produce a quota for each party (a party list with a quarter of votes cast obtains a quarter of seats available), but this leaves a problem of how to treat fractional entitlements. The d'Hondt system is one kind of quota which deals with this problem by dividing votes cast for each party list by successive integers: 1, 2, 3, 4, ... etc. Seats are allocated to the highest quotients resulting. The Saint-Laguë method is similar to the d'Hondt system, but uses integers of the series 1, 3, 5, ... etc., and thus increases the number of seats obtained by the parties with the largest numbers of votes. The Hare-Niemeyer quota, which replaced the d'Hondt quota for federal elections in West Germany from 1987, calculates for each party the result of the product of the total number of seats available multiplied by the votes cast for that party, and this calculation is then divided by the total number of votes cast. The result is the number of seats which that party obtains (further calculations being used to deal with fractional entitlements). For the single transferable vote system of election, the Droop quota is generally used.

The calculation of the quota may be complicated in proportional representation systems by the imposition of a requirement that a party list must secure some minimum percentage of the vote before it qualifies for distributed seats (as in Germany).

The term 'electoral quota' is also used to refer to the standard by which redistricting of constituencies is carried out, based usually on some average number of voters per constituency. See also: *apportionment; d'Hondt method; Droop quota; electoral system; Hare-Niemeyer method.*

Electoral system The method by which votes in an election are translated into seats, for legislatures and other elected institutions. While institutional arrangements such as the franchise, scheduling of elections, the time of day during which polling stations are open, methods of registration of voters, arrangements for proxy and postal voting, etc., may be regarded as part of the electoral system (and, in certain cases, affect turnout, and the outcome of elections), it is more usual to confine analysis of electoral systems to the methods of counting votes and allocating seats to candidates and party lists.

The wide variety of electoral systems, currently in use (see Geoffrey Hand et al., eds, *European Electoral Systems Handbook*, London, Butterworths, 1979), tried in the past or designed for the future, can be classified into three broad categories. Majoritarian systems elect candidates by the simple procedure of counting votes and giving seats to those with the largest number of votes. Either a simple majority suffices (as in elections to the House of Commons in the United Kingdom), or some sort of qualified majority is required (as in the second ballot system used in France for the 1988 elections to the National Assembly and for presidential elections). Preference systems are designed to allow voters to express a preference among candidates, and such preferences are used to redistribute votes as necessary. The alternative vote system used for elections to the Australian lower house and the single transferable vote system (STV) used for legislative elections in the Republic of Ireland and Malta fall into this category. Proportional representation systems endeavour explicitly to relate in an equitable manner the share of votes each party receives, and the percentage of legislative seats each then obtains. Usually, but not inevitably, such systems involve party lists. See also: *additional member systems; alternative vote system; apportionment; constituency; cumulative vote; election; electoral college; electoral quota; franchise; gerrymandering; indirect election; majority; preferential voting; proportional representation; second ballot system; single transferable vote system.*

Electoral volatility The measurement of electoral change between two successive elections, indicated by the sum of changes in votes received by parties, taking into account changes in the total electorate through the addition of new cohorts of young voters and the death of other voters (as well as through migration into and out of the constituency), and the transfer of electors from and to the category of non-voters. An apparently small net change in voting for parties (aggregate volatility) may in fact disguise a high degree of individual-level volatility if mutually cancelling gross changes are large. See also: *party identification.*

Elite Originally meaning the selected or chosen, now the 'select' or 'choice' minority within a social collectivity (e.g. a society, a state, a political party) which exercises a preponderant influence within that collectivity, usually by virtue of its actual or supposed special talents. An elite which exercises preponderant *political* influence is called the ruling or political elite.

New members of elites are recruited by various processes, depending on the culture of the society and the nature and requirements of the ruling elite. Birth, educational attainment, professional ability, the acquisition of wealth, and the control of strategic political resources have all been major recruiting qualifications. Thus the common character of the ruling elite may be that of a caste, an aristocracy of some sort, or a ruling class.

Elite theories (or 'elitism') take two distinct forms, though both may be combined in the work of some writers. The first: normative elitism, argues that only a group possessing special talents can manage the affairs of society so as to maintain order, promote development, etc. The second: empirical elite theory, regards the character and behaviour of elite groups as the crucial factors in political analysis, and maintains that some form of elite domination is inevitable no matter what egalitarian aspirations or democratic forms the society may exhibit.

The general view that political power is always concentrated in the hands of an elite, sometimes referred to as the 'elite hypothesis', is in danger of identification with the uninteresting observation that far fewer people govern than are governed. It is widely, but by no means universally, held that to give the hypothesis some specific empirical substance, three conceptual requirements for the existence of an elite should be imposed: a group must possess self-identity; its members must act together; that action must be in pursuit of some common purpose. These requirements are usually summarized as group consciousness, coherence and conspiracy, or the 'three Cs'. Where those exercising political power fail to exhibit these characteristics, if for instance political power is subject to a continuously shifting division between competing elites pursuing different interests, the term 'the ruling elite' would generally be regarded as inappropriate, though analysis may still be focused on the competing *elites* of various subgroups.

Empirical studies which attempt to test the elite hypothesis, or which attempt to analyze elite behaviour, have often examined the politics of local communities. See also: *aristocracy; community studies; iron law of oligarchy; Marxism; oligarchy; pluralism; polyarchy; ruling class.*

Embourgeoisement A process in which individual members or sections of one class take on the attitudes and life-style of the bourgeoisie. Thus, in the industrialized countries many members of the aristocracy have been assimilated with the bourgeoisie through their participation in commercial activity. Similarly, those with a working-class background who occupy a position within the political elite may come to hold values more strongly associated with the bourgeoisie than with the class from which they have sprung.

In political analysis 'the embourgeoisement thesis' usually refers to the suggestion, in the 1950s and 1960s, that the more affluent of British workers could no longer be regarded as part of the traditional working-class and would therefore fail to support the traditional stance of the Labour party. See also: *capitalism; dealignment; elite; iron law of oligarchy; proletarianization; realignment; social class; socialism.*

Empiricism The belief that experienced phenomena, rather than theories or ideas, are the basis of knowledge, and that, at best, only those hypotheses, theories and scientific laws which are verified by observation should be included in the body of accepted knowledge within a discipline.

'Empiricist' is now often used critically when applied to some example of political analysis, implying that the work is 'merely empirical', lacks theoretical foundation, fails to go beneath the observable surface of phenomena, uncritically and unreflectively reports 'facts', etc. See also: *behaviourialism; positivism.*

Environmentalism An ideology which emphasizes concern for the natural and physical environment, and whose proponents seek to influence governments in order to institute measures to protect and improve the environment. Many environmentalists go beyond a 'first aid' approach, involving the processing of polluting by-products to minimize their adverse effects on the environment, and instead seek to develop a more radical approach to the whole economic and technological basis of society, to deal with sources of environmental hazard before they are produced at all, to develop the use of renewable or recyclable materials, and to encourage conservation of energy and raw materials. Growing out of local and regional interest groups and movements in, for instance, the USA, the Federal Republic of Germany, Britain and Switzerland, environmentalist organizations have in some cases moved more directly into the political arena by forming parties and offering candidates at elections. In the Federal Republic of Germany the Green party won seats in the Bundestag in 1983 and 1987, has been represented in most Länder parliaments, and has participated in coalition governments in Hesse, Lower Saxony and Berlin. The Swiss Ecological party has had electoral successes at national, cantonal and local elections. In Britain, Green party candidates have won seats on local government authorities. In the European Community, several representatives of Green parties have seats in the European parliament. However, interest groups involved with environmental issues, such as Greenpeace, still have a significant political role. Alongside other movements and ideologies, such as feminism and pacifism, environmentalism can be seen as deriving from a growing concern with post-industrial values among the populations of developed states. See also: *interest group; movement; overload (a): government overload; post-materialism.*

Equilibrium The state of balance or stability of elements of a system. A system is in equilibrium when its elements have, in themselves, no propensity to change their relations even though external (or 'exogenous') variations in conditions may produce change. Systems which maintain the same form, or the level of some particular variables, despite external disturbance, are described as 'homeostatic'. An equilibrium may be stable, returning to the same position following disturbance by external factors; unstable, not returning when so disturbed; or metastable, moving to a new equilibrium position.

In so far as the distinction between a system and factors external to it is a product of theoretical construction, not necessarily corresponding to degrees of isolation between a set of variables and its environment, a state of equilibrium may never actually obtain. Nevertheless, the idea of a tendency towards equilibrium may be analytically useful. See also: *adaptation; feedback; functional explanation; political system; structural-functional analysis; systems analysis; variables.*

Essentially contested concepts A term used by W.B.Gallie to clarify difficulties in the explanation of ideas like 'democracy' and 'Christianity', ideas whose histories comprise a series of radical disagreements about their basic meanings. Other writers have broadened the term to cover most, perhaps all, of the concepts used in political analysis.

It is argued that part of the essential meaning of a political concept is its expression of value. To describe something as an exercise of 'power', for example, is to say that it is a bad thing, in need of justification. People disagree about which things are good and which are bad. They will therefore disagree fundamentally about how 'power' is to be defined. According to this view any attempt to study politics objectively will fail because ideological contests are intrinsic components of the basic concepts. See also: *ideology; power; value judgements.*

Étatisme See: *interventionism.*

Ethnocentrism The tendency to analyze and assess aspects of other cultures by use of one's own culture as a frame of reference. In social science research, this may lead to erroneous conclusions being drawn and even to the application of the standards and values of one's own culture to the study and analysis of other cultures in a biased and improper fashion. Such bias may arise from an implicit or explicit belief on the superiority of one's own culture, and may in extreme cases be an expression of racism or xenophobia. In political science, ethnocentrism as a problem is particularly relevant in comparative research, international studies and studies of political development. See also: *racism; xenophobia.*

Eurocommunism See: *communism.*

Exchange theory An approach, often encountered in sociology but also associated with political analysis, which combines concepts and techniques drawn from both economic and psychological analysis. Political relationships are treated as embodying exchanges of valued non-material goods in the form of favours, concessions, ideas, etc., generating reciprocal relations such as those of obligation, esteem and trust.

There are obvious difficulties in using economic models to deal directly with diffuse and ill-defined 'psychological' values. Exchange theory is often criticized for redescribing political and social relations in an inappropriate and naively conceived language.

The approach has been applied to the analysis of political power and authority, and to the dynamics of change in groups such as political parties and bureaucracies. It is particularly associated with the work of George C. Homans and Peter M. Blau, the former placing more emphasis on the individual psychology of exchange, the latter attempting to bring economic concepts and tools more rigorously to bear on the workings of institutions. See also: *bargaining theory; behaviouralism; bureaucracy; clientelism; economic theories of politics; political psychology; utility; values.*

Executive In its broadest usage, the branch of government responsible for the implementation of policies and rules made by the legislature. It thus includes in its membership the head of the government (e.g. the prime minister, chancellor, or, in presidential regimes, the president) and that leader's ministerial colleagues, the political bureaucracy, whether permanent or politically appointed, and the enforcement agencies, such as the police and the armed forces. In a narrower sense, the executive is considered to be the group of politicians and senior civil servants who have responsibility for initiating and coordinating policy, and is thus almost a synonym for one usage of the term 'the government'.

Executives vary in composition, recruitment, powers and degree of responsibility (to a legislature, a constitution, or the people), depending on the regime. In one-party states, the most senior positions, in actuality if not always constitutionally, will usually be those of leaders of the party rather than the state.

In order to implement policies of the legislature, executives in some states and other political organizations (e.g. the United Nations, the European Community, local government authorities, political parties) are frequently given the powers necessary to make implementing legislation, generally called 'delegated legislation'. The executive may also possess quasi-judicial powers, exercised through the operations of administrative tribunals. See also: *administrative tribunal; bureaucracy; delegated legislation; government (a): the institution; separation of powers.*

Exhaustive ballot A method of voting involving successive ballots being held until one candidate obtains a specified majority: usually an overall majority of votes (over 50% of those cast), with the provision that candidates with the lowest votes on any round of balloting are removed from succeeding rounds. See also: *second ballot system.*

Exit One of a triad of ideas used by Albert O. Hirschman to analyze 'responses to decline in firms, organizations and states' in his book *Exit, Voice, and*

Loyalty (Cambridge, Mass., Harvard University Press, 1970). Faced with deteriorating performance, customers, members or citizens have two basic options: 'exit' – stop buying, resign, secede or emigrate; 'voice' – express dissatisfaction. Each of these will generate different pressures on the organization concerned. If 'exit' is easy, this will reduce the incidence of effective voice. To the extent that loyalty is present, exit becomes less likely and the effectiveness of 'voice' enhanced.

Exit poll See: *psephology*.

Explanation Explanations have been described as answers to 'Why?' or 'How?' questions. By itself, this is inadequate since it does not state the criteria for an acceptable answer to such questions. One of the most influential attempts to specify criteria by developing a general form of explanation is known as the 'deductive-nomological' (D-N), 'covering-law', or 'Popper-Hempel' model.

The D-N model consists of a universal law of the type 'Whenever conditions C occur, an event E occurs', together with a statement that conditions C did, in fact, obtain in the case to be explained. If the occurrence of an event can be deduced from these two components, then they comprise the explanation of that event. For instance, a law setting out the conditions under which revolutions occur, together with a statement that these conditions obtained in Russia in 1917, would allow the deduction that a revolution would occur and would thus explain the Russian Revolution.

It has been argued that *all* explanations, in whatever field of enquiry, should conform to this pattern. Even in the natural sciences this claim is implausible: many acceptable explanations do not follow this pattern; statements can be formulated which do satisfy its formal requirements but which clearly do not explain the natural phenomena to which they are directed. But nowhere is this claim more hotly contested than in political and historical enquiry. How, for instance, can one formulate a universal law sufficient to explain the Russian Revolution? If the conditions were formulated in terms sufficiently general to cover a number of other instances then the law would almost certainly be false since there would be cases where those conditions did not generate a revolutionary outcome. If, on the other hand, the conditions were more narrowly defined they might produce a trivial law, applicable only to the single instance of Russia in 1917. In such cases, adherence to the D-N model offers a choice between falsity and triviality. Similarly, political analysis (and everyday discussion) often focuses on one or more conditions which may be *necessary* for a particular event to occur but which cannot be sufficient. Successful revolutionary movements may require strong leadership, and thus strong leadership may be a necessary condition for revolution, but the satisfaction of this condition cannot guarantee revolutionary success and therefore cannot, by itself, provide a D-N explanation for revolution.

These problems suggest an alternative to the D-N model, an alternative frequently encountered in political science. Explanations, rather than being deduced from a universal law, may be inductively inferred from a statement of probability. This inductive-statistical (I-S) model replaces the universal law with a statement like 'conditions C are associated with event E in $x\%$ of

47

cases (and with some other outcome in 100-x% of cases)' or with a less precise statement that an outcome is likely. Thus the choice between falsity and triviality, referred to above, is avoided. Two main objections are raised against this form of explanation. Firstly, that if anything is explained it is our expectations of events rather than the mechanisms underlying the events themselves. Secondly, that if some propensity of the conditions themselves *is* referred to, then the lower probability outcome is as well explained as the higher, since both are claimed by the law to be produced by the given set of conditions.

A stronger response comes from those working within the hermeneutic tradition. The adherents to this position generally accept the D-N model as adequate for the explanation of natural phenomena but regard it as irrelevant to the human or social sciences. Human action is not law-governed (in the natural scientific sense) and explanation should therefore be focused on the reasons and purposes of actors. This focus produces a deep description of action against the background of the beliefs and social conventions of a particular society or epoch, a description which, it is argued, cannot be subsumed under the D-N model.

One of the fundamental difficulties is that models of the structure of explanation are confronted by propositions which *are* accepted as explanatory in some field of natural or social science but which do not fit the requirements of the model. Some philosophers of science have displayed considerable ingenuity in rewording these examples to fit their own preferred model of explanation or in reworking their model to cover the example. Others have responded with further counter-examples and objections.

In short, there is deep disagreement on fundamental questions such as 'What form should explanations take?' and 'Should explanations follow the same pattern in different fields of enquiry?'. In the light of this disagreement it is not surprising to find a range of different explanatory patterns on offer in political science, and also an increasing willingness on the part of individual analysts to be eclectic in their choice of explanations. See also: *functional explanation; hermeneutics; law (a): scientific law; teleological explanation; theory*.

Exploitation Generally, a process or relationship in which one person or group uses another for selfish advantage and without adequate reward.

In political analysis the term is most usually applied to economic relationships in which the labourer receives less than the full value of labour: in Marxist terms, 'surplus value' is extracted from that labour. Thus, under feudalism, a peasant may be required to transfer some portion of the produce of his land to the feudal lord, or to spend some portion of his time working on the estate of the feudal lord without direct reward. Under capitalism the extraction of surplus value, and therefore the presence of exploitation, is less manifest since the portion of unrewarded labour time is not immediately visible but only theoretically represented by the difference between wages and value produced. See also: *alienation; capitalism; communism; feudalism; Marxism; social class; socialism*.

Externality Externalities are costs or benefits that are not subject to market transactions between producer and consumer. For instance, airport operators produce such costs in the form of noise imposed on the surrounding population, and perhaps also produce benefits for local traders selling goods to those travelling to and from the airport. To the extent that these costs and benefits are not reflected in the producer's decisions, the utility of all concerned may not be maximized by market mechanisms. Governments may therefore attempt to regulate the production of externalities, often under pressure from those suffering costs. See also: *public goods; utility*.

F

Fabianism As a general term, any strategy of gradualism and the avoidance of decisive confrontation (after the policy of the Roman general, Fabius Maximus). More particularly, the term refers to the philosophy of the Fabian society in Britain (founded in 1884), which considers the proper strategy for socialism to be the use of existing political institutions, the permeation of existing political organizations, the gradual introduction of reform, and the promotion of a moral consensus. Although in principle anti-authoritarian and certainly concerned with the democratization of both political and economic institutions, Fabians have frequently been accused of viewing socialism as an efficient means of central collective administration with little real need for extensive democratic participation.

Fabianism has been influential in the British Labour party, mainly through the reputation and proposals of its founders and early members, such as the Webbs and G.B. Shaw. Although an affiliated organization from the inception of the party, the Fabian society has never acted collectively as an organized pressure group within the Labour party. It has never, for instance, submitted a collective policy proposal to the party conference. Its chief role has been as a source of ideas. See also: *social democracy; socialism*.

Faction A section of some larger group, usually a political party, which has a separate identity from the larger group without normally possessing separate formal organizational status, and which pursues aims distinguishable from those of the larger organization. Such aims may include a separate set of policies, the advancement of a particular political or electoral strategy, a distinctive ideological position, the bestowal of patronage to supporters or clients of the faction, or the career advancement of a political leader. A faction is usually organized less formally than the main group. It will often cooperate within the main group for the pursuit of collective goals (e.g. in the case of a faction of a political party: electoral campaigning on a united basis, solidarity in opposition to other parties, or subscription to a basic ideology). If, however, differences between a faction and the main group become too great, such cooperation may prove impossible, and the faction may choose, or be forced, to create a separate organizational structure (for example, the extreme left-wing Independent Social Democratic party in Germany during the first world war, which broke away from the Social Democratic party). The extent to which political parties are subject to factionalism varies from country to country and over time. Some parties (e.g. the Japanese Liberal Democratic party and the Italian Christian Democratic party) possess a kind of organized and permanent factional structure, based on personalities more than on policy differences, and this encourages clientelist relations.

Examples of factions: the Liberal-Unionists associated with Joseph Chamberlain in the late nineteenth century; the Bevanites and Powellites in postwar British politics; groupings within the Indian Congress party; 'realist' and 'fundamentalist' factions in the West German Green party.

In the eighteenth and nineteenth centuries faction was also a term used, in criticism, to apply to organized opposition, especially as indication that such opposition was contrary to the public welfare or national interest (e.g. as used in *The Federalist Papers* in the USA, or in British parliamentary rhetoric of the period). See also: *clientelism; party*.

Falsificationism The doctrine that scientific theories should be formulated so as to yield clear and definite propositions which logically could be falsified by observations of the world. Thus the statement 'All ravens are black' is not scientific simply because we may observe many black ravens: any finite number of observations would fail to confirm this universal hypothesis concerning *all* ravens. The statement is scientific because it would be falsified by the observation of a white raven. The most useful theories will be those with the highest degree of falsifiability: those yielding the clearest and boldest propositions. Scientists hope, of course, to develop theories which are, in principle, highly falsifiable but which, in fact, resist attempts to falsify them.

Science, thus distinguished from unfalsifiable non-science or 'pseudo-science', consists of a process of conjecture and attempted refutation of hypotheses. A hypothesis which survives attempts at falsification may be provisionally accepted but remains conjectural and cannot be regarded as the proven truth since its survival is contingent upon the degree of ingenuity displayed by scientists in devising tests, and on the validity of a host of assumptions which must always underlie such tests.

Falsificationism is synonymous with the work of Sir Karl Popper. Political scientists have often paid lip service to his ideas but theories that clearly satisfy the requirements of these ideas are rare. See also: *explanation; hypothesis; law (a): scientific law; positivism; scientific method; theory; verification*.

Fascism A political ideology derived originally from the Italian Fascisti movement led by Benito Mussolini, which took power in 1922. The Italian model directly influenced similar political movements in Germany (especially the National Socialist – Nazi – movement and party), Spain, France, Britain and many other European countries, and movements which have some similar principles to pre-war fascist parties can be found in many industrialized states since the second world war.

The main principles of fascism must be inferred from the policies and activities of the movements, since only rarely can coherent expressions of fascist ideology be found (as contrasted to rhetoric concerning opportunistic aims and policies). Such principles include some form of extreme nationalism, in some – but not all – cases combined with racism; uncompromising hostility to communism; opposition to parliamentary democracy, liberalism and the market economy; glorification of a leader, whose 'will' is regarded as law; a disciplined state order, in which secondary groups are subjected to control by the movement or party; populist political appeals and mobilization of mass demonstrations of support; expansionist foreign policies, in the name of national self-protection or economic betterment; and sometimes a glorification of a past, often mythical, culture in place of the 'bourgeois' culture of modern society. It was essentially and unapologetically an 'irrational' ideology (and here its contrast to Marxism is especially marked), with its emphasis on emotion and feeling as social forces and the elevation of the 'will' of the leader to the status of supreme law. Despite this contrast with Marxism as practised by communist states, observers have remarked on the essential similarity of political methods used by fascist and communist regimes for attaining, exercising and preserving power.

Though seen by some interpreters as a class phenomenon (especially by Marxist commentators, who view it as an extreme expression of capitalist and anti-working-class interests), fascism as an ideology appears to have been hostile to all classes as such, seeing them as disruptive of the unity of the state and society which fascism sought to promote. Other interpreters have viewed fascism as a historical phenomenon, explicable only in terms of the particular economic and social conditions of the inter-war years. It is certainly not applicable as a label for every nationalist, racist or anti-communist movement or party in the twentieth century and perhaps hardly appropriate as an accurate description of any significant right-wing political group since the end of the second world war, though some would regard the Peronist regime in Argentina (1946-55) as fulfilling most of the criteria of a fascist regime. Certainly 'fascist' is often misused as a pejorative term to denigrate political opponents, especially by groupings on the extreme left, through which usage it loses all utility as a description to distinguish a particular type of political movement.

Despite its glorification of the past, fascism has been regarded as a modernizing force in many of the states where it has been influential, in so far as it has challenged entrenched traditional interests and procedures, offered a strong sense of national identity, and emphasized the need for efficient social organization. See also: *corporatism (a): ideology; movement; social class; society; state; totalitarianism.*

Federation A state in which there exists both a central government and a set of provincial governments, and where each of these two levels of government is sovereign within its own sphere, normally according to and safeguarded by a written constitution. This constitution will list the competences of the two levels of government, and will usually make arrangements for allocation of residual powers, and for coordination where competences overlap, as well as allocating adjudicatory responsibility to a constitutional court or other institution to make binding decisions where conflicts arise concerning the interpretation of the constitutional allocation of powers. Generally the national legislature in a federation will possess a second chamber, in which the component provinces (variously called cantons, republics, Länder, states, etc.) will have direct and often equal representation. Both levels of government will possess taxing powers and powers of law enforcement.

The degree or style of federalism differs quite markedly among federal states. Switzerland and the USA are usually regarded as countries in which federalism is most strongly displayed. Australia, Brazil, Canada, Germany and India are other important examples of federal states. Some states possess federal constitutions, but for various reasons (such as the overriding political role of an ideologically based party, as in the USSR) cannot be regarded as being federations in practice.

The federal form of state develops for a number of reasons, among them the need to integrate disparate ethnic, linguistic, religious or other territorially identifiable groupings (e.g. India, Switzerland); to govern a territorially dispersed population (e.g. Australia, Brazil, Canada); or to avoid over-centralization of political power (e.g. the Federal Republic of Germany). See also: *confederation; devolution*.

Feedback A concept utilized in systems and communications approaches to political analysis. Feedback is a term used to indicate the process of conveying information about the state of the political system, or some specific element within it, or about the environment of the system, to structures within the system in such a way that the future action of those structures is modified in consequence. The results of such modification may then in turn, through feedback, produce further modifications, and so on.

A feedback channel is any medium through which information may pass regarding the state of the system or a structure within it, to some other structure which is capable of modifying the behaviour of the system or any of its structures. Feedback channels to and from the adjusting structure of the system combine to form feedback loops: circuits of information channels through which information is conveyed regarding the state of a structure within the system and those through which responsive information is conveyed to adjust the condition of that structure. The pattern of communication between a party headquarters and its component constituency party organizations may constitute such a feedback loop, for instance. See also: *functional explanation; overload (b): communications overload; political system; systems analysis*.

Feedback channel See: *feedback*.

Feedback loop See: *feedback*.

Feminism An ideology involving concern about, and striving for, the equality of women in society, based on the assumption that women are not, and have not been, treated equally in relation to men. Historically, feminism was associated with struggles for voting rights (e.g. the suffragette movement in Britain and similar movements in for instance the USA, France and

Germany) and with abolition of legal, economic, social and cultural barriers to female equality in society.

The contemporary feminist movement contains within it proponents of several different sub-categories of feminism: including, for example, Marxist feminists, who see in class relations and economic exploitation the causes of sex discrimination and in the class struggle the best opportunities for achieving women's rights; liberal feminists, who welcome the emphasis of liberalism on the equality of individuals regardless of sex, race, creed, etc., and who look to institutional change as a means of achieving such equality; and varieties of radical feminism, some of which contemplate the separate development of feminist social organizations as the only way to overcome fundamental biological and psychological barriers (unmodifiable by institutional or economic change) to women's equality, and which have emphasized the political aspects of the private and personal sphere as relevant to feminist concerns.

The feminist movement has acted as a separate political force in many countries, but has also been associated with various parties and political groups (socialist parties; Green parties; the peace movement; etc.). Political reforms (e.g. voting rights for women; constitutional and legislative provision for sex equality), social and economic changes (e.g. greater access to higher education; removal or diminution of formal career barriers to women; the spread of contraception techniques) and cultural developments have stimulated the growth of feminism even as the more immediate aims of the feminist movement have been achieved in many countries, leading to a focus on issues such as the overriding rights of women in relation to reproduction (including the issue of legalized abortion), and the publication or display of pornography. See also: *movement*.

Feudalism A system of social organization found for instance in Europe between about AD 900 and 1500, and in Japan up to the latter part of the nineteenth century. Feudalism is characterized by: an economy based on agricultural production; a complex network of reciprocal rights and obligations, among a hierarchy of classes, concerning matters of land tenure, military service, justice and order; weak monarchical rule; a landed aristocracy possessing wide discretionary powers within its own domains; a peasantry restricted in its freedom of movement, and paying feudal rent in the form of labour, agricultural product, money, or some combination of these.

No actual society exhibited purely feudal relations. In parts of western Europe, for instance, mobility of labour, commercial relations, and a flourishing merchant class, were increasingly marked during the 'feudal period'. The development of these features, together with other economic, political and military imperatives, led to a transition from feudalism to the modern state and commercial society. See also: *capitalism; industrial society; state*.

Filibuster A speech of extraordinary length by a legislator, intended to obstruct proceedings. It has been common in the US Senate and House of Representatives, and in the House of Commons, though revision of the rules in these and other legislative chambers in order to limit the length of speeches or to allow them to be terminated by motions from other legislators, have made the filibuster less available as a means of procedural obstruction.

Franchise The legal right held by an individual or a group to vote in elections. Thus extensions of the franchise beyond the property-owning classes, to women and to people attaining the age of eighteen have been stages of democratization of the franchise in Britain, for example. See also: *civil rights*.

Free trade International exchange of goods and services, unimpeded by protectionist measures (such as customs tariffs, subsidies, import quotas, unnecessarily severe and selective administrative regulations, domestic preference in the awarding of government contracts) designed to favour domestic producers and shield them from foreign competition. Free trade between countries is held by its supporters to maximize the overall advantages gained from specialization in production, though some economists have argued that protectionist measures are, under certain conditions, beneficial. Still more controversial is the question of the share of advantage, if any, gained by individual countries, particularly those countries (e.g. in Latin America) dependent on the production and export of raw materials. Whatever the rights and wrongs of economists' arguments, there may be strong political reasons for protecting some sector or region.

Most countries are now members of one or more trade alliances or customs unions, allowing relatively free trade between members while erecting barriers against non-members. Attempts more broadly to regulate and diminish protection are made through the General Agreement on Tariffs and Trade. See also: *dependency theory; interventionism; liberalism*

Function See: *functional explanation*.

Functional explanation Explanation of a phenomenon by reference to some effect the phenomenon produces where that effect is not necessarily intended by those involved. For example, that giraffes have long necks might be explained by reference to long necks enabling them to feed on the leaves of trees. Here no design is imputed but rather that long necks perform a function crucial to the survival of the organism. Similarly, the existence of liberal-democratic forms of state might be explained by reference to the capacity of such states to promote the interests of the capitalist class. Again it may be that the implied explanation is not in terms of the *pursuit* of interests by the capitalist class but that the satisfaction of such interests is a function necessary for the continuation of the system, and that its performance is brought about by some other force or mechanism. In both examples it appears that any explanatory force, if it is not gained from design or purpose, must depend on explicit or implied reference to some process of selection operating on the system. Biological examples of functional explanation usually depend on some theory of natural selection or law of 'the survival of the fittest'. Since adequate specification of such mechanisms presents considerable difficulties for social science, functional explanations are often regarded as radically incomplete or just non-explanatory.

Functional explanation is sometimes criticized for its alleged tendency to neglect power and conflict in treating existing institutions as contributors to the harmony of the system. While this may be a just criticism of some writers, particularly those who assume that all aspects of society can and must be explained in terms of their functional contributions, it should not be treated as an intrinsic tendency of functional explanation. Marx, for instance, could hardly be accused of stressing harmony or neglecting power and conflict, yet a fairly plausible case can be made for the centrality of functional explanation in his writing.

A more general problem is raised by the relation between 'function' and 'system'. The identification of functions only has meaning in reference to the system within and for which the function is performed. The precise specification of a social or political system, clearly identifying the boundaries between the system and its environment, is a supremely difficult task. To the extent that such specification is lacking, the identification of functions and their performance must lack explanatory power and, at the extreme, be meaningless. 'Functionalism' in social science originally denoted a strong commitment to social explanation in functional form. Over the last forty years it has come to be applied more loosely to any approach which examines institutions and practices in terms of their consequences for the social system, whether or not those consequences are used to explain the institution or practice. Functions that are intended or at least recognized by members of the system are sometimes described as 'manifest', unrecognized or unintended functions as 'latent'. Functions tending to the destruction of the system are described as 'dysfunctional', functions aiding persistence or adaptation as 'eufunctional' or simply 'functional'. See also: *explanation; structural-functional analysis; teleological explanation; variables*.

Functional representation See: *representation*.

G

Game theory Often called an 'economic' theory of politics, but in fact emerging from the discipline of mathematics rather than economics, game theory provides a means by which strategic decisions are modelled and analyzed. A scenario is described in which the outcome is dependent on the choices made by each of two or more players. These players make rational choices between strategies in an attempt to maximize their utility 'pay-off' or to satisfy their highest possible ranked preference. Analysis is primarily directed towards the identification and elucidation of a solution: the outcome that would result from the choices of rational actors. Game theory may involve very sophisticated mathematical techniques but the essence of most games commonly cited in political analysis can be conveyed more simply. A game known as 'prisoners' dilemma' illustrates some of the central features:

Game theory

Two prisoners are held in separate cells, unable to communicate with each other. They have been caught illegally carrying guns, an offence for which they are likely to receive a one year prison sentence. They are also suspected of armed robbery but the prosecutor has insufficient evidence to secure a conviction on this charge. He offers each of them a deal: 'If you confess to your joint involvement in the robbery and your partner does not then you will be released without charge while your partner will carry the whole blame, probably receiving a ten year sentence; if your partner confesses and you do not then you will receive that sentence and your partner will go free; if you both confess you will both receive a moderate sentence; if neither confesses then you will both be convicted on the minor charge and each will receive a light sentence.' The game can be represented thus:

| | | Prisoner B | |
		No confession	Confession
Prisoner A	No confession	-1,-1	-10,0
	Confession	0,-10	-6,-6

Each player has a choice between confessing and not confessing; there are therefore four possible joint outcomes, represented by the four boxes within the matrix. Each box contains the pay-off, for that outcome, to each player (A,B). Pay-offs may be represented as cardinal utilities (as above) or outcomes may be ordinally ranked according to the preferences of each player. Games are described and classified according to certain characteristics, e.g. as zero-sum or non-zero-sum, as fixed or variable sum, as cooperative or non-cooperative. The Prisoners' Dilemma is 'non-zero-sum' (each pair of pay-offs does not add up to zero, therefore one player does not simply gain what the other loses); 'variable sum' (the outcome totals vary from choice to choice); and 'non-cooperative' (the players cannot communicate or make binding agreements with each other).

This game represents a significant problem. Each prisoner will recognize that, whether the other confesses or not, he can reduce his sentence by confessing (from one year to zero, or from ten years to six). It therefore appears individually rational for each to confess. Yet in so doing they will fail to achieve their mutually preferred outcome and will each serve six years in prison rather than one. The same outcome will occur even where communication is possible, to the extent that each cannot trust the other to make the cooperative choice of non-confession. If the same players are engaged in a *series* of such games, cooperative strategies may rationally be adopted. Otherwise, some agency enforcing binding agreements is necessary. Mutual cooperation is a public good which, in this context, is not provided by the voluntary actions of rational individuals.

The game is thought to resemble many situations in politics where the preferences of actors are similarly structured: voluntary restraint in pay claims; cease-fire negotiations; arms control; over-exploitation of natural resources; and, most fundamentally, the need for the state itself.

Game theory's strengths parallel its weaknesses. It allows clear rigorous analysis of some features of strategic choice but often seems to offer a simple abstract and closed picture that must be very imperfectly analogous to the complexity and openness of actual decision-making. See also: *bargaining theory; coalition; conflict approach; decision-making analysis; side payments; simulation; public goods; rational choice analysis; utility*.

Gaming See: *simulation*.

Gatekeepers There are two associated but distinct meanings. In theories of bureaucracy, gatekeepers are those bureaucrats who control access to public services (e.g. discretionary welfare benefits). In systems theories (especially those associated with David Easton) gatekeepers are the intermediary organizations, such as parties and interest groups, which link the public to the authorities, by collating, aggregating and sorting demand-inputs, which those organizations then transmit to the authorities. See also: *systems analysis*.

Geopolitics The study of the interrelationship of the geographic environment (particularly the physical, ethnic, economic, demographic and ecological aspects of that environment) with the state, and especially with the policies of the state. Foreign policies of states , and the conflicts which result from these, are of special interest to those who use geopolitical modes of analysis.

The term can also be used to refer to an ideological view that emphasizes the deterministic effects on politics of geographical factors, including effects on the political development of states and racial groups within states. Such an ideological position was, for example, influential within the National Socialist movement between the two world wars. See also: *determinism; political geography*.

Gerrymandering A term of American origin which refers to the improper and 'artificial' designation of constituency boundaries to increase the likelihood of a party or faction securing more seats in an election than would otherwise have been the case. It has at times been prevalent in various states of the USA, where redistricting occurs after each decennial census, and was used in Northern Ireland local elections to reinforce the Protestant electoral majority prior to the termination of devolved government in 1972. The term derives from a particularly blatant effort to secure such party advantage by Governor Eldridge Gerry in Massachusetts in 1812, where one district in particular was so artificially designed as to take on the shape of a salamander (hence 'gerry-mander'). See also: *apportionment*.

Government (a): the institution Those institutions which make and implement rules in the form of binding decisions for a political community: whether a state, a city, a province, a tribe, or any other organization. The word also refers to the activity of governing: i.e. of making rules, implementing them and providing arbitration concerning their implementation. These activities of government are often referred to as the legislative, executive and judicial functions.

In a narrower sense, the word may refer to the executive branch alone: as in reference to the Conservative government in Britain or a coalition government in the Netherlands, though such a context may include the idea of legislative support for the executive government also.

Government (b): the study area

    The type of government possessed by a state or other political entity is sometimes called its regime. See also: *executive; judiciary; legislature; regime; separation of powers*.

Government (b): the study area The study of government has often been regarded as equivalent to the study of politics, and is often found as an earlier synonym for 'political science'. Indeed, some university departments of political science are still called 'departments of government'. More precise usage limits the word to refer to those aspects of political science concerned directly with the personnel, activities and institutions of government, and usually of state government at that. In contrast, political science may be taken to include, in addition to the study of government, study of parties, interest groups, and various aspects of political behaviour, as well as the politics of non-state organizations.

    The term is also sometimes used to differentiate the study of the institutional aspects of politics from the study of political ideas, whether historically or as political philosophy. See also: *political science*.

Group theory An approach to political analysis based on the premise that the group, rather than the individual or the state, is the basic unit of political activity, since individuals in politics act in groups and their behaviour is affected, some might even say determined, by group structures, norms and goals.

    The first major statement of the group approach was made by A.F.Bentley in *The Process of Government*, (Chicago University Press, 1908). The core ideas were further developed in the political science of the 1950s and 1960s, most notably by David Truman in *The Governmental Process*, (New York, Knopf, 1951). A 'group' may be defined as 'a mass of activity' (Bentley), or a relatively persistent pattern of human activity and interaction. Accidental collectivities such as crowds, or analytic collectivities such as married men or new voters are not groups within the terms of these definitions. 'Interests' are defined as 'activity directions' or 'policy attitudes' of groups; interests which are not manifested in group activity are only significant through their potential for group formation, as the need for certain policy changes becomes greater. The state is seen as a source of policy outputs, the content of which reflects the balance of group pressures at any one time.

    Group theory stresses the dynamic aspects of politics as activity and of government as process. It rejects analysis based on formal, legal and constitutional categories, as well as those concepts like 'national interest' which impose normative standards not necessarily manifest in group activity. It attempts to capture politics 'as it really is' by restricting its attention to the actual group activity taking place, rejecting concepts like Marxist 'class structure' as too narrowly focused on a single reference-point and insufficiently concerned with actual conflict between groups.

    Major criticisms of the approach focus on the difficulty of defining the concept of 'group', without making it so general as to be meaningless; its tendency to treat individuals and the state as channels through which group activities flow; its denial of any unity or reality to society and the public interest; its difficulty in satisfactorily accounting for individual political behaviour, especially in terms of the psychological determinants of that behaviour. Nevertheless, group theory has exerted considerable influence over the development of political science, particularly in the USA. Many of its tenets have been absorbed by the behaviouralist and pluralist approaches, and its impact has been partly responsible for the proliferation of interest group studies. See also: *behaviourialism; interest group; interests; organization; pluralism; political behaviour; social class.*

Guild socialism See: *anarcho-syndicalism.*

Hare-Niemeyer method A method of calculating how seats in a legislature, or other elective offices, should be distributed among candidates from party lists (or lists based on some other criterion, such as territorial divisions) in an electoral system based on proportional representation. It was developed by Thomas Hare, and elaborated by Horst Niemeyer. It was used in the Federal Republic of Germany for elections to the Bundestag in 1987, in the 1990 Volkskammer election in the German Democratic Republic, and in the first all-German legislative elections in 1990, for instance.

The method operates as follows: the total number of seats to be allocated (S) is multiplied by the number of valid votes received by a party (PV), and the product of that calculation is divided by the total number of valid votes cast (TV). The formula is thus:

$$\frac{S \times PV}{TV}$$

Seats are allocated to parties in accordance with the whole numbers resulting from this formula, and any seats remaining unallocated are then distributed to parties which have the highest decimal fractions after the whole numbers. As an example: suppose four parties contest an election for eight seats, with the following votes: Party A = 6600; Party B = 4800; Party C = 3100; Party D = 1500 (total votes cast = 16000). Applying the formula, the results are:

	Party A	Party B	Party C	Party D	
	3.30	2.40	1.55	0.75	
seats per whole number	3	2	1	0	(=6)
two seats for remainders	0	0	1	1	(=2)
totals	3	2	2	1	(=8)

The d'Hondt method in this case would have allocated Party A four seats, Party B three seats, Party C one seat and Party D no seats, because the d'Hondt method tends to favour larger parties at the margin, the Hare-Nie-meyer method smaller parties. See also: *d'Hondt method; electoral quota; electoral system; list system; proportional representation.*

Head of state The occupant of that political office which is responsible for acting as leading representative of the power and authority of the state, as indicated by such functions as the formal declaration of war or a state of emergency, the appointment of the prime minister and other members of the government, the award of honours and formal assent to legislation. These functions vary from state to state, but are basically similar in most cases. In some states, the head of state is also the head of the government (as in the USA and in some autocracies, and, to an extent, in France).

The head of state may attain that position by right of birth (e.g. the British monarch), be chosen by some group (e.g. a general following a military coup), be elected either directly (e.g. the president of France) or indirectly (the president of Germany), or be imposed by an external force. The term of office may be fixed and limited, or be for life. The extent to which the powers of the head of state are limited by law and custom vary from state to state, but also within one state vary over time (e.g. the decline in the powers of the British monarch since the eighteenth century; the expansion of the powers of the US president since Washington's presidency). See also: *leadership; monarchy; sovereignty.*

Hegemony Most simply, predominance of one element of a system over others; for example of one state over others in the same confederation or region. Current usage, influenced by the work of Gramsci, most frequently refers to the position of a dominant class which exercises control through its ability to achieve acceptance of a particular set of cultural values and norms. Such a class need not exercise control through the defeat of political and economic challenges. The accepted world-view of the society may prevent the emergence of such challenges. The incorporation of the concept of hegemony broadens the scope of political analysis in examining the means by which ideological consensus is achieved and maintained through socialization, education and forms of communication. See also: *consensus; ideology; Marxism; norm; political socialization; power; social class.*

Hermeneutics The study of society through the re-interpretation and analysis of the meaning of social action. The subject-matter of the human sciences is, by its very nature, already interpreted by social actors and cannot be regarded in the same way as the natural world. On these grounds hermeneutics rejects models of enquiry and explanation drawn from the natural sciences and attempts instead to understand the social world as the product of human thought and purpose. For instance, instead of attempting to establish the causal factors associated with the rise of German fascism (military defeat, economic slump, political polarization, etc.), the hermeneutical approach attempts to understand the attitudes, beliefs and culture that developed during the fascist period and to make sense of fascist political activity in terms of the motives and reasons of the relevant actors. Work within the hermeneutical tradition has been more common in continental European than in British or American political science but its arguments are of general importance for social science and its influence is significant, particularly in significant, particularly in the analysis of ideology. See also: *explanation; ideology; scientific method; teleological explanation*.

Heuristic See: *theory*

Hierarchy The ranking of persons or political offices on the basis of the authority or political power each one possesses. Thus there are hierarchies within the British cabinet, including the ranking of ministers in the official published list of members of the government, the central committee of the Communist party of the Soviet Union, the party organizations of the US Senate, etc. Informal hierarchies may exist as well as formal ones, e.g. in the political system of international organizations such as the UNO, or in a local community, where the most powerful political actors may hold relatively lowly positions in terms of formal political office (or, indeed, hold no office at all).

The term is also applied in a collective sense to those occupying the most powerful positions within an organization, such as the Roman Catholic hierarchy, which includes the Pope, the Curia, the College of Cardinals, etc. See also: *status*.

Historical sociology See: *political history*.

History of political ideas See: *political thought*.

Human rights See: *civil rights*.

Hypothesis A conjecture, directly or indirectly testable, usually offered as a partial explanation of an event. Thus 'hypothesis' may cover: broadly, both 'theory' and 'law' to the extent that these are offered as provisional explanations and are open to test; more narrowly, a proposition deduced from a theory for the purposes of testing the validity of that theory under a specific set of conditions. The term is also used loosely to describe both an assumption and an imagined, non-actual, set of conditions regarded as 'merely hypothetical'. See also: *axiom; empiricism; explanation; falsificationism; law (a): scientific law; positivism; theory; verification*.

I

Ideal type The main focus of an analytic method particularly associated with Max Weber. The diversity and complexity of the social world is confronted by the construction of ideal types, conceptions expressing a range of alternative forms of thought, action, organization, etc., as a set of extreme limiting cases or pure forms, each embodying different essential principles. Concepts of competition, rationality, capitalism, and forms of authority have all been developed as ideal types.

Actual phenomena are classified according to their greater or lesser correspondence to the idealized conceptions but analysis goes beyond classification in its concern with the nature and significance of differences between actual phenomena and ideal type. Since an ideal type will never purely or simply correspond to actual phenomena it cannot in itself be the subject of empirical laws. This gives rise to difficulties in assessing the validity of such analysis.

The use of ideal types has been criticized for encouraging the researcher to describe the respects in which the actual political world fails to conform to some arbitrary idealization rather than, from the outset, trying to get to grips with the world as it really is. This criticism is countered by the requirement that ideal types should not, in general, depart too greatly from the actual world cases to which they are related and, more tellingly, by the insistence that the explanation of any actual historical event should include an elimination of those factors which initially appear to be possible causes but which are not actually involved. For example, the common pluralist assumption that shared individual interests produce group organization in pursuit and defence of those interests is challenged by ideal type models of rational action which demonstrate the barriers preventing the collective pursuit of shared goals. In practice, it may be difficult to decide whether a particular analysis deals with ideal types or with 'real' theoretical constructs and laws. Thus it is a matter of some controversy whether Marxism (or indeed Marx) depends upon ideal types: the conception of a capitalist mode of production, and the 'laws' governing its development, for instance. See also: *authority; capitalism; classification; law (a): scientific law; Marxism; model; paradigm (a): general usage; pluralism; public goods; realism (a): scientific realism; typology*.

Ideology Originally (in the 1790s) the name for a deterministic science of human thought and ideas, the term now denotes the primary values, assumptions and beliefs which people possess and which enable them to impose some kind of mental order on the diverse individual and social experiences that they meet. Explicit and distinct political doctrines (e.g. conservatism, fascism, liberalism, socialism) are frequently referred to as ideologies but the term may be used to describe sets of ideas more general and less publicly espoused than these. 'Ideology' may be distinguished from simple reference to 'a collection of ideas' by certain features of usage. An ideology is the property of a group (a class, a party, an elite, a society, or the inhabitants of an epoch): a particular and unique ideology is not usually attributed to a single individual. An ideology comprises ideas so basic to the outlook of its holders that they will frequently be unaware of its nature: it engenders habits of thought and perception that impede reflective self-awareness. Ideologies contain values which serve as justifications for action or which legitimate social and political arrangements. The component ideas are sufficiently coherent to leave the mind undisturbed by contradictory judgements and demands. Together these features comprise a description of the kinds of basic beliefs, identification of which may be important for understanding or explaining political activity. Such a description implies that 'ideology' is merely a useful concept, applied neutrally in political analysis.

However, in much political discourse to describe a view as ideological, or an action as ideologically inspired, implies criticism: that the view of the world produced by ideology is false, or partial and one-sided, or serving some particular interest (those holding the ideology, of course, may take the view to be true, complete and neutral). The precise nature of the criticism will vary according to the view (or perhaps ideology) of the critic. A conservative will usually mean that the view or action issues from some all-embracing dogma which aspires to the status of universally applicable theory and is insufficiently sensitive to the particular needs of the moment or the particular traditions of the society. A Marxist will generally focus on the function of the view or action, its tendency to support existing arrangements and to offer a favourable, or at least neutral, picture of class domination, and on its representation of some historically particular phenomenon as if it were universal and unchanging, e.g. the norms of bourgeois society treated as 'human nature'. Some writers, most notably Karl Mannheim, have used 'ideology' to denote sets of ideas that justify and reinforce an existing social order, preferring to describe as utopian those ideas with a transforming effect. It is nevertheless common to find both sorts of ideas referred to as ideology. Despite the commonly implied distinction between science and ideology it is sometimes argued that, since all attempts to understand politics must be rooted in a particular political outlook, all political explanation has an ideological character. See also: *hegemony; legitimacy; norm; utopianism; values; value judgement.*

Impeachment Accusation before a competent tribunal of some public official for crimes of, for example, impropriety, misdemeanour or corruption in the exercise of office. In Britain, where the House of Lords tried such cases following accusation by the House of Commons, the last recorded case was in 1806. In the USA impeachment is provided for under both federal and state law. At the federal level, the House of Representatives prepares articles of impeachment and the Senate acts as the tribunal. The case of the impeachment of President Andrew Johnson (1868) is the most famous. Impeachment is rarely used as a remedy nowadays, being replaced by alternatives, such as action in the civil courts or the resignation of the incumbent from office, which was the method by which President Nixon avoided impeachment proceedings in 1974.

Imperialism The policy or practice of one state imposing its rule over another state or territory, not necessarily contiguous or ethnically similar, for the purpose of economic advantage, military security, international prestige, or in pursuit of some ideological aim. Such an expansion of rule establishes an 'empire'.

Imperialism is usually distinguished from colonialism in one of two ways. Politically, 'imperialism' generally implies some political integration of the subject territory with the sovereign power such that citizenship is extended to all inhabitants of the empire. Economically, 'imperialism' is often used to denote a stage in the development of capitalism when economic conditions in the advanced capitalist countries lead those countries towards expansion abroad. This latter use, particularly associated with Lenin, is better regarded as a particular hypothesis concerning the causes of late nineteenth and early twentieth century colonialism than as a general definition or theory of imperialism.

The term is also extended, loosely following Lenin's usage, to denote economic domination: of former colonies by their respective former colonial powers; and of poorer by richer countries, even in cases where no direct military or political intervention occurs. The terms 'neo-colonialism' and 'neo-imperialism' are frequently, but not always, used in this regard. See also: *citizen; colonialism; dependency theory; sovereignty*.

Incrementalism A style of policy-making marked by its concern with relatively small-scale goals and the solving of immediate problems, paying particular attention to the political feasibility of solutions in the light of existing policy and the strategic positions of affected groups. Change comes about in the form of piecemeal responses to particular tasks, each decision making some small alteration to the context of future decisions and therefore making an incremental contribution to cumulative change. In so far as such a process is not subject to systematic coordination, and decisions do not reflect one specific and fixed set of values, the policy-making style may be described as 'disjointed incrementalism'.

Incrementalism may be contrasted with 'rational' decision-making: selection of the policy which, from an exhaustive list of alternatives, maximizes the satisfaction of an ordered set of ultimate values; and with 'satisficing': the examination of alternatives until one is found which produces a tolerable level of satisfaction. See also: *decision; policy; policy analysis*.

Index numbers The quantification of change in some variable, such as the rate of inflation, gross national product, or a party's share of the vote in a series of general elections, by which the state of the variable as measured at an initial point in time is given a value of 100, and subsequent changes are expressed as percentage increases or decreases on this base (e.g. an increase of 40% from the base date would be expressed as 140). A set of measurements can be taken for periods before the base date, as well as after it. Index numbers can be used for comparing changes in two or more variables over a period by basing them on their state at a base date, and expressing changes as relative percentages, e.g. in population size and national income, or in unemployment rates in two different occupations. Such comparisons can also be made between the states of the same variable in two or more different countries. See also: *misery index*

Indirect election A process of election whereby office-holders are elected by a group of electors (such as the Electoral College for presidential and vice-presidential elections in the USA) who are themselves directly elected: thus the office-holders may be said to be indirectly elected by the larger constituency (in the USA, by the whole electorate). See also: *electoral college*.

Individualism The doctrine that the aim of society should be the satisfaction of individual ends, rather than some notion of the 'public good' or 'collective interest' which is not reducible to individual ends. Or the belief that collective interests or individual ends, or both, can best be satisfied through individual choice, as far as possible unconstrained by collective decision-making or state control. See also: *collectivism; liberalism; reductionist theories*.

Industrial society A society in which the style and shape of social, political, economic, and legal institutions are substantially affected by the dominant position of industrial production in the economic order. In such a society, agriculture has declined as a source of employment; urbanization has arisen from the concentration of large numbers of workers near factories and associated places of employment; family and class structures, and occupational divisions, reflect the influence of industrial production.

Politically, industrial society may or may not be democratic, but the existence of large concentrations of population will mean that the masses become a significant political factor. Generally, politics will reflect the influence of trade unions and industrialists, an extended franchise, and the formation of mass parties. The diversity of industrial society will give rise to numerous political interests, which may be represented by political parties, lobbies, interest groups, or (in one-party states, for example) by informal groupings. From the 1960s onwards, the more advanced capitalist countries appeared to some analysts to be developing features beyond those associated with industrial society. The concept of 'post-industrial society' was developed in an attempt to describe the sorts of conditions and changes present or presaged in these societies. The main features include: a shift away from manufacturing towards service industries; the growing importance of knowledge and technical control; the emergence of relatively widely held values of a non-acquisitive kind; and, consequent on all of these, changes in social and class structure producing a shift away from traditional class politics. See also: *capitalism; convergence thesis; dealignment; mass society; post-materialism; modernization; political development; social class; state socialism*.

Influence See: *power*.

Initiative Proposals for the introduction or repeal of legislation or for the amendment of a constitution, which derive from the electorate rather than from legislators or the executive. Use of the initiative is usually conditional upon obtaining a minimum number of signatures of electors or of a specified fraction of the electorate. A majority – possibly a special majority – of the electorate must then vote in favour of the measure in a referendum for the proposal to be adopted. The initiative is thus a form of direct democracy, and is used in, for example, Austria, Italy, some states and local government areas of the USA, and in the cantons of Switzerland. See also: *direct democracy; referendum*

Institution A network of structures, procedures and shared values within a social system, which persists over a period of time, and which is concerned with some social function or group of functions. Examples of institutions which have political functions are: the Supreme Court of the USA (the functions of conflict resolution and authoritative interpretation of the constitution); the United Kingdom parliament (functions of rule-making and control of the executive, among other things); the electoral systems of democratic regimes (functions of political recruitment and selection for authority roles).

Insurrection Armed resistance against governmental authority and its executive agents, for purposes of, for example, opposing the imposition of legal constraints, overthrowing the government, or weakening its authority. See also: *coup d'état; putsch; rebellion; revolution.*

Integration See: *political integration.*

Interest group An organized group which has as one of its principal purposes the exercise of influence on political institutions, in order to secure decisions favourable to the interests the group represents, or to discourage decisions from being taken which would be unfavourable to those interests. Compared to a political party the major distinguishing features of an interest group are: the restricted range of policies with which it is concerned, compared to the universal range of concerns of a party; the rarity with which an interest group will contest public elections in its own name, and then only as a method of exercising political influence; its intention of exercising influence, whereas a party seeks to exercise political power. But some organizations are on the margin, exhibiting features of both a political party and an interest group.

An interest group – sometimes termed a 'pressure group' to reflect its activity of exerting 'pressure' on agencies of government – differs from a lobby, which has the sole purpose of influencing legislation or the execution of policy, whereas an interest group usually has other purposes as well, such as providing services or news for its members. An interest group differs from an 'interest' in so far as it is organized, whereas an 'interest' (e.g. consumers, old age pensioners, single mothers) may be unorganized yet still politically influential.

The targets of interest group activity will vary according to the political system concerned. Where the power of the legislation is strong in relation to the executive, it will be subject to greater and more varied types of influence from interest groups than in countries where a strong executive dominance exists (e.g. contrast the US Senate with the British House of Commons). The degree of party discipline within the legislature is also an important factor, as strong party discipline lessens the opportunity for interest groups to exercise influence on legislators successfully. Occasionally the judiciary may be regarded as a target for interest group activity, especially where judicial interpretation or judicial review have political significance. An example is the campaign for civil rights conducted, in part, through the US courts by groups such as the National Council for the Advancement of Colored People. In totalitarian systems interest groups will be weak or non-existent, since extra-party political activity will be prohibited, but this will not prevent certain interests (such as the military) from exerting influence.

Methods of interest group activity will also vary, depending as they do on the opportunities afforded for access to political decision-makers. Among methods found in most industrialized countries are: public meetings and demonstrations; personal letters to politicians; letters to the press; committee negotiations; petitions; deputations to government agencies; the election of sympathetic candidates or the recruitment of existing legislators; cooperation with official institutions in return for favourable treatment by those institutions; and various forms of participation in election campaigns. See also: *interests; lobby.*

Interests Individual, group and class interests play an important role in political analysis. An interest is an advantage or benefit gained from some action or outcome. To say that something is in someone's interest may be distinguished from that person's wants or desires: I may want to go to the cinema tonight though it is in my interests to write an essay. Here some notion of prudence, rational calculation or attention to long term goals enters the assessment of interest but may be absent from the feeling of desire. Thus persons may perceive their interest in attaining some goal despite their failure to manifest it in their behaviour. A distinction of this sort would be acceptable to many analysts although some would argue that interests must be treated as revealed preferences, manifested in actual behaviour.

Still more controversial is the idea of *objective* or *real* interests. Unlike the example cited above someone might be unaware of these interests or consciously opposed to them. It might be argued that, as a member of an occupational group or a class, a person shares the interests of that group in pursuing its collective goals irrespective of perceived wants and interests. Analysis in terms of real interests is supported by the view that individuals would perceive such interests if their perceptions were not subject to manipulation by others, or that they will come to recognize those interests at some future time, or simply that objective characteristics rather than subjective perceptions are the more fruitful concepts on which to build political analysis. A number of different objections have been raised against these views: to talk of interests in this way is at best metaphorical, since many of the actual characteristics of the individuals concerned are being disregarded or overridden; more worryingly, the idea of real interests seems to license either tyranny on the part of political leaders or the arbitrary imposition of values by political analysts, or both. In each case the desires and perceived interests of individuals or groups are being discarded in favour of someone else's judgement of what is good. While it may be possible to establish that given individuals would have different perceptions of interests in circumstances at variance with their actual experience it is difficult to justify the selection of *one* set of alternative circumstances that can be said to give rise to perceptions of *real* interests. Finally, notions of class based on objective interests have come under especially heavy attack. To the extent that such interests are not manifested in actual behaviour they are thought by some to be irrelevant to any analysis of the actual political world.

Perceived interests may form the basis of a demand for action within the political system. Shared interests may generate organized groups making joint demands on specific issues (e.g. the Campaign for Nuclear Disarmament) or representing the shared interests of groups over a wide area (e.g. occupational groups like the British Medical Association).

It is common to talk of organized groups as agents of interest aggregation and articulation. The perhaps diffuse and various opinions and resources of individuals are aggregated through group organization and distilled into coherent demands for action, sometimes called 'issues'. See also: *behaviouralism; interest group; issues; power; structuralism*.

Internal colonialism See: *colonialism*.

International politics The political aspects of relationships between states, including the international institutions and processes through which such relationships are conducted. Such relationships may be cooperative, competitive or conflicting.

Various approaches have been developed to study international politics. These include the power approach, conflict approaches, systems analysis, institutional approaches, policy analysis, communications approaches, and the application of formal models such as those used in game theory. Gaming, simulation and case-study methods have also been used as aids to study and for the testing of hypotheses concerning international politics. Subjects of interest in the study of international politics include the making of foreign policy, and the institutions through which it is made operational (formal diplomatic channels, propaganda media, international agencies, etc.); the relationships between diplomatic and military-strategic policies; the functioning of the international political system, and of various subsystems contained within it (e.g. alliances such as NATO; regions such as Latin America or the Middle East); war, including its avoidance, political prosecution and terminal settlements; relationships of power and influence between states (e.g. in bipolar or multipolar power distributions); the organization and functioning of international political institutions; supranational political communities (e.g. the EEC). See also: *alliance; bloc; case-study method; communications approach; conflict approach; game theory; gaming; international relations; simulation; systems analysis.*

International relations The relationships between states and their peoples, which concern the policies they adopt toward each other with regard to their national interests; the methods of contact and communication used (including warfare, economic sanctions, propaganda, etc.); the operation of international institutions; the formation of alliances, coalitions and blocs; the development of international law; and the identification of the economic, social and political customs and conventional practices which exist.

It is an interdisciplinary field of study, involving particularly political science, history, law, economics, social psychology and sociology. The study of international politics is a major part of the study of international relations. See also: *international politics.*

Interpellation A device used in some legislatures for the purposes of obtaining information from a minister by means of a formal, written question regarding some aspects of policy or administration for which the minister is responsible. It is more formal and important than an oral or written question during 'question time' (where such an institution exists). Generally, the question must be notified to the minister several days in advance, and there may be other requirements such as a minimum number of supporting signatures from members of the legislature. The standing orders of the legislature will state whether, and under what conditions, debate or a vote may occur following a reply to an interpellation.

The device was employed in the French Fourth Republic, and is still used in the Italian and Swiss legislatures and, in the form of a 'major question' (*grosse Anfrage*), in the German Bundestag.

Interventionism The policy and practice of government regulation and control of economic affairs, beyond what is necessary for the maintenance of a market framework and for the raising of revenue. Intervention may range from subsidy and price control to nationalization, and may be directed towards domestic production or foreign trade. The French expression *dirigisme* is sometimes used to denote such a policy. 'Statism', or the French '*étatisme*', is similarly applied, but may alternatively refer to a broader emphasis on the role of the state in social change.

The term is also used to characterize a foreign policy of active, particularly military, involvement in the domestic or international affairs of other states, especially where no immediate interest of the interventionist state is directly affected. See also: *corporatism (b): ideal type; free trade; isolationism; liberalism; nationalization; new right; privatization; state capitalism.*

Iron law of oligarchy A proposition, put forward by Robert Michels in 1912, most succinctly expressed as, 'Who says organization, says oligarchy', implying that the forces at work within organized groups will produce elite domination of that group. Although intended to apply to all organization, much of the theory underlying the law is derived from Michels's analysis of political parties: parties pursue complex goals, technical expertise and leadership are therefore essential; command over organizational resources reinforces the position of incumbent leaders who thus escape control by, and accountability to, the membership; parties require mass support, leading to the dilution of doctrine; leaders become ideologically and materially separated from ordinary party members; these tendencies to drift away from the original goals of the party towards the career-oriented goals of the leaders are reinforced by the political apathy and deference of most party members and voters. See also: *elite; embourgeoisement; oligarchy.*

Isolationism The advocacy and practice of a foreign policy of withdrawal from international politics and neutrality in international disputes, at least in so far as these do not impinge on any immediate or vital interest of the nation concerned.

Isolationism has been a recurrent issue in US politics, producing strong opposition to the policies of President Woodrow Wilson after the first world war. As a practised doctrine, isolationism is associated with the foreign policy of the USA, outlined in 1823 by the Monroe doctrine and intermittently followed thereafter. This doctrine was isolationist in a limited sense, being as much concerned to assert rights and responsibilities of the USA over the whole of the Americas, and to exclude European intervention in that region, as to prevent the USA from becoming entangled in global political conflict. See also: *interventionism.*

Issues Matters about which there are two or more different sets of attitudes, and which thus may give rise to conflict. Of course, only a minority of different attitudes will give rise to actual conflict, and in turn, only a minority of these will manifest conflict which is carried into, and is perhaps resolved by, the political system. How 'political issues' should be defined and identified in political analysis is therefore a matter of dispute. In research into political power, for instance, pluralists have tended to adopt a behaviourialist approach, concentrating on political issues identified through manifest conflict which commands the attention of significant elements of the political system. By itself, this seems a narrow basis for research since it ignores the problem of attitudes, wants, interests, etc., which may fail to command attention.

'Issue voting' is a phrase sometimes used to describe voting choice determined by identification with specific policies adopted by the competing parties, contrasted with voting determined by habitual party loyalty. 'Position issues' are those on which competing parties adopt different policy positions. 'Valence issues' are those which embody no ideological disagreements between parties, and where voting choice reflects some judgement of the superior competence or preferred style of the chosen party. See also: *agenda setting: behaviouralism; cleavage; dealignment; non-decision; party identification; pluralism; realignment.*

J

Judicial legislation Rules, declarations or judgements promulgated by members of the judiciary, which have the effect of adding to, or changing, the content of the law. This may be the result of previous ambiguity inherent in a statute, which is then resolved through litigation. Judicial legislation is associated especially with aspects of judicial activism: the tendency of some judges to go beyond declaring a statute or governmental decision to be unconstitutional, and to suggest boundaries within which amended provisions of statutes or decisions would be constitutionally acceptable. An example was the series of decisions of the Constitutional Court in the Federal Republic of Germany in 1958, 1966 and 1968 concerning appropriate forms and levels of state subsidy to political parties. See also: *judicial review; judiciary; law (b): stipulative law.*

Judicial review The process whereby a court or tribunal consisting of members of the judiciary decides on the constitutionality of laws, rules, decrees or actions of the legislative or executive branches of government. It is thus one method of settling disputes concerning the interpretation of written or unwritten constitutions, but is not found in all states, since it depends upon acceptance of the independent status of the judiciary and respect for its decisions. In the United Kingdom the doctrine of parliamentary supremacy prevents such disputes of interpretation arising (though the judiciary may be required to pronounce upon, for example, the validity of ministerial decisions in relation to parliamentary legislation or common law); in one-party states the settlement of disputes is usually by party fiat; in theocracies the priesthood regard themselves as the sole and proper interpreters of the law and hence of its constitutionality. Judicial review is found especially in federal states, where it is used to adjudicate on constitutional disputes regarding the division of central and local powers. It is thus important in the USA (where the Supreme Court assumed the power of judicial review in the important judgement of *Marbury v. Madison*, 1803); in Germany, where the Basic Law (Art. 93) provides for a Constitutional Court to review the constitutionality of legislation and other such matters, such as the constitutionality of political parties; Australia; and India. It exists also in, for instance, Japan and the Republic of Ireland, and in the European Community. Courts exercising judicial review may be either constitutional courts, solely concerned with questions of constitutional law (e.g. Germany) or supreme courts, as in the USA, which also serve as the highest court of appeal for non-constitutional cases. See also: *constitution; constitutional law; judicial legislation; judiciary.*

Judiciary The judiciary is the branch of government responsible for interpreting authoritatively the laws made by the legislature and administered by the executive branch, or adopted under international agreement (as with member states of the European Community), in cases where disputes arise relating to the meaning, validity, or supposed breach of such laws, and then for taking decisions concerning outcomes of such disputes, such as the imposition of sanctions (fines, imprisonment, costs, damages). In most politically developed states, the judiciary consists of professionally trained judges, appointed or, in some cases, elected, though some judicial systems provide also for the presence of lay assessors on the bench. The selection of judges, their relations to the political process, the effects of their decisions on the law, and the factors which influence judicial decision making, have all been topics of interest to political scientists. See also: *administrative law; administrative tribunal; judicial legislation; judicial review; law (b): stipulative law; legislature; separation of powers..*

L

Law (a): scientific law A statement describing invariant and universal, or probabilistic, relations between classes of phenomena, accepted as true on the basis of evidence. Universal laws describe all instances of the class of phenomena without regard to time or place, e.g. 'Whenever or wherever x occurs, then y occurs'. Probabilistic (or statistical) laws identify the frequency of the occurrence of relations, e.g. 'Condition x is associated with condition Y in 95% of cases'. Probabilistic statements are often treated as laws even when less precisely formulated, e.g. 'The development of democracy is usually associated with early moves towards commercial agriculture'. Laws constitute a basic component of most forms of explanation; sets of laws, systematically combined, form the core of theory.

Laws of nature may be distinguished from analytic statements, statements true by definition rather than by the nature of the world, e.g. 'All governments exercise political power'. Scientific laws are also distinguished from empirical generalizations, statements identifying only accidental properties of a class, e.g. 'All American presidents are (happen to have been) male'. Such distinctions may appear plausible but in fact raise a host of problems in the definition and identification of scientific law. In particular, it may be very difficult to distinguish between statistical *laws* and accidental statistical generalizations.

Political science has produced few, if any, propositions that clearly meet the formal requirements for a scientific law and are sufficiently well corroborated to command general acceptance. See also: *explanation; falsificationism; hypothesis; theory; verification.*

Law (b): stipulative law Rules stipulated or posited within a political system, prescribing conduct for the whole community or some identified part of it, and recognized as legitimate. Laws of this kind, sometimes referred to as positive laws, do not describe (contrast *Law (a): scientific law*), but command, and are supported by coercive sanctions such as imprisonment or loss of property, as imposed by judicial authorities. Law may emanate from the will of an individual sovereign, from a legislative assembly, or from the custom and practice of the community. See also: *authority; coercion; custom; judiciary; legislature; legitimacy; positivism; rule of law; sovereignty.*

Law (c): natural law A system of moral rules, held to be binding on all humankind irrespective of the laws and conventions of particular communities, universally recognizable through the use of reason. Natural law theories, from those of ancient Greece to those of the present day, have been used to provide external criteria for assessing the legitimacy of positive laws. In the modern period, natural law theories have been frequently associated with ideas of natural rights and the development of liberalism. See also: *civil rights; legitimacy; liberalism.*

Leadership Leadership is a pattern of behaviour which has as its purpose the organization and direction of the efforts of a group towards desired ends. Political leadership is found where those desired ends are political. It is situational behaviour, in that leadership is dependent on specific configurations of a leader, followers, goals and methods of goal attainment within a particular environment. The acceptance of leadership by followers depends on their regard for the legitimacy of the leader, as well as on, for example, the likely efficacy of leadership, and this legitimacy may depend upon the leader's occupancy of a formal authority role. Weber's classificatory scheme of ideal types of leadership underlines the varieties of bases for leadership acceptance. Weber distinguishes charismatic leadership, when leaders are obeyed because they are thought to possess extraordinary or magical attributes; traditional leadership, when the leaders are obeyed because they occupy some status in society which has previously been entitled to obedience, for instance by birth into a dynasty or some ruling class; and legal-rational leadership, based on authority arising out of a rationally established set of rules and procedures.

As well as the basis of leadership authority, leadership styles also vary. Some leaders are persuasive, others forceful, yet others conciliatory, and the study of such different styles is one field of political psychology. Efficacy appears to depend less on the possession of any one style than on an ability to choose and adapt styles in the context of task, means available, and attributes of followers. The differences between Trotsky and Stalin, Churchill and Attlee, Roosevelt and Truman, Brandt and Kohl, illustrate the varieties of leadership style and levels of leadership success available in modern states.

Recruitment of political leaders is provided for in different ways in different political cultures. Patterns of education, differences of social class, types of leadership position available, and limitations imposed on would-be recruits (women, members of ethnic or religious minorities, people under a certain age): all affect the availability of leaders. But it is important to note that both formal and informal processes affect leadership recruitment, and also that the demands of a crisis may permit the rise of leaders who otherwise might not have been considered for such positions, e.g. Hitler, Churchill, de Gaulle. See also: *authority; charisma; dictatorship; elite; ideal type; legitimacy; political psychology; ruling class*.

Legislature The institution of government which has the power of making, amending and repealing laws for a society. It may be elected, appointed or hereditary in composition, or some mixture of these. It may consist of one or several chambers: in most states a bicameral form of legislature is preferred. Having regard to the principle of the separation of powers, many states have different principal institutions for legislation and administration; politically, however, it is difficult to maintain an absolute distinction of function, and delegated legislative powers are often given to executive bodies. See also: *bicameral; delegated legislation; executive; separation of powers*.

Legitimacy A characteristic of the exercise of political power when that power is believed to be in accordance with certain principles and practices. The term may be applied normatively, positively, or descriptively: normatively when power is judged worthy of acceptance according to some coherent set of standards, such as right or justice; positively when power is exercised within the limits laid down by law and constitution, by the persons and according to the procedures so prescribed; descriptively when power is more or less generally accepted, by those over whom it is exercised, to be in accordance with whatever principles they happen to hold. Political science is primarily concerned with the beliefs and practices actually present within a system, and so uses 'legitimacy' principally in the descriptive sense. The exact nature of the principles and practices that confer legitimacy vary from society to society, and over time: divine authority, natural law, constitutional settlement, the rule of law, democratic decisions or elections, and hereditary descent, being common examples.

Legitimacy is crucial for the operation of government, and for the survival of the political system. All government depends on some belief in its right to exercise power, even though that belief may never be unanimous and may sometimes be limited to key elements of the state apparatus. Governments will therefore seek to justify the form and content of their rule by reference to those principles that seem most cogent. The production of appropriate beliefs, whether by the conscious creation of ruling groups or by unintended social processes, is referred to as 'legitimation'.

Legitimation is never finally achieved. For legitimacy to survive legitimation must be a continuous and continually modified process, as new generations are socialized into political life, and as circumstances change. This raises problems. A regime may, for instance, derive legitimacy from its consistency with some particular ideological principle concerning the proper relationship between government and economic institutions. But faced with economic difficulties, certain otherwise satisfactory measures may threaten the legitimacy of the regime: for instance, when liberal-democratic governments pursue interventionist policies, or when communist governments attempt to liberalize the economy. If pursued, such policies will weaken legitimacy, increase the visibility of inequality, exploitation, and the tendency of government to favour particular interests, and, in extreme cases, engender a 'legitimation crisis' that threatens the very basis of the regime. Like legitimacy itself, the legitimation process enables political power to be routinely exercised, but also imposes constraints on its exercise. See also: *authority; constitution; contradiction; hegemony; ideology; law (b): stipulative law; law (c): natural law; leadership; political socialization; power; state.*

Leninism See: *bolshevism.*

Liberalism A tradition of political thought centred on the value of individual liberty and its relation to the state. Individuals are said to hold rights, often 'natural rights' having an existence independent of government or even of society, forming the basis for constitutional limits on the powers of government. Such rights typically comprise the secure enjoyment of life, liberty and property, and freedom of speech and association. The task of government is to respect and protect these rights, allowing individuals to pursue their own chosen goals with due regard to the rights of others.

The core of classical liberalism is recognizable from the late seventeenth century onwards, most notably in England in the writing of John Locke, and parallels both the development of limited government and the removal of state restrictions on production and trade. Liberalism in this sense is strongly associated with minimal state power, government being merely an instrument for the maintenance of the social and political framework necessary for free individual action. However, liberalism in the latter part of the nineteenth century adopted the more positive view that government should enable democratic participation and extend health, welfare and educational rights in order to encourage the development of the individual citizen, capable of rationally selecting proper goals.

This shift in the meaning of 'liberalism' illustrates the broad and ambiguous nature of the tradition. Liberalism has tended to take its direction from those ideas and problems with which it has developed. In continental Europe, for instance, liberalism has been associated with nationalism, this association being more dependent on the contingent presence of forces opposed both to liberalization and to national independence than on any necessary connections between the two traditions. Similarly, it may be helpful to distinguish between economic and political liberalism which, though commonly associated in both theory and practice, focus on different spheres of activity and individual rights. A government (e.g. Chile in the 1970s and 1980s) may seek to maintain an open market framework in the economic sphere while severely restricting political liberty. See also: *citizen; conservatism; contract theory; ideology; law (c): natural law; nationalism; new right; pluralism; radicalism; social contract; utilitarianism; welfare state*.

List system A system of election based on proportional representation of parties or similar groups, each of which presents a list of candidates. The voter then casts a vote for one of these lists, and candidates are declared elected normally according to their ordering on the list. In some systems the voter can amend the content or the ordering of the list (or both). Various methods of calculation to produce the result in terms of numbers of seats per list can be used, including the Hare-Niemeyer method now employed in Germany, and the d'Hondt method. The list system is used for example in the electoral systems of Belgium, Finland, Israel, Italy and Switzerland. See also: *cumulative vote; d'Hondt method; electoral system; Hare-Niemeyer method; proportional representation*.

Lobby The term has several associated meanings. As a verb, 'to lobby' is to attempt to exercise influence directly on legislators in order to persuade or coerce them into taking some decision favourable to those lobbying. In the context of British parliamentary practice, the 'Lobby' refers to the area within the confines of Parliament, but not in the legislative chambers, where members of parliament and peers may meet with those journalists to whom the privileged status of 'lobby correspondent' has been accorded (and who are collectively referred to as 'the lobby').

Despite a tendency among some authorities to prefer a wider use of the term to serve as a synonym for interest groups (e.g. see S. E. Finer, *Anonymous Empire: A Study of the Lobby in Great Britain*, Pall Mall Press, 1958, esp. chapter 1: 'What is the Lobby?'), a more restrictive definition is preferred by others. Such a definition would distinguish a 'lobby' from interest groups by using the term to refer to groups specifically organized for the purpose of influencing legislators, though such groups may be composed of other groups which would qualify for the title of interest group because their activities were not confined to such attempts to influence legislators. Examples of lobbies would include those formed to promote and to resist the introduction of commercial television in Britain; the road transport lobby in Britain; the road haulage lobby in Germany; the fisheries lobby in Norway; the war veterans lobby in the USA; the wine producers lobby in France.

A lobbyist or lobby agent is a person who directly represents the views of a lobby to legislators: in the USA, for instance, many paid lobbyists are registered under the Federal Regulation of Lobbying Act (1946). In Britain, there is no such regulatory provision, though professional lobbyists and lobbying firms (sometimes called 'parliamentary consultants') exist. See also: *interest group; interests*.

Local government Local government is the process whereby certain public functions and services are carried on within a given set of territorial units which are administrative and political subunits of a state. The extent of these functions and services differs from state to state and over time, but they will generally consist of the exercise of certain mandatory and discretionary powers given to local authorities by the state in accordance with the constitution and under provisions of legislation. It must be noted that certain other local functions may be carried out by field agencies of the state rather than by departments of local government authorities.

Important variables in local government include the organizational structure of local authorities; the range of functions associated with those authorities (in particular, the distinction between multi-purpose authorities and single-purpose authorities which deal with a particular function, such as in Britain regional health authorities, or school boards in the USA); whether members of local authorities are elected or appointed, and, if elected, the form and frequency of election; the forms and sources of local government finance; and the structure of authority within the local government unit. In federal systems such variables may be different as between one province and another (as in the states of the USA or the Länder of Germany, for example).

Local government systems, in which the local units possess no powers independent of the central government, should be distinguished from federal systems, in which the federal units do possess such independent powers. See also: *devolution; federation.*

'Log-rolling' A process of tit-for-tat bargaining among members of a legislative body (e.g. the US Congress and its committees) whereby a legislator promises to vote for a project – whether an item of legislation or an appropriation – favoured by another legislator, expecting some equivalent act of support in return at some future date. It is a term chiefly applicable in the US context, but the phenomenon may occur in any legislative body where there is both a degree of freedom of voting choice available to legislators, (rather than a high degree of party discipline), and recorded votes (rather than secret voting) to ensure that bargains are kept. 'Log-rolling' may apply also to votes on allocation of distributive projects known as 'pork-barrel'. See also: *'pork-barrel'.*

Longitudinal studies Studies of persistence and change in the condition or value of some phenomenon over successive periods of time, e.g. of the opinions and attitudes of voters during an election campaign or across a series of elections by means of a panel study. See also: *cross-sectional analysis; panel study.*

'Machine politics' Political situations where the influence of a highly organized local party structure, controlled – possibly corruptly, perhaps with the aid of violence – by a 'boss', is exercised over patronage appointments, electoral campaigns, selection of candidates, and the policy agenda as this affects local affairs. The party machine operates in the political interests of its local leadership and their clients, rather than the interests of the party membership as such, the general public or the national party organization.

'Machine politics' is associated particularly with urban politics in the USA, but the term sometimes can be applied appropriately to local politics in other countries where control is in the hands of a small, self-perpetuating elite of a local party. See also: *clientelism.*

Macro-sociology See: *political history.*

Majority The term 'majority' can be used to refer to that section of a group constituting more than one-half. Alternatively, the term may refer to a 'relative majority' or plurality, i.e. the largest number of, for example, votes or voters when there is a selection among more than two choices (e.g. candidates in an election), but a number less than 50% of the whole. Some procedures require an 'absolute majority', i.e. over 50% of those entitled to vote on an issue in an election, whether they all cast a vote or not.

Special majorities are those requiring some higher proportion than 50% plus one: two-thirds or three-quarters are common examples (e.g. as in the amendment process of the US constitution). The United Nations Security Council and the Council of Ministers of the European Community are institutions which require certain forms of special majority on particular types of issue.

Other usages of the term 'majority' are: to indicate the quantitative differences in votes between, for example, the winning candidate in an election and the runner-up, or those favouring and those opposed to a legislative proposal in parliament; and to refer to the group, coalition or party constituting more than half of a legislature or other such body. See also: *minority; plurality.*

Mandate The commission regarding policy given by the electorate to a legislature or a legislator, or else claimed by a government by virtue of its success in an election on the basis of a declared programme or manifesto. The existence of such a mandate is difficult to establish through normal electoral procedures, except in the most general terms, since most governments and members of legislatures are elected under party labels and on the basis of complex, multi-policy manifestos. It is more legitimate to use the term in a negative sense, to deny that a mandate exists to introduce some policy not foreshadowed in the electoral programme, and for which no emergency need has arisen.

A second usage of 'mandate' is to refer to the decrees issued by the League of Nations to certain member-states after the first world war, requiring them to administer on behalf of the League certain territories, formerly colonies of defeated countries in that war, on a temporary basis and under specified conditions. See also: *referendum; representation.*

Manifesto A published statement of political beliefs and policies, originating from an individual or, more usually nowadays, a political party or political movement. It may be intended as a fundamental guide to some movement or group concerning its aims (e.g. the Communist manifesto published by Marx and Engels) or as a statement of intentions on the basis of which an electorate can decide for which party it wishes to vote: e.g. the manifestos of

British parties at general elections, or the platforms of American parties in presidential elections. See also: *platform*.

Market socialism See: *socialism*.

Martial law A situation in which regulations and decrees originating from the military replace civilian rule, either by means of the grant by the civil authorities of governing power to the military, involving the suspension of civil government and of ordinary laws and court procedures, or by the assumption of power by the military through a *putsch* or revolution. Martial law may refer to a state of military rule in the country to which the military itself belongs (e.g. Greece 1967-74) or to rule of an occupied country by the military of another state (e.g. Germany immediately after the second world war). Martial law may be provided for in a constitution, to be instituted in a state of emergency. See also: *putsch; revolution*.

Marxism A theoretical tradition based on the work of Karl Marx (1818-83). Marxism was one of the major influences on the development of socialism in nineteenth century Europe, and provided the main theoretical source of a distinctive communist movement. As adapted and modified by Lenin, Marxism (or 'Marxism-Leninism') became the official ideology of communist regimes from 1917 onwards, though this has not prevented major conflicts of interpretation.

The most important aspects of Marx's work, from which the tradition developed, include these views and ideas, collectively described as 'historical materialism':

- that human nature comprises a set of needs and capacities, particularly the capacity to transform the natural world, manifested in various forms through different sets of social relations. The possibility of a full realisation of human capacities and a full satisfaction of human needs only occurs when alienation is overcome and class division transcended through the abolition of private property. (This position is most easily identifiable in Marx's early work. There is some controversy concerning the consistency of this 'humanist' position with Marx's later writings, but the weight of scholarly opinion is now on the side of its consistency).

- that social being determines consciousness, and not the other way around: that is, the norms, values and understanding that people possess are conditioned by their experience of the particular set of social relations present in society. The form of consciousness (or 'ideology') prevailing in any class-divided society will be that which justifies and serves the interests of the dominant class.

- that the most significant differences between societies can be understood by reference to their class structures, which in turn derive from their form of economic organization, e.g. feudal, capitalist, socialist. Thus the primary explanation for social and political activity must refer to class configurations, and the primary explanation for social and political conflict must be conflict between irreconcilable class interests.

- that labour is the source of the value of a commodity, that profit and the accumulation of capital must involve the extraction of 'surplus value' from labour, and therefore that social relations enabling such a process to occur must be exploitative.

- that each system of production develops productive forces which conflict with its productive relations (the system of ownership and control of production), and that this conflict eventually results in the overthrow of one system of production and the new predominance of another. Thus capitalism, like all previous systems, is doomed to be destroyed by the contradictions developing within itself (e.g. over-production, under-consumption, a decline in the rate of profit, the impoverishment of the proletariat, the polarization of class conflict), the significant difference between the destruction of capitalism and the destruction of earlier systems being that the new dominant class (the proletariat) will have an interest in abolishing class division, rather than perpetuating it in a new form.

- that in a communist society, class interests will disappear, and with them class conflict, leading to the 'withering away' of the state as a coercive regulator of exploitative social relationships.

Marx's ideas have served as a source for the ideology of the communist movement, and have also been adopted as a specific analytical approach in history and social science. The connection between these two roles is generally regarded as a virtue by Marxism's exponents, who stress the unity of attempts to understand the world and attempts to transform it, but as a vice by its opponents who suggest that the quest for understanding may be compromised by political commitment.

The influence of Marxism on the development of the historical and social sciences has been profound. Although there is a perceived division between Marxist and non-Marxist approaches, some of those most opposed to Marxism as an orthodoxy have conceded that, 'In many respects we are all Marxists now'. In other words, a willingness to look for explanations in terms of the conflicting economic interests of class groupings, and to view historical epochs in terms of their dominant mode of production, is at least a part of the approach adopted by many non-Marxists. In political analysis the distinctive character of the Marxist approach lies in the view that relations of production and associated class relations are to be given *primacy* in explaining political relations, most particularly when explaining the character and activity of the state. But, just as Marxism has influenced other traditions of enquiry, it has itself not been immune from change. During the early decades of this century, Marxism largely comprised materialist explanations of historical development, often thought to be of a rigid and determinist character, and, linked to these, various views of the role of trade unions and workers' political parties in the struggle to create socialist society. The first of these owed much to the elaboration and interpretation, some would say distortion, of Marx's ideas by Friedrich Engels, Marx's friend and collaborator; the second is primarily associated with Lenin's ideas, and with those of his critics, such as Rosa Luxemburg, Karl Liebknecht and Karl Kautsky. Although an interest in these questions remains part of the core of the Marxist tradition, since this period Marxism has taken many turns. The Stalinist position of most communist parties, the conduct of the Soviet Union towards its east European satellite countries, and the availability of Marx's early writings, led to a rethinking of Marxism's philosophical and moral roots, and the growth of a cluster of theories known as 'humanist Marxism'.

By the 1950s European Marxism was as much concerned with questions of ideology and class consciousness as it was with the direct links between economic and political development. The pursuit of this line of enquiry, together with other factors, has led some writers away from the materialist and scientific approach with which Marxism has traditionally been associated. In the 1960s and 1970s European Marxism, as part of a reaction against both humanist Marxism and Stalinism, fell under the influence of structuralism, particularly through the work of Louis Althusser. In contrast, despite the opposition of many Marxists to methodological individualism, there is now a flourishing branch of Marxism which employs the methods of rational choice analysis.

The picture of Marxism as rigidly deterministic and reductionist in its explanatory strategy has, perhaps, always contained a degree of caricature. It has certainly been a false picture of western Marxism for some time. Across the whole tradition, it would now be hard to find work which treated the activities of the modern state as rigidly determined by the interests of a dominant class, or historical change as rigidly following a predetermined pattern of development. Contingency, the importance of temporally and spatially specific conjunctions of factors, and the relative autonomy of the modern state, are all generally accepted.

Developments within the tradition that are thought to mark a radical break with Marxist orthodoxy are often referred to as 'neo-Marxism'. In academic work, the terms 'Marxian' and 'Marxist' have distinct meanings, the former denoting the work of Marx himself, the latter denoting the broad tradition developing from his work.. See also: *alienation; bolshevism; capitalism; communism; contradiction; determinism; exploitation; ideology; industrial society; rational choice analysis; reductionist theories; revolution; social class; socialism; state; structuralism.*

Mass media Those media of communication which are channelled toward a large and undifferentiated audience, which send uniform messages by methods which preclude personal modification during transmission of the message by sender or receiver (in contrast to, for instance, person-to-person phone calls or a political speech to a small audience). Thus, in industrialized societies, the mass media include radio and television broadcasting, mass-produced sound or video recordings, the cinema, posters, leaflets, newspaper production and book publishing. As a result of aiming messages at a large and undifferentiated audience, the production of such messages by use of the mass media is relatively inexpensive in relation to the size of the potential audience reached. See also: *mass society; political communication; propaganda.*

Mass society A society in which individuals have no highly valued attachments to social groups or traditional norms. The major institutions, processes and communication patterns deal with the population as an undifferentiated aggregate. Power is centralized: regional and local autonomy are discouraged.

In contemporary political analysis, these features have been associated with a high level of urbanization, division of labour, industrialization and density of population. Under these conditions the population tends to be very mobile, and thus has relatively few opportunities to develop social relationships of more than a transitory character. Political participation through voluntary organization is low, partly because the opportunities for political influence appear to be few, partly because of the difficulty of developing voluntary political organization in a mobile society. The media are organized for, and their communication based on, a national and undifferentiated audience.

In the nineteenth century, the concept of 'mass' generally embodied a bleak and pessimistic view. The term continues to be used pejoratively: sometimes in connection with the ease with which the mass can be manipulated and controlled, either by fanatical leaders or by conservative elites; sometimes as a part of an argument about the decline of culture and civilized values in modern society. Generally, the concept suggests an absence of democratic participation and a tendency towards totalitarian rule.

Clearly, modern societies exhibit some of the features of mass society, but the term embodies a pessimistic view of some of the trends in modern society, contrasted with a somewhat romantic view of earlier forms, rather than a neutral description of the modern social condition. See also: *alienation; anomie; industrial society; mass media; pluralism; totalitarianism.*

Methodological holism See: *reductionist theories.*

Methodological individualism See: *reductionist theories.*

Methodology The study of the methods of investigation within a discipline or area of inquiry. The term is also used to denote the particular methods adopted by an analyst or within some more general approach. Thus 'Marxist methodology' may refer to the *study* and *discussion* of methods appropriate to Marxist analysis, or simply to the methods generally used by Marxists.

Methodology in political analysis is concerned with all aspects of the research process, from theoretical argument about how best to conceptualize the subject matter to be investigated, to examination and selection of techniques for gathering and analyzing data, the main purpose of such discussion being the assessment of the utility and validity of methods and the identification of their limitations and bias. See also: *political analysis; scientific method.*

Minimal-winning coalition A coalition which would no longer possess a winning majority of votes if any one of the parties belonging to it withdrew. An example would be a coalition made up of: Party A = 30% of parliamentary seats; Party B = 15% of seats; Party C = 8% of seats. If that coalition contained any additional party (e.g. Party D with 6% of seats) it would no longer be minimal-winning because at least one party could then withdraw without robbing the coalition of its majority of seats (in this example either Party C or Party D). See also: *coalition; minimum-winning coalition.*

Minimum-winning coalition A coalition made up of parties in such a way as to be the smallest possible (in terms of seats in the legislature, for instance) which would still exceed 50%. Given a legislature made up of five parties: A = 35% of seats; B = 28% of seats; C = 17%; D = 12%; Party E = 8%; then the minimum-winning coalition is one made up of Parties A and C (52%), whereas coalitions of parties B, C and E (55%) or A and B (63%) would not be minimum-winning. On the assumption that the parties were ranged along a policy dimension (e.g. the 'left-right' dimension) in alphabetical order, from Party A at one extreme, all the above coalitions would be 'open' with the exception of A and B, which would be a closed coalition. See also: *coalition; closed coalition; minimal-winning coalition; open coalition.*

Minority A group which constitutes less than half the total membership of some larger aggregate of which it is part. In voting, a minority is the voters or votes constituting less than 50% of votes cast. In a society, the term refers to an ethnic, regional, religious or other group possessing distinctive identity and outnumbered heavily by the rest of the population (e.g. the Catholic minority in Northern Ireland, the Danish minority in Schleswig-Holstein). See also: *majority.*

Misery index A measure consisting of the aggregate of the percentage rate of inflation and the percentage rate of unemployment, used for example for purposes of comparing the socio-economic condition of states, or of one state over time. See also: *index numbers.*

Mobilization The process by which members of a political community are brought into situations which involve them directly in political affairs. One form of such involvement is voluntary participation in politics, by means of membership of parties, of movements or of interest groups, by voting at elections, involvement in political discussion, and similar activities. However, especially in totalitarian, modernizing or non-democratic 'mass' societies, mobilization may well involve forms of coerced participation in demonstrations, rallies, political campaigns, etc., attendance to vote in elections where choice is absent and turnout compulsory, forced membership of political organizations (e.g. the professional party groups for teachers and for lawyers in Nazi Germany), etc.

A related use of the term is in the context of preparation for a military conflict: mobilization of the armed forces or of the reserves, meaning bringing them to a state of readiness for war by moving them to positions for attack or defence, and arming them for such military action. See also: *participation.*

Mobilization of bias See: *non-decision.*

Model An interpretation of a theory so as to provide a representation or illustration of the relations theorized. In political analysis, models are often presented diagrammatically or by drawing analogies between politics and other more familiar or better understood processes. In such cases the chief purpose of the model is to present an easily visualized sketch of the theorized processes.

'Model' may also be used to describe a theory, the elements of which are not supposed precisely to correspond to actual political phenomena, but which offers a formal, simplified or idealized explanation of the relevant processes. See also: *analogy; ideal type; methodology; simulation.*

Modernization The term is often used as a close synonym for 'development', but is often preferred to that concept on the grounds that it more readily draws attention to the holistic nature of social change, and that it avoids presuppositions of 'improvement' or teleological views of the modernization process often associated with concepts of development.

Modernization may be defined as the process of social change which involves economic advancement, specialization of political roles, the pursuit of rationality in policy formation, technological development, and fundamental alterations in social patterns involving urbanization, social and geographic mobility, educational development, and the formation of secondary groupings. All these transform a society based on traditional values and institutions into one able to assume the characteristics of developed, or modern, societies (i.e. societies with highly complex, specialized economic systems, bureaucratized political institutions, advanced technologies, etc.).

Because of the nature of the modernization process, its study and analysis involves a sensitive appreciation of relevant aspects of the cultures of modernizing societies, an integrated knowledge of concepts, theories and techniques of several of the social and behaviourial sciences, and an awareness of the complex interrelationships of social, economic, political, psychological and cultural factors involved in social change. See also: *political development; third world*.

Monarchy Rule by a single head of state with the title of king (or queen) or its equivalent, in which the office of head of state usually is acquired by hereditary succession, though some monarchies (e.g. Poland) have been elective. It is usual for a monarch to be believed to be possessed of religious or traditional symbolic importance for the state and its institutions.

Associated more especially with feudal or medieval periods of history, the monarchy today is regarded as possessing political significance in only a few states, primarily in Africa and Asia. A series of revolutions, from the American war of independence and the French revolution, replaced monarchies or totalitarian dictatorships, or else, as in the United Kingdom and the Netherlands, for example, monarchies became transmuted into constitutional monarchies. In such regimes, the monarch acts as head of state, but has little or no political discretion; rather he/she confirms political decisions for which the government takes political responsibility. Spain, after the death of Franco, provides one of the rare recent examples of a monarch being restored as head of state. See also: *head of state*.

Movement A collective grouping that seeks to bring about, through political means, major changes in policy or social institutions, or else, in the case of revolutionary movements such as a separatist movement, to produce an entirely new political order. Movements may attract relatively large mass support, or be confined to a small number of adherents. They are distinguishable from interest groups because of the fundamental nature of their aims, their lack of reliance on a single organizational base, and their disregard of subtle political tactics. They differ from political parties because they do not normally seek to exercise the functions of government and because they lack a unified organization; however, they may support candidates in elections for public office. Yet a movement is more permanent than a mere crowd, and more purposeful than an unorganized interest.

A major feature is the possession by a movement of some very basic common purpose, or even an ideology, which generates a strong sense of group identity, and which may encourage the emergence of charismatic leadership. A movement may transcend existing divisions of social class, religion, party affiliation and even nationality. Examples of movements are: the suffragette movement, the working-class movement; the civil rights movement in the USA; the environmentalist movement; the peace movement.

A movement may change into a political party, or may be captured by a party (e.g. the Populist movement in the USA), or it may produce a political party as a 'vanguard' organization without losing its character as a movement (e.g. the Green parties which have developed in Germany, the United Kingdom and other European states). Alternatively, a movement may become organized as an interest group, losing some of its ideological quality but gaining a sharper political profile and embracing a more deliberate and sophisticated set of political tactics. See also: *environmentalism; feminism; interest group; pacifism; party; Zionism.*

Multi-party system A party system in which more than two relevant parties compete with each other. Sartori (*Parties and Party Systems*, Cambridge, Cambridge University Press, 1976) makes a significant typological distinction between 'moderate' multi-party systems and 'polarized' or 'extreme' multi-party systems, indicated by the latter having usually six or more relevant parties, and by an associated syndrome of other properties, such as the existence of anti-system parties, bilateral and irresponsible oppositions, and a tendency for voters to desert centre parties in favour of parties located towards the extremes of the party spectrum. The Weimar Republic of inter-war Germany is usually regarded as the classic case of a 'polarized' multi-party system, though the French Fourth Republic and post-war Italy may also be considered to fall into this category. Some authorities have attempted to distinguish between 'true' multi-party systems and 'two-and-a-half' party systems, claiming that Britain and the Federal Republic of Germany, if in different ways, have recently had such 'two-and-a-half' party systems. See also: *opposition; party system; two-party system.*

N

Nation A group of people who share a common historical and cultural tradition usually associated with a defined territorial area, which provides the group with an identity vis-à-vis other such groups. The idea of 'nation' stimulates claims to the right to a common political organization for the group if that does not already exist, and serves as an integrative force if the nation already possesses its own state organization.

The force of the idea of 'nation' is often sufficient to persist in the face of occupation, partition, dispersal of the population of a nation, incorporation of the people into a federal or imperial state, industrialization and other changes associated with modernization. The Jews, Poles, Lithuanians, Irish, Basques and Germans are examples of nations which have persisted in such circumstances.

There is also a definition based on a more subjective set of criteria, which holds that a nation is any group of people who believe (correctly or incorrectly) that they possess a common historical and cultural tradition. This is found in, for example, some African states, which depend on the creation and fostering of a sense of nationhood to preserve political integration. See also: *nationalism; political integration; state.*

Nationalism An ideology based on the premise that states should be organized on the basis of nationality, and that, for any specific nationalist movement, some particular nation has not yet achieved statehood or has not achieved it as completely as it should. It is this link to incomplete statehood which distinguishes nationalism from patriotism, xenophobia, etc.

Historically, modern nationalism has roots in the eighteenth and nine-teenth centuries, and was especially influenced by the French Revolution, Napoleonic conquests, and the nationalist revolutionary movements of the first half of the nineteenth century. The post-war settlements of 1918-19 with their emphasis on 'national self-determination' and the anti-colonialism of the period following the second world war were also influential in stimulating nationalist movements, especially in areas of the world undergoing modern-ization, such as Africa and the Middle East.

Nationalism can be allied to other doctrines and ideologies, e.g. commun-ism (as in several third world states), democracy (in pre-unification German and Italian states for instance), militarism (as in Prussia), and religious beliefs (as in Northern Ireland).

While relying on such factors as a common language, a shared history, territorial contiguity, ethnic similarity and a shared culture, nationalism defies definition in terms of precise objectively identifiable components, depending more on a subjective belief in belonging to a common 'nation' than on objective tests of nationhood. See also: *nation; xenophobia.*

Nationalization The process of taking under the ownership and control of the state some commercial enterprise previously under private ownership and control. The enterprise is then normally operated either directly by a government department or indirectly through a public corporation.

Nationalization is associated with political ideologies of a socialist or collectivist type, though in Britain has often been implemented by Conser-vative governments, and throughout western Europe has been supported at times by parties of the right. It is usually directed first at public utilities (e.g. water, electricity and gas supply, transport undertakings) but may extend to any type of economic activity. See also: *collectivism; communism; privatiza-tion; socialism.*

Neutrality A legal condition in international relations, whereby a state declares its intention not to be a party to a conflict, either by hostile actions against one or other of the belligerents or by extending privileges of trade etc. to either belligerent without also extending them to the other. In return, the neutral state expects its territory to remain inviolate, and its trade and other activities to be unhampered, as far as possible, by the actions of the conflicting powers. Such neutrality can be declared in advance, either with regard to a potential conflict between identified parties, or generally with regard to any external conflict. Neutrality may be imposed on a state as a condition of a treaty, for example; this process is termed 'neutralization'. An example of a neutralized state is Austria, following the second world war and the four-power agreements in 1955 regarding her future status..

New right In everyday parlance, a term loosely applied to right-wing critics of socialism and social democracy in the 1970s and 1980s. Such criticism is 'new' by virtue of its prominence and vehemence, but more particularly through its rejection of traditional conservative values. Specifically the 'new right' describes two ideological positions, mutually opposed in many of their policy preferences, basic values and styles of analysis.

The first position has been most apparent in the USA: the new right in the form of the self-styled 'moral majority', stressing the need for strong moral values, often rooted in arguments from religious fundamentalism, and opposing the alleged social fragmentation encouraged by more liberal attitudes. Such arguments support an active authoritarian state in the moral sphere, though they may seek to reduce state intervention in matters of economic and welfare policy.

The second position, comprising a resurgence of liberal and libertarian ideas, has been more widely apparent. Taking individual choice to be basic, as both moral value and unit of political analysis, a powerful critique of socialist and corporatist tendencies within the modern state has been developed. This view is most often applied to economic policy, seeking to restrict state activity to the maintenance of a framework within which market forces may freely operate, intervening only to prevent the power of sectional interests from distorting those operations. State intervention is regarded as inefficient, self-defeating and an affront to individual liberty. At the extreme, this idea of the 'minimal state' is extended to all social policy, opposing state attempts to prevent the supply of commodities like pornography and drugs. See also: *anarchism; conservatism; corporatism (b): ideal type; free trade; liberalism; privatization; rational choice theory; socialism.*

Nomenklatura A Russian word employed in the Soviet Union (and later, by extension, in other communist political systems) to refer both to the positions in the party, the state, the economy and society to which nomination is made by – or subject to the approval of – the Communist party in the Soviet Union, and to the set of persons considered to be proper and suitable candidates for those posts..

Non-decision A concept developed to criticize 'pluralist' studies of power and to extend their scope. Research like Robert A. Dahl's *Who Governs?* (1961) had concentrated on the decisions made within issue-areas being formally considered by city government. Critics such as Bachrach and Baratz argued that power might also be exercised by thwarting or suppressing demands, thus preventing an issue from arising. The preventing action was said to result from a 'non-decision', an unfortunate choice of expression.

The regular occurrence of non-decision-making may support, and be legitimated by, a set of dominant values and procedures which systematically benefit some persons and groups at the expense of others. This set of accepted rules is often referred to as the 'mobilization of bias'. See also: *decision; decision-making analysis; ideology; legitimacy; norm; pluralism; power; values*.

Norm A rule of conduct or shared value which regulates or is used to judge the social behaviour of group members. Some norms are explicit, such as laws and regulations, and are enforced by legitimate formal sanctions; some, still relatively explicit, such as customs, morals and manners, are enforced by more informal sanctions; others may be implicit in the practices of the group and effective sanctions may be the unintended consequence of commonly held attitudes. Women, for instance, may be legally excluded from holding political office; or the role and status of women might be at odds with those expected of a politician; or the organization of work and training may make it difficult for women to develop the expertise regarded as necessary for effective political action. In each case it would be proper to talk of a norm excluding or inhibiting women from full political participation.

The term is also used, in statistics, to refer to a measure of central tendency (such as an average, a median or a mode) and, more loosely, to refer to the 'usual' or 'normal' case of some class of phenomena. See also: *ideology; law (b): stipulative law; role; status; values*.

Normative theory A systematic explanation of values or standards of conduct, including the reasons why they are held, their effects on behaviour, their relation to other values and rules, etc.

A distinction is sometimes made between theories that seek to explain the shared values of an actual group and theories that seek to establish the proper or reasoned grounds for the prescription of values. Thus a theory of legitimate government may be centrally concerned with the types of rules, values and goals underlying various *beliefs* in the legitimacy of a political system (e.g. Weber's treatment of legitimate authority), or it may set out standards that claim to be universal criteria for ascribing legitimacy to government (e.g. Rousseau's treatment of the social contract). See also: *authority; contract theory; legitimacy; norm; political philosophy; political theory; value judgement; values*.

Oligarchy A form of government consisting of rule by a small, unrepresentative elite group which governs in accordance with its own interests, especially in terms of the accumulation of wealth and privilege. It is one of the basic forms of government identified by Aristotle. More loosely, the term is sometimes used as a synonym for any ruling elite. See also: *aristocracy; iron law of oligarchy; plutocracy; political elites*.

Ombudsman Originally a Scandinavian office (where the term meant 'Procurator'), the institution has now been adopted in various countries beyond the Scandinavian area, though generally with a change of name. The United Kingdom has a Parliamentary Commissioner for administration, for the health service and for local administration; New Zealand also has a Parliamentary Commissioner; Germany has a Parliamentary Commissioner for military affairs; post-Franco Spain has a *Defensor del Pueblo*; etc. While details concerning the powers and jurisdictions of the institutions vary from state to state, in general the task of the Ombudsman is to receive complaints from citizens aggrieved by some alleged decision or action of public servants, and for whom perhaps the normal channels of legal redress are not appropriate (perhaps because the decision or action complained of is not in itself illegal). If a prima facie case of 'maladministration' (e.g. improper use of powers, unsuitable criteria applied to decision making, erroneous interpretation of the law) is established, the Ombudsman and the staff associated with the office investigate the case and report their findings, usually to the legislature. In some countries the Ombudsman may initiate legal proceedings if thought appropriate.

The term may also be used, in a non-governmental context, for officers or institutions dealing with complaints and grievances of the public in relation to, for example, the legal profession, banking or insurance.

In some countries, the function of the Ombudsman is carried out by a system of administrative courts, but these, in contrast to the Ombudsman, are not agencies of the legislature. See also: *administrative law; administrative tribunal*.

One-party system A party system in which one, and only one, relevant party exists. It may be the only relevant party because of legal or constitutional provision, or because its monopolistic position is maintained by violence or the threat of violence (as in a military regime, for instance), or, rarely, because communal, tribal or national feelings are channelled through just one party, during and immediately after a struggle for independence, for instance. One-party systems must be distinguished from what Giovanni Sartori (*Parties and Party Systems*, Cambridge, Cambridge University Press, 1976) terms 'hegemonic' or 'dominant' party systems, where other relevant parties exist, though a 'hegemonic' party system in which other parties are totally dependent on the hegemonic party (the German Democratic Republic until 1989, for example) may in effect differ but little from a one-party system. See also: *hegemony; party system; totalitarianism*.

Open coalition When parties represented in a legislature are ordered along some relevant policy dimension (such as the left-right dimension) and at least one party that is not a member of a governing coalition is located on that dimension between two parties which are in coalition, the coalition is said to be 'open'. See also: *closed coalition; coalition*.

Operationalization The process of translating concepts in order to develop empirical propositions, amenable to observation, test and sometimes measurement. For instance, political power may be conceptualized as 'the capacity of a class to realize its objective interests'.

If actual cases of political power are to be identified, if laws and theories involving political power are to be developed and tested, 'class', 'realization' and 'objective interests' must be related to indicators of their incidence in the actual political world, and some means of measurement must be attached to the notion of 'capacity'. Most analysts hold that not all the concepts used within a theory need be operationalized so long as the operational capacity of the theory as a whole is sufficient to generate some empirical propositions. The procedures for operationalizing a particular theory are sometimes called correspondence rules or rules of interpretation. See also: *concept; theory.*

Operational research A term originating from the use of statistical and other scientific techniques to analyze and resolve complex problems in the second world war. Operational research now refers to the application of quantitative techniques, often on a multidisciplinary or cross-disciplinary basis, to the decisional or functional problems of any organization, including government..

Opinion leader A person who is influential within a community or other social collectivity in forming the opinions of others, by virtue of being regarded as an authoritative or reliable source of information and advice, and whose own views are often taken as models by others in that social group. An opinion leader need not necessarily hold a position of formal authority, or control communications resources, though both may be relevant to establishing a reputation as an opinion leader.

The notion of opinion leaders is included in the two-step theory of communication flow, which postulates that most people obtain their information and form their opinions about social matters via intermediary agencies such as opinion leaders, rather than directly from news services or other sources of direct information. See also: *political communication.*

Opposition In its most general usage, the term 'opposition' in politics refers to any group or other set of individuals who are in disagreement with the government – usually on a consistent, long-term basis though the term can apply to issue-related opposition in the context of a single item of legislation or policy proposal. More specifically, the term is applied to those parties in a legislature which disagree with the government and wish to replace it. In some legislatures, such parliamentary opposition is formalized and institutionalized: in the United Kingdom, the USA and Germany, for example, there exist provision of public money and defined political status for the opposition, as well as its right of reply to public statements by the government and the right to be consulted on certain bipartisan matters such as legislative schedules and procedures, declarations of war, and arrangements for state ceremonies. In other states (as in Britain before the mid-nineteenth century) opposition may be regarded as 'faction', and even seen as opposition to the state as well as to the government of the day, and so, especially in one-party states, as being near-treasonable. Extra-parliamentary opposition may also be important in some states, especially where parliamentary opposition is absent, or is perceived to be ineffectual.   The term can also be applied to groups within parties or other organizations which systematically disagree with the leadership of that organization. See also: *faction.*

Organization A social group, possessing identifiable boundaries and a common subculture, which has been deliberately formed for the purpose of pursuing some goal or objective by joint effort of its members. A political organization is therefore a group which has been created to pursue political objectives. See also: *movement; organization theory*.

Organization theory The framework of concepts by which the study of organizations, their characteristics, behaviour, membership, etc., is conducted.

The main interests of organization theorists have been: the interaction among members of organizations, including their roles, hierarchical patterns, intercommunication, etc., styles of organizational structure and types of leadership; the norms and cultures of organizations; decision making in organizations; conflict resolution; relationships between formal and informal structures within organizations; interaction among organizations. The study involves the use of concepts and methods derived from several disciplines, such as game theory, small group theory and systems approaches. In political science organization theory has been used principally for the study of committees and other small groups, parties, and legislative bodies. See also: *organization*.

Overload (a): government overload The term refers to the condition where governments are burdened by increased demands from the public to resolve problems or provide political benefits, coupled with growing complexity of the technological, economic, ecological and social environment in which the political system operates. Overload has been offered as an excuse for the apparent failure of governments to cope with crisis, and as a reason for the growth both of 'alternative' political activities such as 'new social movements' concerned with environmentalism or feminism, and citizen-initiative groups, and of apolitical affiliations of citizens, as responses based on mistrust of government's capability to 'deliver', especially in states such as Germany, the USA, Sweden and the Netherlands..

Overload (b): communications overload A term employed in the communications approach to political analysis, which refers to the state of communications channels when they are used to convey messages at a rate greater than their optimum capacity. Overload, if it persists, can lead to channel failure, garbled messages, and perhaps even the breakdown of the communications system. It is a signal for either the development of new or additional channels of information, or a reduction in the load on existing channels. See also: *political communication*.

P

Pacifism The belief that violence, including war, cannot be justified by the ends intended or achieved. As the destructive potential and reality of modern warfare have increased, pacifism has played a greater role in various peace movements, inside both political parties and pressure groups. Such belief has also influenced political activity in other ways: as a part of the move towards various forms of international consultation and adjudication, including the League of Nations, the United Nations, and the World Court; through its association with programmes of passive resistance, such as that led by Gandhi in India; and in its implications for political obedience when conscientious objectors refuse to comply with conscription orders, or more positively oppose mobilization for war. See also: *war*.

Pact An agreement between persons, groups or states, usually concerned with the undertaking of joint action, or the readiness to do so in specified circumstances. A pact is usually less formal and more limited in content than a treaty, though some treaties are referred to also as 'pacts' (e.g. the 1939 treaty signed by Molotov and Ribbentrop on behalf of the Soviet Union and Nazi Germany). In British politics, for instance, the agreement in 1977 between the Callaghan Labour government and the Liberal MPs led by David Steel, which maintained the Labour government in power despite its lack of a single-party majority, was called the 'Lib-Lab pact'. See also: *protocol (b): treaty; treaty*.

Palace revolution A change of ruler brought about by the threat or application of force, generally by associates of the ruler or by politicians with ready access to the ruler. It usually involves an element of surprise, only the minimum of actual violence, and little or no public disturbance. It is a form of coup d'état. See also: *coup d'état; revolution*.

Panel study A type of longitudinal study, employing the technique of repeated interviews, or other methods of data acquisition (such as diaries filled in by the respondents). It usually utilizes a sample of the population which, it is hoped, will remain unchanged, though, varying with the time span of the panel study, attrition will result in a smaller sample being available at each successive use of the panel. The purpose is to study alterations in the attitudes, opinions or behaviour of respondents – and hence, by extension, of the population which the sample represents – over a specified time period. It has been used as a method in sociology, in social psychology, in broadcasting audience research and in market research. In political science, its best known applications have been in psephological studies, to discover changes in voting intention, and to relate those changes to other attributes of the voter, e.g. changes in exposure to electoral propaganda, changes of occupation or residence, or change in family status. See also: *longitudinal studies; psephology; sample; survey*.

Paradigm (a): general usage A relatively pure or advanced case of some phenomenon under investigation, clearly exemplifying certain important and relevant features and therefore useful as a pattern for the analysis of other instances. A paradigm is used in the same way as an ideal type but differs from that concept in constituting an actual case. British political development might be used as a paradigm of liberal-democratic development; the United States might serve as a paradigm of federalism; physical coercion might provide a paradigm of the exercise of power. See also: *ideal type*.

Paradigm (b): Kuhnian usage A more restricted sense of 'paradigm (a)' employed by Thomas Kuhn for the analysis of the development of science. According to Kuhn, scientific research in any given area is marked by an alternation between periods of 'normal' and 'revolutionary' science. Normal science is dominated by a single view of the sort of theory to be developed, the kinds of experiment to be performed, the procedures for measurement, and so on. A scientific community sees its field of enquiry only in these particular terms; no alternatives are seriously contemplated. But, sooner or later, the adequacy of this agreed paradigm is called into question and a revolutionary period ensues during which fundamental argument takes place and a variety of alternatives are proposed to replace the old paradigm. No fixed rules can be applied to judge between the competing alternatives but eventually opinion coalesces around one candidate. This victorious view becomes the paradigm dominating a further period of normal science.

The idea of science as a succession of paradigms raises questions about the nature of scientific progress. If science is periodically ruptured by revolutions which redefine and transform perceptions of the world, appropriate methods of enquiry, and the criteria for identifying significant problems, then science cannot consist, in any simple sense, of a continuous process of accumulation of knowledge.

In the absence of a single dominant theoretical perspective the application of this 'Kuhnian' usage to political science is bound to be suspect. Nevertheless the term is often used to identify competing approaches to political analysis: e.g. the 'Marxist' or the 'pluralist' paradigms. This usage implies that the two approaches construct for themselves such radically different views of the political world and its problems that no meaningful dialogue can take place between them. See also: *falsificationism; positivism; problematic; scientific method*.

Parameters In analysis, parameters are the dimensions or states of relevant external conditions which are held constant for any given series of tests, experiments, measurements, etc., but which may be varied for other series of such tests or measurements.

The term is also used figuratively to denote boundaries or limits beyond which something cannot or should not move, as in the statement: 'Constitutions define the parameters of political power'. See also: *variables*.

Pareto optimum A term, derived from economics, denoting an allocation of resources where no possible reallocation of those resources can benefit anyone without making someone else worse off. The idea is used in assessing the distributive efficiency of systems, and in identifying possible equilibrium positions in bargaining. Its main difficulty lies in deciding the limits of 'possible' reallocations, a decision that often appears arbitrary. See also: *bargaining theory; equilibrium*.

Participant observation A method in social science research where either a member of a group or organization, or a participant in some activity such as a coup d'état, becomes also an observer, recording or transmitting pertinent information about the behaviour of the group or the course of events, or else an outsider becomes a member of the group or organization for the same purpose.

Several advantages are obtainable by participant observation rather than external observation or interview techniques. The situation under observation is likely to be less affected by the investigation if members of the group are unaware, or less aware, of the fact that they are being observed. The observer is capable of gaining a more sensitive notion of the group and its activities by participating than by remaining external to it. However, ethical and practical problems are raised concerning any concealment of the 'dual role' of the participant observer.

The technique has been used mainly in anthropology; industrial, organizational and community studies in sociology; and in small group studies in social psychology. Applications in political science have been mainly in the areas of community and small-group politics, decision making, and electoral studies.

Participation The term is usually applied to voluntary, rather than coerced, activities, though this is a distinction not implicit in the concept.

Participation, as used in political contexts, is thus the voluntary activity of an individual in political affairs, including inter alia: voting; membership and activity connected with political groups such as interest groups, political movements and parties; office holding in political institutions; the exercise of political leadership; informal activities such as taking part in political discussions, or attendance at political events such as demonstrations; attempts to persuade the authorities or members of the public to act in particular ways in relation to political goals. The term is therefore closely associated with democratic political systems, in so far as non-democratic systems tend to limit participation by the general public, or to channel it in predetermined ways. However, the term is not applicable solely to conventional or even legal forms of political activity; unconventional and illegal political activities must also be comprehended by its definition. See also: *mobilization*.

Party A political party is an organized group, made up of members who subscribe to some common set of values and policies, which has as its fundamental aim the attainment of political power and public office in order to implement the policies. It seeks such power normally by constitutional methods, especially by contesting public elections, though revolutionary or anti-system parties may engage in extra-constitutional political activity to achieve their goals.

A party differs from lobbies or interest groups, since these are concerned with influencing government decisions or legislative proposals in some specific case, or over a limited range of cases, whereas a party seeks to participate in government and thereby to implement its policies, at least potentially, over the whole spectrum of public affairs. A party differs from a movement by virtue of its more formal organizational structure and the more specific nature of its aims.

The exercise of governmental power is not the only function which a political party seeks to fulfil. It is an agency for political recruitment, an instrument of political socialization, a channel for political communication, etc. In terms of the political system, it has, among others, functions of 'gatekeeping' and interest-aggregation, filtering the demands of those it represents and shaping those demands into coherent proposals for action by the authorities.

Parties in one-party states have the same fundamental aims relating to the control of governmental power as do parties in competitive party systems. The sources of political competition and rivalry may differ (e.g. there may be, as in China and the Soviet Union in the past, competition from the military or the bureaucracy).

Specialized parties, and minor parties with little hope of participating in government, are marginal cases within the definition outlined here. Some might be better described as interest groups using electoral campaigns as a strategy of influence: the Refugee party in West Germany in the nineteen-fifties, for example; others might more properly be described as 'single-issue parties', such as 'Green' parties in the early period of their existence.

Political scientists, in studying parties, have focused in particular upon aspects of organizational structure, leadership, recruitment methods, policies and policy-making processes, and the social background and political behaviour of members and supporters. In addition, there have been many studies of aspects of party systems. See also: *faction; interest group; interests; iron law of oligarchy; lobby; movement; party identification; party system; political system.*

Party identification A feeling of attachment to some particular political party. This attachment tends to be self-sustaining through its production of a partisan view of political events, and to predispose voters in their electoral choice. Individuals may identify with a party even when they are ignorant of the detail of its current policies.

In empirical research, party identification is most simply established by asking individuals whether they generally think of themselves as, for instance, Conservative, Labour, Liberal Democrat, etc. Such questions seek to establish the existence of attitudes which may or may not match actual voting behaviour. For instance, a voter in the USA may identify with the Democratic party but fail to remain loyal to that party when holding a strong preference for the personality, style or competence of a Republican presidential candidate. Empirical research focuses on the incidence and intensity of identification, its association with voting behaviour, the implications of variations in its incidence and intensity over time or between different systems, and on its social and psychological sources.

The 'party identification model' of electoral behaviour assumes that through socialization, particularly within the family, most voters come to identify themselves with one or another of the major parties, and that these attachments give stability to the political system over generations.

'Party identification' bears a different interpretation in rational choice models of voting where it is treated as a means by which voters predispose themselves to choose a party in rough ideological conformity to their own views, thus avoiding the costly process of gathering detailed information about policy proposals and past performance at each election. See also: *attitudes; dealignment; electoral volatility; ideology; issues; party; political socialization; rational choice analysis; realignment; values*.

Party system The complex interrelationship among political parties in a state or other political organization (e.g. local government; the European parliament). Attempts to create a classificatory scheme to distinguish among types of party system have traditionally focused upon the number of parties in a party system (e.g. Duverger, *Political Parties: Their Organization and Activity in the Modern State*, London, Methuen, 1954). The analytic inadequacy of this crude criterion led to attempts to develop a more refined and complex typology, of which the most influential has been that of Sartori (*Parties and Party Systems*, Cambridge, Cambridge University Press, 1976). Starting from the division between one-party and multi-party states, he introduces two important refinements. One is the importance of having explicit 'counting rules' in order to establish the number of parties, using electoral and legislative strengths of parties to develop the concept of 'relevant' parties in relation to the formation of governments (such 'relevance' varying empirically according to the political context). The other is the 'unpacking' of the simple one-party categories to distinguish among a total of seven types of party system: three basically non-competitive types (one-party; hegemonic; predominant) and four competitive types (the classical two-party system; limited pluralism; polarized pluralism; the atomized system). By combining considerations of relative size and ideological distance with the basic property of number of parties, a sensitive and useful typology of party systems emerges.

Two other significant considerations are emphasized by Sartori. The first is that, in a very important sense, it is illogical to speak of a 'one-party system', since the term 'system' implies interaction among two or more elements or units. However, the one-party case is such a useful limiting case in the universe of party systems that the term 'one-party system' is likely to remain in use. Second, party systems are not immutable, and the paths of change from one party system to another is an interesting topic for analysis. Events in Eastern Europe and Latin America in the late 1980s seem to challenge assumptions that non-revolutionary change from non-competitive to competitive party system types is inherently impossible. See also: *cleavage; multi-party system; one-party system; party; two-party system*.

Patronage The exercise of the power to appoint persons to office or to nominate them for the award of honours on the basis of the opinion of the authority exercising the patronage (e.g. a prime minister, president, senator). Such patronage power may be restricted by, for example, tradition, legislative requirements, or necessity for confirmation of nominations by some external institution, such as the monarch or the US Senate. However, the essence of patronage is the discretionary choice available to the authority, in contrast to the need to appoint strictly by merit or according to some other externally determined criterion. Patronage may still operate even when some specific minimum condition or requirement exists (such as possession of a professional qualification by appointees).

The term is chiefly applied to appointments to political or administrative posts, such as Cabinet office, membership of public boards, or ambassadorships. It also includes, in the British political system, appointments to judicial office, to certain educational posts (headships of some Oxford and Cambridge colleges, for instance), and to some religious appointments in the Church of England, such as archbishoprics and bishoprics, as well as the bestowal of titles, peerages and orders of chivalry. In the American political system patronage is widespread at the federal, state and local levels, and the president, senators, members of the House of Representatives, state governors, mayors, etc., all have patronage powers. Recently an increase in the proportion of 'non-patronage' posts in the federal civil service has diminished the availability of patronage posts available in the federal administration.

The term 'patronage' does not itself imply venal or corrupt use of appointive powers, though in some contexts the suggestion of improper motives is obviously involved in the choice of this word. See also: *clientelism; nomenklatura*.

Peer group A group characterized by the possession of some shared factor, e.g. age, educational attainment, or social status, believed to be relevant to the values and interrelationships of members of the group. Peer group membership may, for instance, be influential in the formation of political attitudes, determination of the level of political participation of an individual, or the acceptance of various forms of authority. See also: *primary group*.

Personation The attempt to pass oneself off as another person by deceitful means. In politics, personation usually refers to a fraudulent attempt to vote in place of someone else..

Platform A series of policy proposals produced on behalf of a candidate or party in anticipation of a forthcoming election campaign. The word may refer to the whole of the proposals of a particular party (e.g. the Conservative party platform) or to a section of such proposals (e.g. the environmental protection platform of the Republican party). A single proposal from such a platform is sometimes called a 'plank'. See also: *manifesto*.

Plebiscite A vote in which the electorate gives its verdict on a proposed change of regime, or ratifies such a change if it has already occurred. It thus differs from a referendum, which is a vote on an issue of policy. Examples of plebiscites include those conferring the status of Life Consul (1802) and Emperor (1804) on Napoleon; the separation of Norway from Sweden (1905); and those held in the Saar in 1935 and 1955 concerning the return of the Saar area to Germany. A referendum may acquire the qualities of a de facto plebiscite if a ruler or the people link it to issues of a change of regime: the 1969 referendum in the French constitution was so regarded by de Gaulle in advance of the vote, and he resigned as president when the proposals were defeated.

The word derives from the Latin term which referred to a vote by the 'plebs': the non-noble section of the citizenry in ancient Rome. See also: *referendum*.

Pluralism Sometimes used to describe a society composed of a range of different groups (ethnic, religious, etc), the term has acquired more specific connotations in political science. Pluralism is often used in an explicitly normative or prescriptive fashion. A pluralist is someone who believes that power should be shared among the diverse groups and interests in society and that political decisions should reflect free-flowing bargaining and compromises between such groups. The state itself should therefore be an agent for this process, acting as a neutral referee or arbiter, rather than as a contestant with specific interests of its own.

But a somewhat similar position is often maintained, ostensibly without the normative foundation alluded to above. Some analysts have argued that, irrespective of any moral preference for a pluralist society, it is this aspect of modern societies which provides the most fruitful basis for political analysis. It is the variety of actual values, interests, beliefs and preferences together with the way these are socially integrated and pursued by groups that provides the basic material for analysis. Again the state is seen as an agent in this process, with different pluralist analyses taking different views of the precise nature of state involvement. Because of its emphasis on the fragmentary nature of society and politics, pluralists have been accused of adopting an approach biased towards the conclusion that political power is pluralistically dispersed. See also: *behaviouralism; elite; interests; issues; polyarchy; power; state*.

Plurality The proportion of votes secured by a candidate which is (a) more than the proportion obtained by any rival candidate, and (b) less than a majority of votes cast, i.e. is a proportion smaller than 50% plus one vote. See also: *majority*.

Plutocracy A word derived from Greek, meaning a constitution based on property qualifications, in which the rich rule and the poor have no share in government. Application extends beyond explicit constitutional requirements to include systems where high expenditure is in fact necessary to hold or gain office, for instance in modern democracies (such as the USA) where a successful election campaign generally requires substantial private funds.

The term is not often used in modern political analysis, although wealth is frequently identified as one of the factors sustaining elites or oligarchic rule. See also: *aristocracy; elite; oligarchy*.

Polarization The clustering of elements around one, two, or several points on some scale. In international politics, for instance, it can refer to the forming of alliances around two major powers (bipolarity) or several (multipolarity). In psephology, it is often used – rather imprecisely – to refer to the tendency for votes to be given to two major and opposed parties, rather than to parties located between these. It may also be used to refer to a general tendency toward support for extreme, rather than moderate, parties. See also: *bipolarity*.

Policy A set of decisions taken by a political actor or group, concerning the selection of goals and the methods of attaining them, relating to a specified situation. These decisions should, in principle, be within the power of the policy-maker to achieve.

A policy may be simple – consisting, for example, of a single decision – or it may be a complex set of contingency plans. It may be a decision to postpone decision (a policy of 'wait and see'). It may be relatively concrete (e.g. a decision to reduce direct taxes and increase indirect taxes), or relatively abstract (e.g. a policy of non-intervention in the affairs of other states).

Four elements of this definition of policy require special attention. The *selection of goals* implies that the policy-maker possesses an explicit value-system and an ordering of values. Such goals may be positive (e.g. economic growth) or negative (e.g. freedom from aggression); they may be of various levels of specificity (e.g. a policy of nationalization in general; a policy of nationalization of public utilities; a policy of nationalization of the electricity supply industry). The *methods* of attaining the goals must involve, at least in part, the purposeful management of human behaviour, thus distinguishing policy from technology involving control and manipulation of inanimate objects. The *specified situation* is one of future interaction between the policy-making process and the social and physical environments, interaction which imposes constraints on the attainment of goals. The element of *control* by the policy-maker may be through authority, persuasion or coercion, but if it is not present, at least in principle, then it is inappropriate to use the term 'policy', since the selection of goals is merely a statement of preference or intention. See also: *decision; incrementalism; non-decision; policy analysis.*

Policy analysis The study of the formation, implementation and evaluation of public policy, the values of policy-makers, the environment of the policy-making system, the costs of policy alternatives (e.g. by the use of techniques such as planning-programming-budgeting, normative economics, game theory, etc.), and metapolicy – the study of policies for improving policy making.

Policy analysis draws on many of the approaches and methods of political science, such as the systems approach, decision-making approaches, and aspects of the study of political behaviour, but may also incorporate concepts and approaches from other disciplines, such as economics, administrative theory and psychology.

In a secondary usage, policy analysis may be used as a term to describe the detailed examination of a particular policy or policy-making system. See also: *policy.*

Policy community See: *policy network.*

Policy network A set of political actors, governmental and non-governmental, sharing an interest in a policy issue and exerting influence upon decisions concerning outcomes relating to that policy issue, sometimes by means of the initiation of new policy proposals. Such a network tends to be relatively impervious to influence from the public, the legislature or other policy networks. A typical policy network may include staff from several ministries and representatives of affected interest groups, as well as, in some countries such as the USA and Germany, members of legislative committees concerned with the policy area in question. Where such networks persist over time and develop a consciousness of their shared interests in a policy area, they may be termed policy communities. See also: *interest group; policy*.

Political analysis In its loosest sense, a term that might be used to describe any more or less rigorous enquiry into matters political. More strictly, that part of political enquiry which resolves political phenomena, problems, etc., into their component elements, expressed abstractly, for the purposes of definition, classification and explanation. Different forms of analysis include: analysis of some aspect of the political process (e.g. policy analysis, electoral analysis); of some aspect of the process of enquiry (e.g. conceptual analysis, methodology); or analysis using some particular approach, method or technique (e.g. comparative analysis, rational choice analysis). See also: *concept; methodology; policy analysis; political science; rational choice analysis; systems analysis*.

Political anthropology Anthropology, the science of humankind, comprises aspects of many other disciplines and areas of enquiry, from human biology and evolution (often involving archaeological techniques), through the cultural and social sciences and history, to philosophical study of human nature. Within this range, *social* anthropology may often appear to merge with sociology, but social anthropology has directed much of its attention towards relatively primitive and isolated tribal groups and, more generally, towards groups within which custom, myth, tradition and other apparently non-rational characteristics predominate. Political anthropology is the study of the political relations in such groups, often attempting to uncover the political significance of culture, symbol and ritual, and to explain how political functions, common to all societies, are performed in the absence of formal political structures. See also: *custom; functional explanation; hermeneutics; political culture; politics; structural-functional analysis*.

Political asylum The practice of granting refuge and protection to inhabitants of some foreign territory when their political beliefs or actions have rendered them liable to punishment or persecution. In deciding whether to grant asylum, governments usually try to distinguish such dissidents from those who are 'economic refugees', fleeing only from material deprivation. The place of refuge is usually the host territory itself but asylum may also be granted within some other area of jurisdiction exercised by the host country, such as an embassy or ship..

Political behaviour An area of study within political science, concerned with those aspects of human behaviour that take place within some political context. Its focus is the individual person – as voter, leader, revolutionary, party member, etc. – rather than the group, political system, institution or structure. Philosophy and the social sciences use the term 'behaviour' to denote, strictly, that aspect of activity that can be simply observed, not including the dispositions and inner states of the individuals concerned. Behaviour is, in this sense, action shorn of the beliefs and intentions of the actor. But studies of political behaviour are often centrally concerned with political socialization, culture, ideologies, attitudes and opinions, as well as the relationships between individuals and groups, the constraints of the system on the individual's opportunities for action, and the methods of political communication employed by individuals. Such studies are not, therefore, concerned only with 'behaviour' in the strict sense, but more generally with individual activity and its relation to other factors.

'The study of political behaviour' may thus be distinguished from behaviouralism. The former denotes the initial focus of enquiry on individual political behaviour, while allowing a wide range of concepts and techniques to be brought to bear on such questions. Within the latter, a much wider range of topics may be tackled but the methods of analysis and evidence are more narrowly circumscribed. This distinction does not, of course, preclude the study of political behaviour through behaviouralism. See also: *behaviouralism; group theory; political culture; political psychology; political socialization; political system.*

Political communication Political information which is transmitted and received, or the process by which this information is transmitted and received, by the various elements of a political system. Information may be regarded as political by reference to its content, its intended effect, or its utilization by the recipient. The concept is not limited to attempted political persuasion, indoctrination or propaganda; the information may be of any type, transmitted through any medium: e.g. statistical reports, statements of individual opinion, opinion polls, reports of decisions, news coverage, education, etc.

Political communication can be studied in a variety of ways. Its content may be analyzed; the predominance of different forms of communication in different political systems may form the basis for comparative analysis; the relationships between communications subsystems and political systems generally may be investigated, some species of systems analysis coming close to reducing the notion of a political system to a pattern of communication. Many recent studies have drawn attention to the way the style of modern media coverage, particularly radio and television coverage of electoral politics, reduces the political message to a few fragments of speech and image, from which meagre information the general character of politician and policy is inferred. See also: *content analysis; feedback; mass media; political socialization; propaganda; rhetoric; systems analysis.*

Political culture The overall pattern of orientations, values, attitudes and beliefs, held by the individuals who are members of a political community. The intuition informing the idea of 'a political culture' is that cultural patterns will shape and constrain the political system and that certain patterns of belief will be strongly associated with corresponding types of political system, with implications for future stability, consensus and development. Aspects of political culture which have been regarded as being of particular importance include: the agents and styles of political socialization; the relationships between political values and the procedures of the political system; attitudes towards leadership and authority; the focus of political identity of individuals and groups.

While it is likely that in nearly all political systems there are some basic norms that are broadly, if not universally, shared, the degree of homogeneity of political culture must vary considerably between systems and over time. A political culture will generally contain identifiable subcultures, based on religion, region, ethnicity, social status, etc. These subcultures will consist of political attitudes and values distinct from those of the general political culture. Strong and markedly distinct subcultures may weaken, or even threaten to destroy, the political integration of the community. Examples of such subcultures include the nationalist subcultures in Northern Ireland and the Soviet Union, and the linguistic subcultures in Belgium.

During the 1970s, much of the earlier work on political culture came to be viewed with suspicion. It had been common in the 1950s and 1960s to find the *English* political culture identified as the only significant culture in the United Kingdom, and the homogeneous character of this culture used to explain the relative stability, flexibility and success of the UK political system, the political cultures of non-English groups being treated as peripheral differences which had made no difference to the modern outcome. Such treatments were regarded by some as historically flawed in their tendency to dismiss the contribution made to British political development by the need to accommodate different cultures and, following the resurgence of nationalism in Scotland, Wales and Northern Ireland, these treatments appeared to offer a poor and complacent depiction of the present.

More broadly, the use of the concept of political culture is sometimes attacked as pseudo-explanatory, inferring the content of the culture from political behaviour and then purporting to explain that behaviour by reference to the underlying culture. While this may be a valid criticism of some work in the area, there are also studies which are not guilty of this obvious circularity and which, particularly when pursuing comparative analysis, have produced hypotheses worthy of further research and discussion.

One of the most important studies of political culture, *The Civic Culture*, by G. Almond and S. Verba (Princeton, Princeton University Press, 1963) examined five democratic political systems. This study continues to attract critical attention: see, for instance, G. Almond and S. Verba (eds), *The Civic Culture Revisited*, (Boston, Little Brown, 1980). See also: *attitudes; norm; political integration; political socialization; post-materialism; values*.

Political development The processes of rapid political change which occur in traditional societies, often in association with other processes of modernization, and which result in a more complex and differentiated political system and a more defined, integrated political community. It is a term particularly, though not at all exclusively, applied to those states of the third world which were formerly colonial dependencies of European states, and so is often linked to the processes of decolonization and attainment of political independence.

A major conceptual difficulty arises over the application of the term 'development'. It is fallacious to suppose that all states will somehow follow the course of political development which western democratic states or European communist states have taken. On the other hand, political scientists have claimed that some uniform trends can be identified which appear to be associated with processes of political development in most, if not all, cases, such as: increased social and political complexity; specialization of political roles and institutions; enlargement of an educated political elite; politicization of the population (through mass parties, for instance); the increased saliency of national, rather than parochial, political issues; and the increasing interrelationship of political, social and economic spheres of society. See also: *modernization; third world.*

Political economy Originally, the science of the wealth of nations, or the economics of polities. The term is particularly associated with eighteenth and nineteenth century works concerned with the national economy, the subsistence of the people and the revenues of government. More recent usage refers to, in political analysis, the study of economic policy and the linkage between political and economic factors in public policy, and, in economics, a critical interest in the various social and political frameworks within which economic systems operate. See also: *economic theories of politics.*

Political elites See: *elite.*

Political geography The study of the relationship between political areas, institutions or processes, and their physical environment. Its origins can be traced to early modern speculation about the effect of terrain and climate on culture and customs. More recent areas of interest include geographical influences on the formation and political growth of states; the nature of frontiers and boundaries; the relations between core and periphery within states and in international state systems; the structure of communications networks; demography as affected by geographic factors; the distribution of natural resources. See also: *apportionment; geopolitics.*

Political history A term usually denoting historical study which focuses on continuity and change in government, rulers, constitution, forms of the state, etc. Works of this type comprise the bulk of historical writing before the emergence of economic and social history. More recent examples include biographies of politicians, accounts of periods of government or of the development of political parties, etc. Of course, a great deal of the work generally regarded as political science uses historical materials. This raises questions about the distinctiveness of the category 'political history', and about the more general relation between history and social science.

The traditional view of the difference between the study of history and the social sciences might be expressed thus: while both historian and social scientist may be concerned with the events of the French Revolution, the historian's principal concern is with those particular past events purely in themselves, in the sense that their coherence is simply given by the fact that they happened as a related complex of occurrences; the social scientist's concern is with these events as a particular incidence of a more general phenomenon, revolution, a phenomenon for which theoretical explanation may be provided.

It is increasingly difficult to draw boundaries in this area, and most practitioners are reluctant to do so. A lot of recent work combines the explicitly theoretical concerns of social science with historical focus and method. Recent examples include Barrington Moore, *Social Origins of Dictatorship and Democracy* (Boston, Beacon Press, 1966), Theda Skocpol, *States and Social Revolutions* (Cambridge, Cambridge University Press, 1979), Douglas E. Ashford, *The Emergence of the Welfare States* (Oxford, Basil Blackwell, 1987). Much of this work is 'political' in that it focuses on forms of the state, but terms like 'historical political science' are not generally used. Work which attempts to construct general theory in terms of economic and social forces tends to be known as 'historical sociology' or 'macro-sociology' (e.g. Moore and Skocpol). When work is described as 'political history' (e.g. Ashford) the usual implication is that it pays more detailed attention to events at the level of political institutions and policy processes. Such distinctions are somewhat arbitrary and always debatable. See also: *comparative analysis; explanation; political science; political thought; theory*.

Political integration The state of cohesion which exists in a political community (such as a state, a province or a confederation), as demonstrated by a high degree of mutual political interaction among the members of that community, both individuals and groups, interaction which is based on consent rather than coercion. While distinguishable from other aspects of social integration (e.g. economic integration or cultural integration) by this emphasis on political interaction as its expression, political integration is obviously closely linked to such other forms of integration.

The degree of integration of a political community is related to several factors, including the dominance of the political culture of the political community as a whole over any distinctive subcultures within it; the efficacy of political institutions and processes in meeting expectations; the ease and frequency of political communication among members of the political community; etc. Malintegration occurs when the range of shared political values is diminished, coercion increasingly becomes necessary to obtain compliance with the law, and demands are made by sections of the political community for secession. Stresses which lead to a weakening of political integration must be reduced by appropriate responses from the political authorities, otherwise the system will tend to divide, or may collapse entirely. Such stresses may result from societal change, external threat, failure to remove or reduce sources of social cleavage, inability to satisfy members of some salient subculture, economic deprivation, etc. Examples of such malintegration stresses in recent history include the rise of Scottish and Irish nationalism in British politics; the demands of 'black power' movements in the USA; the institutionalized malintegration of apartheid in South Africa; claims of the French-speaking population in Quebec; the problems of nationalities in the USSR; Tamil separatism in Sri Lanka. Some authorities have suggested that the division between elites and the mass of the population is the major problem of malintegration, but others have pointed to failures of consensus within elites as equally likely to give rise to malintegration. Though not a problem confined to modernizing states, political integration is a pervasive issue in the processes of modernization.

The European Community has been a special case for the analysis of processes of political integration, where the integration of member-states, as well as sections of their populations, is a central problem. See also: *cleavage; consensus; political culture; political system; secession*.

Political party See: *party*.

Political philosophy Systematic analysis and critical evaluation, at a high level of abstraction, of normative, methodological or metaphysical aspects of politics and political enquiry.

In English-speaking countries the greater part of modern political philosophy is concerned with the analysis of theories and concepts used in normative discourse and empirical enquiry. For instance, various conceptions of 'justice' might be analyzed to uncover their relation to other concepts, their relation to matters of fact, the sort of normative judgements they license, their consistency with other values and standards of judgement, and the general grounds for holding to one conception rather than another. Similarly, conceptions of 'power' might be analyzed in terms of their normative implications, and also in terms of their susceptibility to operationalization and use in empirical research.

Political philosophy also deals with matters related to metaphysics and the philosophy of history: the nature of the state and civil society; the nature of political life; the basic presuppositions underlying thought about history and society, either universally or in a particular epoch. Hegel, for instance, held that the state must be understood as part of a process of realization of 'mind' (or 'spirit'), a claim that appears to be neither a moral imperative nor an empirical hypothesis. See also: *concept; normative theory; political science; political theory; political thought; theory*.

Political psychology Enquiry, by both political scientists and psychologists, into the relationship between political behaviour and conscious or unconscious mental states and processes.

In the earlier part of the twentieth century attempts were made to reduce explanations of politics to some mechanistic basis in individual human nature, or to pursue behaviourist research into stimulus and response. Work in the 1950s and 1960s concentrated on the relationships between personality factors and political behaviour; the classification and scaling of political attitudes; the socialization process; and the psychological bases of leadership styles. More recent studies have turned towards group psychology; cognitive models of decision-making; the 'psychodynamics' of social and political change; the social creation of ideology; and the workings of political rhetoric. See also: *attitudes; behaviouralism; determinism; ideology; political socialization; reductionist theories; rhetoric; values*.

Political recruitment See: *recruitment*.

Political science The term 'political science' has at least two meanings. It may refer broadly to the study of political matters. Or it may be used to distinguish the study of political institutions and processes from the study of political ideas, particularly denoting those aspects of the study of politics that are based on empirical theory and which aspire to produce grounded and validated knowledge. The academic study of politics is not a single 'discipline' in any strict sense of the word. Its orientation to its subject, its methods and techniques, are drawn from a wide range of disciplines and subdisciplines: philosophy, history, mathematics, law, economics, anthropology. These, and many others, have seemed to bear some relevance to political events and have contributed to the development of political science and its emergence as a specific, if hybrid, form of enquiry.

The use of the term in its more specific form, to refer to empirically directed political enquiry, raises a host of problems and arguments about the nature of science and the actual or possible scientific status of political explanation. 'Political science' is currently used to describe the work of those who reject the idea of a single scientific method or any mimicry of the methods of natural science, as well as those who embrace such ideas and methods. See also: *explanation; government (b): study area; political analysis; political philosophy; political theory; political thought; politics; scientific method; theory.*

Political socialization Political socialization is the process through which, on the one hand, an individual acquires information, attitudes and orientations concerning political phenomena, and, on the other hand, society transmits political norms and beliefs both from one generation to the next and to immigrant newcomers. These two aspects may be in contradiction where an individual apparently acquires deviant attitudes and orientations.

The socialization process tends to be gradual in normal circumstances, and to extend from early childhood into, and throughout, adulthood. It appears that basic political attitudes are acquired first: loyalty towards society (or the state, the race, the nation, etc.), recognition of authority, and predispositions towards its exercise; then come more specific attitudes such as broad identification with a political party; and after that follow attitudes towards political issues, stances on political programmes, etc. While this process normally occurs in sequence through the lifetime of an individual, major societal changes or the entry of an individual into a new society (e.g. through migration) may involve a new socialization process at a relatively late age.

Political socialization can occur through direct or indirect processes. Direct processes include formal political education and indoctrination (though some definitions would distinguish political socialization from overt political education), as well as personal political participation. Indirect processes include extension of non-political socialization to political situations (e.g. the acquisition of general social attitudes such as social efficacy), participation in non-political situations which nevertheless may involve bargaining, decision making or the exercise of authority, and imitation.

The agencies of political socialization include the family, peer groups, educational institutions, and organizations, both political (such as parties) and non-political (such as churches or social clubs). The attitudes and values of these various agencies change in content and direction over time, and may well be dissimilar relative to each other. Thus an individual may experience problems of reconciling various socialization processes: e.g. the working-class university graduate; rural inhabitants in modernizing societies when taking up residence in a city; immigrants from a traditional culture moving to an industrialized society. See also: *political culture; political integration.*

Political sociology The study of the relationships between society and politics: between the social and political aspects of structures, institutions and behaviour. Areas of interest include the social basis of political ideology; the effects of social change on political institutions and policies; the social basis of voting behaviour and political participation; social and political culture, political integration, and the social causes of consensus and conflict; the analysis of elites; the relation between social structure and political power. Political sociology thus ranges from micro-research into the social attitudes associated with individual political behaviour to macro-research into the relationship between state and society. No specific level of research can properly be described as typical of political sociology, and no particular assumption concerning the causal priority of social factors over the political is implied by the term. See also: *political analysis; political history; political science; politics; society; state.*

Political system Loosely, the term is often used to refer to the political arrangements of a society, and thus is almost a synonym for the word 'state', but does not have the legalistic and philosophic connotations which the word 'state' carries, and in any case societies without state structures can nevertheless be regarded as possessing political systems. More specifically, in political science the term means the set of structures, processes and institutions which interact with each other, and across the boundaries of the system with the environment, to 'allocate values authoritatively for a society' (David Easton) and generally perform those functions, such as conflict resolution and political recruitment to positions of authority, which may be defined as political. The political system is itself a subsystem of the wider social system, be it of a state, a local community, a tribe or an institution such as a university, a hospital or a prison. It is usually conceived as being an open system, involved in exchanges with its environment, and an adaptive system, capable of responding to changing circumstances, regulating its own component units, responding to stress, and, through feedback mechanisms, adjusting its outputs to input conditions. It has been most thoroughly analyzed in the systems approaches of David Easton and Karl Deutsch. Because the term is defined by its functions, it can refer to non-state, as well as state, political arrangements. See also: *feedback; society; state; systems analysis.*

Political theory Sometimes used broadly to cover all study of general and abstract aspects of politics and political analysis: in a university department of politics, for instance, the courses offered under the general heading 'political theory' will probably include courses in political philosophy and the history of political thought. However, the term is also used more narrowly to denote causal and explanatory theories of politics. Political theory, in this sense, consists of empirically based theories about political systems, processes and behaviour. See also: *political analysis; political philosophy; political science; political thought; theory.*

Political thought A very general term for all types of political theories, philosophies, ideologies, mental processes concerning politics, etc., and their expression. In this broad sense political thought encompasses all political philosophy, political theory and ideology. The term is, however, usually encountered in the narrower context of the *history* of political thought. Here the principal concern is either to trace the source, development and influence of political ideas and forms of argument through history, or to decipher the meaning of particular ideas and forms of argument within their immediate historical and political context. Controversy exists over whether these two endeavours are mutually exclusive, which is to be preferred, whether either is really possible, and so on. But in neither case is the interest of the historian of thought the same as that of the political philosopher or theorist. The historian of thought is not primarily interested in the truth, consistency or practical usefulness of the ideas, but in their meaning and relation to other historically connected ideas or actions. However, undergraduate courses with titles like 'The History of Political Thought' often go beyond any strictly historical treatment in bringing philosophical questions to bear on the material. See also: *hermeneutics; ideology; political philosophy; political theory.*

Politics Derived from the classical Greek word 'polis' (meaning a political community of citizens identified with a city-state, such as Athens or Sparta), in modern usage 'politics' has come to denote the activity in the social system, whether the social system of the state or of other communities or institutions, by which the goals of the system are selected, ordered in terms of priority (both temporally and in terms of resource allocation), and implemented. It thus involves also the ways in which the political authorities (those who have the power to decide on such goal-related matters) are chosen and changed, the value system of groups involved in politics, such as parties, interest groups and movements, the behaviour of individuals, such as their participation in politics and the electoral choices they make, and the organization of the machinery of government by means of which political decisions are implemented. Politics necessarily involves the existence of both conflict and consensus: without conflict, there would be no need for politics, and without consensus concerning norms and political procedures the political process could not function, and other methods of arriving at outcomes, including violence and coercion, would replace it. Politics is distinguished from other social processes by its concern with the 'public' goals of a society, i.e. those intended to be of general concern (decisions about the law relating to divorce, for example, but not a decision in a divorce case for any particular marriage); whereas, for instance, economics may be concerned with private or public allocations of goods and services, and law with the application of a code of decisions drawn up from a constitution or legislation, which thus are decisions derived from a prior political process.

Controversy concerning definitions of politics have abounded in political science. Some regard politics as defined only in relation to the state, regarding the sovereign claims which a state, and only a state, can make as so distinctive and such a significant aspect of politics as to render invalid any use of the term 'politics' for activities of organizations other than the state. Others focus upon the political process as a function first and foremost, and therefore as a function which can be identified as existing, however tenuously, in any society or organization. Some focus their definitions upon power, others upon decision making, yet others upon the conflict and conflict resolution which are inherent in the political process. See also: *government (a) the institution; society; sovereignty; state.*

Polity A politically organized society regardless of its form of government. The word usually refers to the civil organization of a state, but may also be used to refer to an empire, an international political community, a township, etc. See also: *politics; society; state.*

Poll A procedure for obtaining expressions of opinions. This may be by means of a formal ballot (e.g. an election or referendum), or by means of a survey based on questionnaires and interviews (sometimes called an 'opinion poll'). A 'straw poll' is an informal test of opinion on some issue, often concerning a proposal which is still tentative.

A derived meaning of 'poll' as the place where voting occurs is found in contexts such as 'half the voters went to the polls before noon'. See also: *election; plebiscite; referendum; voting.*

Polyarchy Literally meaning 'rule by many', this term has acquired a more precise connotation in political science. It might be argued that, in modern representative democracies, power is not exercised directly by the people but by elites. However, these elites may compete for power by appealing to shifting coalitions of interest present in the electorate. To the extent that this competition is open and no group interests are wholly disregarded, power is indirectly exercised by the many and polyarchy may be said to exist. See also: *democracy; elite; pluralism; power.*

Populism One usage refers to political ideas founded upon the value of direct communication with, and political participation by, 'the people', including the creation of institutions of direct democracy, such as the initiative, referendum and recall. It can thus be linked to any political ideologies of the left or the right, to nationalism, to religious, racial or linguistic movements, etc. Many contemporary political movements and organizations (e.g. Green parties; student movements) emphasize such populist procedures and goals. A populist politician is one who uses direct appeals to the people as a political instrument, but without necessarily approving populist goals and methods of political participation. In this sense, Goebbels, Hitler, de Gaulle, Peron, Senator Joseph McCarthy, Gaddafi and Castro can all be regarded as populists.

A more specific usage refers to movements or parties which seek to organize 'the common people' (including, and sometimes especially concentrating upon, the peasantry), as a counterforce to more sophisticated, cosmopolitan and seemingly corrupt political forces such as landlords, apparently wealthy ethnic minorities, financiers (in the USA), the court (in Tsarist Russia) – perhaps even regarding these as in conspiracy against 'the people'. In the USA a Populist party (the People's party) was founded in 1891 and survived as a regional and national political force until its fusion with the Democrats in support of the presidential candidacy of William Jennings Bryan in 1896. See also: *conspiracy theories; direct democracy; initiative; recall (a): the institution; referendum.*

Pork-barrel A term chiefly used in US politics to refer to the allocation of government projects such as military installations, harbour developments, location of field offices for federal government agencies and other public works, which legislators seek to have located in their state or congressional district. If they are successful, the legislators acquire personal credit beneficial to their chances of re-election, and their constituencies acquire new sources of tax revenue and employment. Though the term itself is not often employed outside the US context, the phenomenon which it describes exists in other – especially federal – states, such as Germany, Canada, Brazil and Mexico. See also: *'log-rolling'*.

Positivism A term applied to a range of positions on questions of scientific method, knowledge and progress, on the relationships between different branches of scientific enquiry, and on the role of scientific knowledge in social and political development. The two sets of ideas most often referred to are those of Comte and of the Vienna Circle. Adopted in the nineteenth century by Comte, the term denotes a unity of approach to be shared by all sciences, natural and social, and by philosophical enquiry. Theological and metaphysical speculation are rejected in favour of reason, experiment and calculation concerning observed phenomena. All knowledge must be reduced to facts and laws, enabling accurate prediction and human control over the natural and social world. Science restricts itself to a description of *how* things happen and does not concern itself with *why* they happen (in the sense of their real or essential nature). Newton, for instance, is applauded for establishing the actual quantitative relations of motion and gravitational attraction without attempting to explain *why* these relations obtain.

In the early twentieth century the Vienna Circle developed a view known as logical positivism. According to this view the meaning of all propositions is, and only is, the procedure that can be adopted to verify the proposition through experienced perception of the world. Propositions not verifiable in this way must be discarded as meaningless.

The influence and attempted application of these criteria in political science is clearly restrictive. Attention is concentrated on observable facts and any broader approach will be rejected as mere theoretical speculation or moral posturing. In political science the term 'positivism' is now encountered most commonly as a critical condemnation of political analysis which is too narrowly concerned with gathering directly observable facts about politics, and lacking theoretical orientation. However, since positivism comprises a variety of different views on a number of separate questions, the unqualified use of the term conveys no very precise meaning.

The superficially similar term 'legal positivism' is also frequently used. This denotes an approach to the study of law and legal systems. No ideal or independent justification of law is sought. Attention is concentrated on laws as they are, conceived as an integrated system of commands made by sovereign authority, backed by sanctions. See also: *authority; behaviouralism; empiricism; falsificationism; law (b): stipulative law; operationalization; realism (a): scientific realism; sovereignty; verification*.

Post-industrial society See: *industrial society*.

Post-materialism A general term for the attitudes and values apparently developing in some sections of post-industrial societies. Those generations born after the second world war, having undergone political socialization during a period of peace, rising prosperity and educational opportunities, and through exposure to internationalized mass media, display a weaker interest in traditional issues of individual material well-being and national security. Such individuals typically express concern for environmental issues and the 'quality of life', and are likely to pursue their aspirations through non-traditional forms of political participation, protest and direct action. The term invests what may be a localized and transitory phenomenon with a sense of generality and permanence. However, these attitudes appeared to survive, though in diluted form, in the face of the economic uncertainties of the late 1970s and early 1980s.

It has been suggested that the emergence of these non-acquisitive values poses significant problems for the political system, in that they are at odds with both the economic requirements and the political structures of modern society, as they are currently constituted. See also: *dealignment; environmentalism; industrial society; political culture; political socialization; realignment.*

Power A concept so central to social science that its role has been compared to that of energy in physics. Most broadly defined, power refers to the capacity of a person or group to act or to achieve something: a person may for instance have the power of speech and the power to achieve certain goals by the use of speech. Political analysis focuses on the capacities of persons or groups to act or achieve goals through securing the compliance of others. Political analysts have used the concept of power for three main tasks: to describe the general distribution of power within a political system; to assess the relative powers of opposed groups in specific conflicts; to identify the nature and limits of power available to groups or institutional offices.

Many different conceptions of power have been suggested and used in analysis. There is disagreement about how best to delineate the distinctions between power and closely related concepts. Power is often treated as the umbrella under which authority, influence, manipulation, coercion, etc., are gathered. Thus each of these is treated as a type of power, distinguished by a specific resource or means of exercise. But power is itself sometimes treated as a more particular relation, distinct from rather than including some of these other concepts. Power is, for instance, sometimes distinguished from influence, the former indicating the determination or control of another's action, the latter some less conclusive effect. The choices on offer do not end here. It has been suggested that 'influence' best describes a relation of continuous or frequent effect but that power refers to resources which may or may not be used to affect others, according to the will of the agent.

More substantive disagreements exist concerning the necessary features of an exercise of power. Must power involve conflict? If it must, is this conflict between wants, perceived interests or real interests? Must an exercise of power include the successful realization of intention, or may power also be exercised if only unintended consequences result? Is power exercised only through actions, or may power be exercised by inaction? Different answers to these conceptual questions yield different notions of power which, in turn, produce different pictures of the political world.

The foregoing discussion has concentrated on variations most usually referring to the subjective features of individual agents: intention, interest, etc. But some analysts regard explanation at this level as superficial and unhelpful, preferring to investigate the structural features of a system. Here power may be used to describe the determination of agents and political institutions by structure, or the consequent capacity of classes to realize objective interests.

The difficulties of definition are heightened when it is realized that most uses of the concept of power require a method of measuring or comparing a number of opposed sources of power. No generally accepted method exists. Some progress has been made in developing indices for comparison of the powers of political actors in decision making through different voting systems. Attempts to measure power in situations not defined by such clear formal rules must confront the problem of quantifying dimensions such as costs of exercise, extent of opposition overcome, and interest-satisfaction. Controversy surrounding matters like these has led some writers to identify 'power' as a prime example of an essentially contested concept. See also: *authority; essentially contested concepts; interests; issues; non-decision; reputational approach; structuralism*.

Pragmatism Philosophically, the belief that the meaning, justification or truth of ideas and propositions should be assessed only in the light of their practical implications for matters of human interest. This belief has been particularly influential in the United States and has had an effect on political science similar to that induced by empiricism and positivism.

The term is also used more generally, often in referring to political practice, to describe a readiness to adapt to the particular needs and possibilities of the moment, without strong regard for theoretical or ideological consistency. See also: *empiricism; positivism; realism (b): political realism*.

Precedent A previous decision or action used as a guide or model for a current decision or action, which can be either binding precedent, as in many legal and administrative contexts, or advisory precedent, as in various areas of political practice. Thus, in constitutional law, a previously decided case may be taken as setting a precedent for a current case; in the civil service, a decision in the past may be a persuasive precedent for settling a similar matter now pending; in the legislature, a matter of procedure may be settled by referring to a similar past example as a guiding precedent, etc. The important feature of all these examples would be the close degree of similarity of the precedent to the current issue.

Preferential voting A system of election which requires the voter to list candidates in order of preference (1, 2, 3, ... etc.), rather then selecting one candidate to the exclusion of others by placing a cross opposite one name. The Alternative Vote and Single Transferable Vote systems both use preferential voting, as do certain flexible variants of list-based proportional representation systems. See also: *alternative vote system; electoral system; proportional representation; single transferable vote system*.

Prerogative The collection of customary powers, only sometimes enshrined in law, enjoyed by a ruler (e.g. a monarch or a president) which are subject to no formal check or veto, nor to surveillance by the courts, though in practice in a constitutional state such powers, if exercised arbitrarily, would almost invariably lead to political difficulties. Prerogative powers may, in effect, be transferred to other persons: e.g. many of the prerogative powers of the British monarch are in fact exercised by the prime minister. Examples of prerogative powers include the right of the US president to recognize foreign governments, and the right of the British monarch to dissolve parliament before the expiry of its five-year maximum term. See also: *monarchy*.

Pressure group See: *interest group*.

Primary election A form of preliminary election for the purpose of selecting a candidate of a political party to be presented as that party's nominee in an election for some public office. It is distinguishable from election by a selection committee of the party by the fact that a primary election is open to all party members, or even to self-designated 'supporters' of the party in some cases. Primary elections may be entirely organized by the party concerned, or – as in the USA – may be controlled by public law and subject to restrictions in the same manner as are public elections. The rules governing entitlement to vote in primary elections may be a matter for the party or for definition by public law. A small number of informal, party-controlled primary elections have been held in Britain. Primaries are associated otherwise almost exclusively with elections for local, state and national office in the USA. See also: *election*.

Primary group A group, often of a relatively small size, characterized by frequent and intimate intercommunication and interaction, often based on face-to-face contact, in which members identify with the group in terms of their total personality, rather than with respect to some specialized role only. The family, peer groups, work gangs and in some cases small committees are examples of primary groups. See also: *peer group*.

Prisoners' dilemma See: *game theory*.

Privatization The process of transferring ownership of enterprises or holdings of shares in enterprises from state ownership and control to private ownership and control, as has occurred with for example the gas, steel, and telecommunication industries and with state-owned shares in British Petroleum in the United Kingdom, the sale of Volkswagen shares to the public in West Germany, and the transfer of numerous enterprises in East Germany since economic and monetary union with the Federal Republic of Germany on 1 July 1990. Privatization can take any of several forms: a share issue to the general public; a management 'buy-out'; a directly negotiated sale to one or a few private investors; or direct transfer of property rights to private citizens, as in the sale of local authority-owned housing to tenants under the Conservative governments of Mrs Thatcher. See also: *nationalization*.

Problematic The basic theoretical and methodological assumptions underlying enquiry. The term is loosely equivalent to one sense of 'paradigm' and usually identifies assumptions made by a group of writers working within a common framework. Thus criticism of some example of political analysis may focus on a particular alleged weakness in 'the Marxist problematic' or 'the pluralist problematic'. See also: *methodology; paradigm (b): Kuhnian usage*.

Proletarianization A process in which elements of some class or classes, for instance the middle class and the peasantry, come to occupy the social or economic position of the proletariat, or to display proletarian attitudes and values.

The term is sometimes used by Marxists to describe an aspect of expected class polarization under capitalism. More usually it forms part of some Marxist explanations of fascism where the petite-bourgeoisie and elements of the peasantry, threatened with proletarianization in conditions of economic crisis, turn against democracy. See also: *fascism; Marxism; social class*.

Proletariat See: *social class*.

Propaganda Persuasive communication by means of any or all available media, designed to change or reinforce in predetermined directions opinions on certain topics held by its audience, particularly through emotional rather than objective message content. Some authorities would include in a definition of propaganda the idea that it should be directed towards the stimulation of action as well as the reinforcement or alteration of opinion. The term is now normally used in pejorative, rather than descriptive, contexts. See also: *political communication; rhetoric*.

Proportional representation A system of voting designed to produce a result which reflects as accurately as possible the proportional support given to some specified characteristic of the candidates (in public elections, this characteristic is normally party affiliation).

In national elections, proportional representation systems of election are generally based on multi-member constituencies, ranging in size from about half-a-dozen seats to a single, nationwide constituency as in Israel. The larger the constituency, in terms of the number of seats to be filled, the more exact will be the equation between share of the vote and share of the seats which each party will obtain. Electoral systems based on preferential voting, such as the single transferable vote system in the Republic of Ireland, may in fact produce results more proportional in terms of party representation in the legislature than do majoritarian systems, but most preferential systems are not designed to secure close correspondence between shares of seats and votes obtained by parties.

There is controversy concerning the degree to which proportional representation systems of election increase the number of parties obtaining seats in the legislature, and thus contribute in some countries to government instability (e.g. the Weimar Republic in Germany after the first world war; Italy; Belgium). In any case, the electoral system is but one factor among many influencing the number of viable parties in a political system. The existence of electoral thresholds in many countries which operate proportional representation electoral systems (such as the 5% hurdle in Germany) reduces the number of small parties able to secure seats in the legislature.

All west European states with the exceptions of the United Kingdom, the Republic of Ireland, and France use some version of proportional representation for national elections, as does Israel. See also: *d'Hondt method; Droop quota; electoral quota; electoral system; Hare-Niemeyer method; list system; preferential voting; single transferable vote system*.

Protectionism See: *free trade*.

Protectorate A territory possessing, in international law, some of the attributes of independent statehood, but which in other respects is subordinate to a 'protecting power'. This subordination is especially concerned with the foreign relations of the protected state. The relationship between a protected state and its protecting power is often regulated by a treaty between them. Tunisia, for example, was a protectorate of France until 1956. See also: *state; treaty*.

Protocol (a): ceremonial Agreed patterns of etiquette for state or international ceremonial purposes, including, for example, the accreditation of ambassadors, state visits, forms of address of state officials, and tables of precedence (for example for state processions). See also: *convention (a): the institution*.

Protocol (b): treaty A form of agreement between representatives of states, which either precedes more formal expression of such agreement in a treaty, or constitutes items of the treaty itself, possibly forming a secret appendix to a published treaty (e.g. the secret protocols of the 1939 treaty between the USSR and Germany, relating to the future disposal of Polish territory, the Baltic states, etc.) See also: *pact; treaty*.

Proxy A person authorized to vote in place of another, generally according to the previously expressed choice of the absent person. The term can also apply to the vote cast by the proxy.

Psephology The study of voting and elections, particularly with regard to quantifiable factors, though in its wider usage the term can apply also to legal, procedural and other aspects of elections. Psephology is one of the most developed areas of political science, because of the discrete and often dramatic nature of elections, plebiscites and referenda, because of the high degree of public and journalistic interest in voting and elections, and because of the suitability of voting and elections for both comparative and statistical analysis.

There are two main sources of information for psephological studies. Official published sources are important, though the degree of detail of these varies from country to country: the United Kingdom publishes only aggregate constituency results, the USA and Germany, for example, provide data at ward level, and, through official representative statistics, the German authorities also publish statistics of voting decisions subdivided by age, sex and region. The other main source is survey data, including polls of voting intention and recall of voting decision (those taken immediately outside the polling station, in order to obtain responses while the voting act is still fresh in the memory of respondents, are called 'exit polls'). Various forms of statistical analysis are then used to extract meaningful data concerning relationships of voting choice to, for instance, socio-economic characteristics of the electorate, to derive classifications and to evolve theories. See also: *election; panel study; survey; voting*.

Public administration Public administration is the name given to that part of political enquiry which is concerned with the process of organization and management carried on within the institutions which execute the decisions of the legislative and judicial branches of government, and the relationships between the legislative, judicial and administrative branches. The term usually denotes an area of study, though it may be used to describe the activity of public administration itself.

The differentiation between 'politics' and 'administration' is one of theoretical convenience rather than practical relevance. The activity of public administration is intermeshed with politics at most of its stages, and is closely related to policy making, for example in legislative drafting or in connection with delegated legislative powers.

Public administration, as a nominally distinct area of enquiry, flourished in the middle decades of this century. In Britain the principal impetus came from within political studies, derived from a concern to examine the detailed working of governmental bureaucracies. Such a concern arose in part from the increasing scope and complexity of modern government but, more particularly, from the growth in importance of a full-time civil service, and from the perceived need to develop incentives, and criteria for judging efficiency and accountability, in the public sector. These considerations appeared especially pressing where previously private economic organizations (such as the coal and electricity industries) had been placed under the control of national government. In the USA, the study of public administration owed its growth more to the attempt to develop a general science of administration and management, applicable to both public and private organization. By the 1960s, the focus of analysis in both countries had expanded to incorporate the role of bureaucracy in the developing world. More recent developments include the application of public choice theory, and Marxist analyses of public administration in the context of social forces and constraints.

Among the core problems studied are: the organization and control of administrative services; the recruitment, training and promotion of personnel; budgeting and planning of resource allocation; executive-legislative relations; and problems of bureaucracy. See also: *bureaucracy; delegated legislation; executive; nationalization; policy; policy network; political development; public choice theory*.

Public choice theory The application of the methods of neoclassical economics to non-market decisions in order to explain the creation and maintenance of the fundamental elements of state and society (bureaucratic forms, systems of property rights, etc.), through rational choice analysis of group interests. See also: *public goods; rational choice analysis; social choice theory*.

Public goods A public good is a benefit which, if provided, cannot be withheld from individuals who do not contribute to its provision. Market forces will fail to provide such goods since free-riding consumers offer no incentive to producers. The stock example of a pure public good is a lighthouse: a ship gets vital navigational information from the light whether her owners contribute to its provision or not. But there may be no goods that are purely public (or purely private). Various steps *could* be taken to reduce the public nature of even a lighthouse; however, these would themselves be costly. To the extent that a good cannot *feasibly* be withheld it is described as 'non-excludable'. A lighthouse would also be described as 'non-crowdable': the enjoyment of its benefit by one ship does not reduce the benefits enjoyed by others.

Public goods are of considerable importance for political analysis. The most basic concerns of government (national defence, the economic framework, law and order, the political system itself) are all public goods. Beyond these, much political argument is concerned with the identity of other goods which cannot feasibly be provided by private activity and the level at which public provision should take place. The possibility of free-riding on public goods also raises fundamental questions about the nature of political activity. To the extent that collective action (by parties, trade unions, pressure groups, etc.) aims to affect the provision of public goods, then the direct benefits achieved will be available to all, whether contributing resources to the organization or not. This may explain the absence of collective action in pursuit of certain interests, but it also casts doubt on many of the usual explanations for the existence of organizations which do pursue public goods. For a seminal discussion of these issues see: M. Olson, *The Logic of Collective Action: Public Goods and the Theory of Groups* (Cambridge, Mass., Harvard University Press, 1965). See also: *externality; game theory; public choice theory; rational choice analysis.*

Public opinion Views shared by members of some 'public', i.e. the members of a community, society or other political unit, relating to a matter of controversy. Some definitions limit the term to opinion on matters of political – therefore of 'public' – concern. In any case, any issue about which public opinion exists in sufficient measure may enter the realm of the political. It is recognized that sections of the public may hold opposing views (in which case one might refer to a 'balance of public opinion in favour of issue *X*'), and that many members of the public may neither be informed concerning some issues, nor, if informed, be sufficiently concerned to hold an opinion. The processes by which public opinion is formed, measured and communicated to the political authorities, and the responsiveness of the authorities to public opinion, are all matters of interest to political science. The role of opinion leaders, the use of sample surveys and studies of political communication are examples of topics related to the study of public opinion. See also: *opinion leader; political communication; propaganda.*

Purge A process by which members of a group (e.g. a political party, a conspiratorial movement, a legislature, a committee) are expelled on the grounds that their actions or opinions have been deemed to be undesirable or even treacherous by the group itself, its leadership, or some important subgroup. Such expulsion is generally justified as necessary to preserve the values or organizational cohesion of the group. The purge may be implemented through use of court proceedings, the use of a group adjudication process, leadership decree, execution, or other methods.

Though usually associated with the politics of authoritarian, especially totalitarian, regimes, purges are not found only in such regimes. The Labour party in Britain has from time to time instituted purges against groups which were regarded as incompatible with the party's aims and beliefs. Other examples include Hitler's actions against the SA in 1934, various purges instituted by Stalin in the USSR, and changes in the leadership of the Hungarian and Czechoslovakian communist parties following invasion by the Soviet Union in 1956 and 1968.

Putsch An attempt to seize political power by violent and illegal means, often involving elements of the armed forces, on the basis of a secret plot.

Unsuccessful attempts include the 'Kapp *putsch*' in Germany (1920) and the Hitler-Ludendorff *putsch* in Bavaria (1923), as well as several attempts in the Philippines during the presidency of Mrs Aquino. The Egyptian officers' *putsch* (1952) is an example of a successful *putsch*. See also: *coup d'état; palace revolution; revolution*.

Q

Questionnaire A series of standardized questions for use in, for example, sample surveys, panel studies, depth interviews and similar forms of social inquiry. The questions on the questionnaire may be 'open-ended', allowing absolutely free response, or 'closed-ended', permitting only a choice of response from a limited and pre-selected set of answers.

A questionnaire generally provides for the recording of answers (this recording may be a tape-recorder or mechanical means, or by writing) either by the interviewer, an assistant, or, with self-administered questionnaires, by the respondent. The questionnaire, in addition to allowing for the recording of answers, will usually require the notification of certain identifying details concerning the respondent: name, age, address, gender, occupation, etc., and the interview situation, such as date, time and place of the interview.

Design of the questionnaire is a critical factor, as poor design may affect the reliability of results obtained. In particular, the wording of questions (to avoid ambiguity and bias), the use of internal consistency check questions, and the calculation of optimal length of interview time are all important. Before a questionnaire is adopted, it is sometimes tested on a small number of respondents. This process is known as a 'pilot survey', and is designed to expose unforeseen problems, such as ambiguous questions or over-lengthy questionnaires. See also: *survey*.

Quorum A specified minimum number of members of a political body (such as a legislature) necessary to be in attendance in order to constitute a valid meeting of that body. In the event of a challenge, a count must be taken to discover whether the body is quorate or inquorate. In some cases a session may continue with a lesser number present unless the quorum is challenged, or the body may continue debate, but not take decisions or votes whilst it is inquorate. In the US Senate and House of Representatives, the quorum is a simple majority of the membership; in the British House of Commons it is 40 MPs and in the House of Lords it is three peers.

R

Race A group of people supposedly sharing some common lineage, generally having a common geographical origin, often somewhat similar in physical appearance, and usually sharing some common history, culture and language. This hotchpotch of features allows 'race' to be identified with a wide range of types of group, from a family to all humankind. In common usage the intended sense is often difficult to discern but is frequently associated with the 'racist' belief that cultural differences are strongly influenced by genetic factors.

The term is sometimes used in political analysis to distinguish groups by using rough indicators of origin. British census forms, for instance, have used the categories White, African, Arab, Chinese, Indian, etc. Many political actors and analysts avoid using the word 'race', preferring to speak of 'ethnic groups', a term similar in basic meaning and application but thought generally to suggest cultural difference without the connotation of genetic determination.

Often the term refers to political issues arising from the presence of a number of different 'racial' groups in a society, e.g. in the phrase 'the politics of race'. Such issues include race relations, racial discrimination in both the public and private spheres, immigration policy, the extension of citizenship to immigrants, and electoral appeals to racist sentiments. In many countries, governmental and government sponsored organizations have been established to promote harmonious race relations, investigate complaints of unlawful discrimination, etc. In the UK these tasks are pursued by the Commission for Racial Equality. See also: *fascism; nationalism; political culture; political integration; racism.*

Racism The belief that the differences between 'racial' groups license discriminatory treatment of those groups and their members. Such a belief, if it is more than just an attitude of hostility to the unfamiliar, is usually supported by some elaboration of the significance of 'racial' differences. Typically, some of the following might be offered: that racial differences reflect deep-seated variations within the human species; that such differences are genetically determined; that they represent different levels of development, or adaptation to different physical environments; that their presence in a society prevents any proper political integration; that racial differences between societies 'block' the development of any common political understanding. Further support for such assertions is sometimes sought in pseudo-scientific ideas dating back to the nineteenth century.

'Racialism' is often used synonymously with 'racism'. Where some distinction between the two terms is implied, the former usually denotes a belief in racial difference, while the latter denotes the further belief that racially discriminatory action is justified. 'Racialism' is also used, however, to designate racially discriminatory behaviour, whether or not this arises from a belief in racism.

Explanations of the phenomenon range from psychological investigations of personality and learning experiences, through historical accounts of colonialism, to functionalist hypotheses in terms of the need for certain types of subordinate groups in particular forms of social and economic system. Empirical studies suggest that racial tension and racist activity are heightened during periods of economic crisis and recession, particularly within groups whose status is threatened. As a prominent and explicit feature of politics, racism is most commonly associated with systems and institutions such as those of Fascist Germany, *apartheid* in South Africa, and the USA (at least until recent times). But racism and racialism are notable features of many political systems, manifest in discriminatory immigration controls and institutionalized barriers to equality of participation between ethnic groups, and also significant in prompting responses such as race relations programmes and anti-discriminatory legislation. See also: *ethnocentrism; fascism; nationalism; political culture; political integration; race; xenophobia.*

Radicalism From the Latin *radix*, a root, 'radicalism' describes any doctrine that opposes the currently dominant traditions, pursues a programme of fundamental change, and rejects existing procedural restrictions on the achievement of that change. Thus, radicalism may be a feature of right-wing, left-wing or even centrist ideologies, depending on the nature of the society and regime in which change is sought. See also: *conservatism; ideology.*

Random sample See: *sample.*

Rational choice analysis The explanation of social and political events as outcomes of the rational choices made by individuals or, more contentiously, by collectivities such as households, corporations or states. The features of an initial situation are outlined incorporating: the constraints (physical, economic, etc.) existing independent from the choices currently and feasibly available to individuals; the perceptions of that situation by the various individuals concerned; the order of preferences held by individuals over the range of possible outcomes. Individuals will be assumed to choose actions in order to maximize the satisfaction of their preferences in the perceived situation. The outcome will be explained by showing how it arose from the interplay of rationally selected actions on the part of individuals, though the overall outcome may not be that anticipated, intended or desired by any of those individuals.

In the broadest terms, these features may be present in many ordinary narrative accounts of politics and in much everyday discussion. But the label 'rational choice analysis' is usually reserved for analysis focusing self-consciously on this form of explanation and concerned to apply abstract formal techniques. The approach is most strenuously opposed by structuralists and by those who regard human rationality as infrequently encountered and almost never determinant of political events. More generally shared are worries about the status of rational choice explanation. For instance, in many applications of the approach it is not clear whether the intent is normative or descriptive: whether we are being told what individuals should do or whether we are being offered an explanation for what they in fact do. For this (and other) reasons it is hard to assess the approach in the light of standards like falsifiability. Some writers use 'rational choice', 'public choice', 'social choice', 'collective choice' and 'economic theories of politics' as interchangeable labels for the same general approach to political analysis. Usually, however, the selection of a particular label designates something distinct in the central problems or the means of dealing with them. See also: *economic theories of politics; falsificationism; game theory; public choice theory; public goods; social choice theory; structuralism; utility.*

Realignment A process whereby groups of the electorate identified with some social cleavage (such as social class, ethnic or linguistic particularity, religious denomination, or regional loyalty) transfer their long-standing electoral support from one political party to another on a relatively long-term basis, as a result of some other social cleavage becoming salient. This transfer produces a changed power relationship among parties in the party system (e.g. the process whereby the Labour party replaced the Liberal party as the main opposition to the Conservatives in British elections after the first world war). See also: *critical election; dealignment; electoral volatility; party identification.*

Realism (a): scientific realism The view that scientific theories can and should be judged as true or false representations of the world, not merely as more or less efficient instruments for making predictions. The realist position is hotly contested by those, for instance, who argue that there are no grounds for inferring the truth of theoretical systems from their predictive accuracy, or that the replacement of one, previously accepted, scientific theory by another cannot plausibly be described as an increase in true knowledge. The debates between realist and instrumentalist views centre on the status of scientific knowledge, but they also have implications for the conduct of scientific enquiry. Realism shifts the focus of enquiry from directly observable phenomena to the underlying mechanisms that generate such phenomena.

It has been argued that a realist view is crucial for political and social science. Political systems consist of a complex array of interacting mechanisms such that no regularities will be displayed between directly observed phenomena. Making predictive accuracy the main point of political enquiry will therefore be self-defeating. The major difficulty of this view is that it must provide some means of isolating and identifying the underlying mechanisms in the absence of opportunity for controlled experiment. See also: *behaviouralism; falsificationism; paradigm (b): Kuhnian usage; positivism; verification.*

Realism (b): political realism The view that politics is about power and the pursuit of interest, not about law, rights and duties, and that political analysis should be conducted according to the dictates of this insight. 'Realism' is most commonly encountered in the analysis of international relations where the absence of a sovereign international order may suggest that legal and moral considerations can only provide a mask for self-interest.

The German word *realpolitik* is sometimes equated with the broad characteristics of political realism but is more accurately applied to a pragmatic concern for the political art of the possible. See also: *pragmatism.*

Recall (a): the institution A device by which the electorate can terminate a period of office of an incumbent prior to the date of its conclusion laid down in the constitution or by legislation. Along with such devices as referenda and legislative initiative, recall is thus a method of supplementing indirect, representative democracy through elected representatives by allowing the electorate certain direct powers.

Generally, recall is required to be preceded by a petition from a minimum number or some specified fraction of the qualified electorate. produced within a given time period. If this precondition is satisfied, a recall election is held, to decide whether to terminate the incumbency of the office-holder in question, and, if so, who to elect in place of the incumbent.

It is a device contained in some state, and many local authority, constitutions in the USA; it was found in various forms in the Athenian and ancient Roman political systems; some Swiss cantons have devices for dissolving the legislature by a recall vote. See also: *direct democracy; initiative.*

Recall (b): remembrance The ability to remember events or attitudes from the past; thus, in politics, a term employed principally to refer to the ability of respondents to reply to questions in surveys regarding their opinions, attitudes, activities, etc., at some past time (such as how they voted at the previous general election). See also: *survey.*

Recruitment The process by which political groups obtain members, either as additions to the group or replacements for other members. Such recruitment processes may include personal contact and persuasion, initiation ceremonies, formal examinations, election, cooption, appointment and promotion. Recruitment processes are of interest to political science especially in relation to the study of elites, leadership groups, bureaucratic organizations, political parties, interest groups, etc. See also: *party participation.*

Redistribution See: *apportionment.*

Redistricting See: *apportionment.*

Reductionist theories Theories which attempt to explain relatively complex phenomena by reference to simpler elements, often alleged to be 'more basic' or 'more real'. The most common form of reductionism in political analysis tries to reduce 'social wholes', e.g. the state, social groups, society itself, to statements describing the set of individual actions of which they are composed. This attempt will usually be backed by the claim that nothing is lost by the process of reduction since social wholes are, and only are, sets of individual actions, or that social wholes do not really exist, being merely a convenient label for certain aspects of individuals. Thus a methodological individualist may argue that questions about armies must be reduced to and properly answered in terms of the actions of the individuals comprising the armies. The holist may respond that these individuals are, irreducibly, soldiers and that the very idea of a soldier makes no sense without an understanding of the idea of an army.

Marxist analysis is also alleged to be reductionist in so far as it portrays complex events and relations within the political sphere in terms of class conflict. See also: *behaviouralism; determinism; explanation; Marxism; positivism; social class; state; theory.*

Referendum A vote by an electorate of a state or other political unit on a specific policy proposal, or on the ratification or amendment of a constitution, usually as provided for in the constitution of the political organization concerned. For some policies (e.g. to increase the public debt through bond issues; amendments to the constitution) decision by referenda may be compulsory. In other cases, the referendum may be used at the option of the legislature or on demand of a specified number or proportion of the electorate, as indicated by petitions. A referendum on an issue concerning the regime or the identity and boundaries of the political community is more usually termed a plebiscite, though this distinction of usage is not always adhered to. The result of a referendum may be either binding on the legislature or only advisory, depending on circumstances.

Examples of the provision for referenda may be found in the constitutions of the French Fifth Republic, Austria, the Irish Republic, Italy, many of the states of the USA, the cantons of Switzerland, and some of the German Länder. See also: *direct democracy; initiative; plebiscite; recall (a): the institution.*

Regime A term referring to the particular form of government possessed by a polity, e.g. parliamentary, theocratic, totalitarian, republican. It refers especially to the set of procedures and arrangements for government, the location of authority, and the style of decision making. The term is used to distinguish such patterns of government from the authorities which constitute the government at any given time. Thus the authorities may be changed by peaceful means without the regime changing (by an election, dynastic succession, replacement of one dictator by another), but a regime is usually only changed by some form of revolutionary upheaval or its threat, or by external intervention.

The classification of regimes according to various principles has long been a primary task of political analysis. Plato, Aristotle and Machiavelli among the classical philosophers, Marx, Lipset and Crick among more modern political scholars, have all produced typologies. These have drawn on such criteria as the number of effective participants in political rule; stability of the regime; the economic system of the regime; and the attitudes of the authorities to law and politics.

In popular usage, sometimes the term is used to refer to a period of government (e.g. 'the Thatcher regime'), though even in such usages there is an implication that the period of government is marked from its predecessors by some significant difference of style of government. See also: *constitution; government (a): the institution.*

Reification The view or treatment of something as if it were an object. Use of the term often implies that the view or treatment is misleading or mistaken. Thus one person, conceiving of 'power' as a relationship between actors, might accuse another, conceiving of it as a resource, of reifying 'power'. In political science the term is most often invoked in connection with Marx's view that market relations come to be seen as relations between things (the commodities exchanged) rather than between persons. See also: *ideology; Marxism.*

Reliability See: *validation.*

Replication The repetition or duplication of a set of procedures: hence, in social science, the duplication of a previous experiment, as far as possible under the same conditions and within the same parameters, as a means of checking the reliability of procedures, results, or both. See also: *experiment; validation.*

Representation A process in which one person or group has the capacity, usually formally established, to speak and act on behalf of a larger number of other persons or groups, e.g. in a legislature, at a party convention or conference, in negotiations with a committee. Individuals and groups may be represented by reference to any of their aspects or attributes: geographical location; gender; occupation; party affiliation; etc.

The method by which representatives are selected, and their relation to those represented, may vary considerably. One common method is election by those to be represented, as in competitive legislative elections, or in the election of the Speaker of the House of Commons, and the Speaker of the House of Representatives. But the method of selection may not involve the expression of choice by those represented: the process of election may be indirect, as in the case of the election of the president of the USA through the Electoral College; representatives may be appointed by some higher authority (e.g. Crown or government) for their presumed capacity to speak on behalf of those represented, for instance in the nomination of members of certain public boards in the UK and USA. Moreover, the doctrine of 'virtual representation' holds that a section of the community may be represented so long as its interests are heard, whether or not it has some designated representative of its own. The argument was applied to the new industrial towns in eighteenth century England, some of which elected no parliamentary representatives, on the grounds that some industrial areas were represented and that industrial interests therefore had a voice, and to the claims for 'no taxation without representation' made by the American colonies in the years preceding their independence. The term was also used in debates about the proper extent of the franchise, for instance in arguing that women were virtually represented by male heads of households, and that younger members of the community were represented by their elders. A representative may be free to exercise judgement as to the interests of those represented, or the best means to promote those interests, but this discretion may be limited or removed by the process of delegation or mandate.

Representatives, taken individually or in aggregate, often do not share the principal characteristics of the populations they represent. Representative assemblies such as the House of Commons in the UK do not comprise a 'representative sample' of the electorate, particularly with reference to gender and ethnic background. In this sense, women and ethnic minorities may be said to be under-represented in parliament. See also: *constituency; delegation; democracy; election; electoral college; mandate; proportional representation; recall (a): the institution; sample; voting.*

Republic The term derives from the Latin *res publica*, signifying public affairs. It has come to mean a form of government in which the head of state is not selected on a hereditary basis, but is elected or appointed, often directly or indirectly through choices made by citizens or their representatives (the presidents of the Fifth Republic in France and the USA are so elected, for instance). However, there is no necessary implication that a republican form of government will be democratic. Republicanism is an ideological belief which favours the abolition of some specified monarchy, though there is also a more archaic meaning, applied to attitudes of civic humanism, stressing the desire for balanced government and attention to civic obligations.

Reputational approach A method for studying political systems, most commonly employed at the initial stage of a study of power. The opinions of supposedly informed participants are sought concerning which individuals or groups possess significant power within the system. The approach is criticized for its tendency to rely on the imprecise concepts and incorrect information that the participants may use in their judgements. See also: *power*.

Revisionism See: *social democracy*.

Revolution In political science there are three distinguishable but closely related meanings associated with the term 'revolution'.

The most restrictive definition limits use of the term to describe a relatively sudden and radical change in the political, social and economic order, generally involving violence or its threat, originating from, or closely involving, large sections of the population. Such revolutions are relatively rare; the French revolution (1789), the Bolshevik revolution in Russia (1917), and the Chinese revolution (1949) are examples.

A more common usage retains the ideas of sudden, radical and violent change in the political order and the involvement of large sections of the population, but does not require associated radical changes in the economic and social order as qualifying conditions. Thus the American revolution (1775-81), the French revolutions of 1848 and 1870-71, and various revolutions in Latin American states this century, would be included in this broader definition.

Both the above definitions distinguish revolution from other forms of violent change of the political order. It differs from civil war, in which large sections of the population are involved on both sides, though revolution may be the cause or the effect of such a civil war (e.g. the American and Bolshevik revolutions). Revolution is more broadly based than a coup d'état in any of its various forms (a *putsch*, or palace revolution, for example), which in any case may be aimed at only bringing about a change in the personnel of government, and not a change in the system of government or in social relationships, though some authorities regard any violent change of government – whether involving a change of regime or not – as a revolution.

The third definition of revolution is at least partly metaphorical. In such usages as 'the industrial revolution', 'the agricultural revolution' and 'the cultural revolution' the focus is upon relatively sudden and radical social, technological or economic change, involving large sections of the population, but change not necessarily in itself productive of concomitant political change. See also: *civil war; counter-revolution; coup d'état; insurrection; palace revolution; putsch*.

Rhetoric Eloquence, or the art of persuasion. The rhetorical aspects of political communication appeal to the emotions rather than to reason, and the meaning communicated lies in the style of communication rather than in its factual and theoretical content. Central elements of rhetoric include: the use and choice of metaphor, analogy, etc.; the use of euphemism; slippage between two quite different meanings of words or phrases employed; the obfuscation of basic assumptions; the use of gesture and modulation of tone.

In modern politics, rhetoric is often referred to in the context of manipulation: the implication is that truth and the interests of the audience are displaced by the sinister interests of the rhetorician. This is a somewhat simplistic view because all political communication has some rhetorical content, and because an audience may be the self-consciously enthusiastic recipient of rhetorical appeals, at political rallies and party conferences, for instance. The use of rhetoric might be viewed as a necessary part of mutual engagement between orator and audience.

In classical times and in the early modern period, rhetoric formed an important part of the study of politics. It has been neglected in modern political science, but related matters have had some place in political psychology. Interest has recently been revived through the analysis of ideological discourse, and by increased concern with the role of political advertising and mass media coverage of politics. See also: *hermeneutics; ideology; political communication; political psychology; propaganda.*

Role The patterns of behaviour and clusters of attitudes expected of persons occupying some position in a social structure. 'Role' is often distinguished from 'status' such that the latter merely describes relative social positions while the former denotes the kinds of acts to be performed within each position. Knowledge of roles, and the ability to perform them, are acquired by individuals through socialization.

Political roles are thus the behaviour and attitudes associated with political positions, e.g. party leader, president, 'elder statesman', revolutionary agitator, international conciliator. Such roles, particularly those which correspond to some formal office, may be partly circumscribed by law, convention, custom, etc., but, as roles, they are more loosely defined by implicit norms. See also: *attitudes; norm; political behaviour; status.*

Roll-call analysis The analysis usually of the record of votes of legislators, committee members, judges, etc., though it might also be used to study stated recorded opinions or attitudes of decision-makers such as judges of the Supreme Court in the USA. Roll-call analysis uses as data the voting records of such decision-makers for the purposes of establishing and measuring sets of underlying factors relating to voting decisions, and the analysis can be utilized to compare the behaviour of groups of such decision-makers (e.g. men and women; regional groups; generational cohorts by age or by year of first election). See also: *attitudes.*

Rule of law Government conducted through legislative procedures, contrasted with the arbitrary will of rulers. Although no constitutional restraints may exist to limit the *content* of law, rule must be *through* known laws and punishments, binding on ordinary citizens and governmental officials alike. See also: *absolutism; autocracy; constitutionalism; due process; judicial review; law (b): stipulative law.*

Ruling class A class that enjoys a position of domination in the exercise of political power, either directly through the occupation of political office by its members, or indirectly through the control of those holding office. The term is used most often within Marxist analysis and elite theory.

Since the 1950s, many non-Marxists have avoided using the term, taking the view that 'class' is strongly associated with the economic interests of a particular group and 'ruling' with political action: thus the term may too readily assume an invariant relation between the two phenomena and obscure the possible autonomy of the political. Marxists, recognizing a similar problem, often distinguish between a dominant or hegemonic class and a ruling or governing class. While these two positions may frequently be occupied by the same group, sometimes they will not: for instance, the interests of a dominant class may constrain the political agenda while the actions of the governing class may provide the detail of political decisions within those constraints. See also: *class; elite; hegemony; Marxism; pluralism; state*.

S

Salience The quality of obvious prominence. In the context of political issues and agendas, a salient issue is one which is particularly prominent, perhaps because of current circumstances. In conflict and bargaining theory, a salient solution is one which is clearly distinguishable from other possible solutions to both actors involved, though it need bear no relation to equity (e.g. a 50-50 division, the existence of a river dividing disputed territory, or the existence of a line of latitude as the basis for an armistice settlement). See also: *bargaining theory; conflict approach*.

Sample A fraction of some collectivity, known as the 'population', selected in some manner so that it can be taken to represent certain required characteristics of the collectivity, within acceptable degrees of probability. The size of the sample relative to the population concerned affects the degree of probability with which the data obtained about the sample can be assumed to be valid for the 'population'. The design of the sampling procedure is also of great importance in this respect.

In survey research random samples are used extensively, as it is possible in this way to assess accurately the probability that the data obtained is representative for the 'population'. Random samples are obtained by using some randomizing device (such as books of random numbers or computer generation of random numbers). Such samples may be drawn directly from the whole 'population', or drawn in several stages: e.g. a sample of voters drawn from a random sample of wards, drawn in turn from a random sample of constituencies, with the wards and constituencies weighted in terms of probability of being chosen according to the size of their electorates. This is called multi-stage sampling. Another method of obtaining a sample for a survey is quota sampling: where the 'population' is categorized in pre-determined categories (e.g. gender and age-group), and respondents are added to the sample according to those categories (e.g. by approaching members of the public in a shopping precinct) until a category is full, after which no further respondents in that category are interviewed. Each category in the sample (e.g. men in the age group 40-65) is given a size representative of its share of the 'population'. See also: *survey*.

Satisficing See: *incrementalism*.

Scientific method A set of procedures and principles designed to facilitate the development of knowledge and the elimination of error. There are many bodies of knowledge called 'sciences', many methods associated with each science, and even more disputes about method, but the procedures most often denoted involve: the development of theory; the derivation of hypotheses; the design and implementation of tests to confirm or falsify hypotheses; the acceptance, revision or rejection of theory in the light of these tests.

The terms 'scientism' and 'scientistic' may also be encountered. These denote a commitment to the use of only natural scientific methods in social science, with the pejorative implication that the commitment is mistaken; or that the particular idea of natural scientific method is unduly narrow; or that the methods cited in fact bear little resemblance to those of natural science. See also: *experiment; explanation; falsificationism; hypothesis; law (a): scientific law; political science; theory; verification*.

Secession An act of separation from an existing state by a section of the inhabitants of an area within that state, who wish either to create their own autonomous state or become part of some neighbouring state. Secession is associated more usually with federal states, being based on the supposed rights of the secessionist province to withdraw from the federation, or their claims that the nature of the federation has become disadvantageous to them in some way.

In the Soviet Union under Gorbachev, the formal right of secession originally stated in the Stalin constitution (1936) has become a constitutional issue in relation to the Baltic states, the Ukraine, etc. Examples of secessionist attempts: the eleven confederate southern states from the USA, 1860-61; Singapore from Malaysia, 1965; Biafra from Nigeria, 1967. See also: *federation; separatism*.

Second ballot system A system for the election of members to a legislature (or similar body) involving the possibility of two ballots, separated in time, usually on the basis of single-member constituencies. Though the detailed arrangements will vary from system to system, basically the requirements are that a first ballot is held in which any candidate securing over 50% of valid votes cast is declared elected. If no candidate secures such a majority, a second ballot is held at a later date, possibly with nominations restricted to the two or three most successful of the candidates on the first ballot, and a simple plurality suffices to elect. The interval between ballots allows time for electoral bargains to be arranged. The second ballot system should not be confused with the two-vote system of election used in federal elections and some Land elections in Germany, where the voter has two votes, but which are cast simultaneously for a constituency candidate and a party list respectively.

France has used this method in the Fifth Republic to elect its president and (with a brief exception in 1986) the National Assembly. It was also used to elect the president in the German Weimar Republic. See also: *electoral system; exhaustive ballot.*

Sedition Acts which, while not falling within legal definitions of treason, are regarded by the constitution, laws or judicial authorities of the state as being likely to promote public discontent or incite rebellion against the state and its rulers. See also: *treason.*

Separation of powers The normative principle that different functions of government should not be entrusted to the same person or institution. The modern version of the principle is derived from the writings of John Locke and Baron de Montesquieu. The powers usually referred to are: the legislative power to make rules; the executive power to implement and administer these rules; and the judicial power to provide authoritative interpretations of rules, in cases of dispute, and for the purpose of trying alleged offenders. The separation of these powers is intended to ensure that liberty and the rule of law are maintained, by preventing power from becoming concentrated, by balancing one power against another, and by providing institutional means by which the use and abuse of power may be checked.

No separation of powers can be complete. If it were, the underlying intention would be defeated since there would be no opportunity for one branch of government to correct the misuse of power by another. What is separated is not simply 'power', but the different forms of its routine and constitutionally proper exercise. The USA has a high degree of this formal separation written into its constitution. In the UK, the separation of powers is much less clear: the executive is formed from members of the legislature; the House of Lords and the Lord Chancellor occupy judicial positions as well as having legislative or administrative roles. See also: *authoritarianism; dictatorship; executive; judicial legislation; judiciary; legislature; rule of law; sovereignty.*

Separatism The claim that a physical area within a state, generally one inhabited by an ethnically distinct population and often one that is territorially peripheral, should be allowed to part from the political community to which it belongs, in order to govern itself or to join some other political community with which it has ethnic or other important ties.

Separatism is closely associated with the concept of political integration, reflecting the idea that political communities will not remain integrated if there is a lack of consensus concerning the proper identity and composition of the community. The separatist claim is often based, more or less explicitly, on the idea that separation in this particular case would help to create better integrated political communities both for the original state and for the separated area. Separatist movements this century have received impetus from the ideas of national self-determination (e.g. Woodrow Wilson's Fourteen Points) and anti-colonialism.

Separatist movements are usually prepared to employ any strategies that might advance their cause, including electioneering, rhetoric, demonstrations, violence (including terrorism), civil war and secession.

Examples of separatist movements in the twentieth century: the Basques (Spain); Irish republicanism (Northern Ireland); the Biafrans (Nigeria); the Quebecois (Canada); the Tamils (Sri Lanka). See also: *autonomy; nationalism; political integration; secession*.

Side payments In game theory, payments made by one player to another outside the 'core structure' of pay-offs. Most simple games allow no bargaining or transfer of benefits: the pay-offs are fixed by the terms of the game and cannot be varied by the payment of benefits in return for cooperation. In other words, no side payments are allowed. This assumption is at odds with the political situations to which game theory may be applied. Politics almost always involves bargaining and is seldom a matter of reaping fixed rewards for unilateral action. A large party may, for instance, offer to include an item in its legislative programme in return for a smaller party abstaining from electoral competition in some strategically chosen constituencies. In order to represent such possibilities, the opportunity for side payments must be included within game theory. See also: *bargaining theory; game theory; model*.

Simulation Any process in which the key aspects of some hypothetical or actual political situation are artificially created or represented, and in which the interactions of these aspects are investigated by proceeding from the situation, on the basis of a scenario worked out in advance. 'Gaming' is a form of simulation frequently applied in the study of international politics and military strategy, e.g. when an international crisis is simulated and participants take on relevant roles for the duration of the simulation. The technique can be used as a device for learning about possible processes and outcomes, or for research into the values and actions of the players, or both. Televised exercises of this sort have become known as 'hypotheticals'. In gaming, each player attempts to maximize her gains, in terms of her own values and, therefore, not necessarily at the expense of the other players. Some other forms of simulation, e.g. of ceremonies, may not involve this motivational element. Abstract models can also be simulated by computer, with or without the interactive participation of human players. This enables complex relations and the effects of changes in variables to be more rapidly calculated. Ranges of alternative simulations can then be easily compared. Models of bargaining, and of voting behaviour, are among those most frequently constructed. See also: *model; prediction; variables*.

Single party system See: *one-party system*.

Single transferable vote system (STV) An electoral system, used for legislative elections in the Irish Republic and Malta (and for European and local elections in Northern Ireland) which utilizes preferential voting in multi-member constituencies.

Each elector has one vote; but that vote is cast by listing candidates in order of preference (1, 2, 3,... etc.) rather than by selecting just one candidate to the exclusion of all the others. In the Republic of Ireland, there are 3-, 4- and 5-member constituencies. Constituencies with more than about five members become inconveniently large, and the process of calculating the result of an election becomes excessively time-consuming. Under STV, a quota is determined for each constituency. This is usually the Droop quota (i.e. the total number of votes divided by one *greater* than the number of candidates to be elected, plus one vote). First preferences are counted; any candidate achieving the quota is elected. If insufficient candidates are elected in the first calculation, any votes surplus to the quota of elected candidates are redistributed candidate-by-candidate according to the ratio of the second preferences of *all* the votes for those candidates. When no surplus votes are available to redistribute, candidates with the least first preferences are eliminated, and the votes given to those candidates are redistributed according to second preferences. These redistribution processes are repeated, using third and later preferences as necessary, until all the seats available in the constituency are filled.

The STV system is not designed explicitly to attain proportional representation of parties (though in the Republic of Ireland a more proportional distribution of seats to parties is normally realized than would be the case using the British simple-majority system). Nor is STV necessarily beneficial to small parties: if votes were cast homogeneously in every constituency, a party would need over 20% of first preferences to be sure of winning any seats in 4-member constituencies, for instance. The system does ensure that elected candidates have been preferred by a majority of voters to unelected candidates, and permits parties or cross-party alliances to nominate two or more candidates in constituencies without 'splitting the vote' and thus damaging their chances of getting any candidate elected. STV is a system which increases the influence of the voter vis-à-vis the party in determining who gets elected. See also: *Droop quota; electoral quota; electoral system; preferential voting*.

Social choice theory An area of rational choice analysis centred on the problem of the 'social welfare function', the means by which individuals' preferences can be aggregated to produce a collective preference (e.g. by various voting systems). Kenneth Arrow has developed a mathematical theory (referred to as the 'General Possibility Theorem', the 'impossibility theorem' or just 'Arrow's Theorem') demonstrating that, given some commonly accepted assumptions about individuals' preferences, there is no way in which these preferences can be aggregated without violating conditions which, it is argued, embody reasonable requirements of non-arbitrariness and fairness. Formally this shows that decisions emerging from groups do not share the characteristics of the individual choices of which they are composed and that the same assumptions and techniques may not properly be applied to both phenomena. Practically, it suggests that, even in political systems which take account of the preferences of citizens, it may be impossible to reach any decision that does not embody inconsistent or unfair treatment. In fact, of course, 'social choices' are made, and may often appear acceptable, on some terms. Attention is then paid to the means by which some of the strict requirements of the formal theory might be relaxed so as to achieve acceptable policy. See also: *public choice theory; rational choice analysis.*

Social class A section of a community which possesses similar cultural patterns based on social status, associated prestige, income levels, values, social power and, in some usages, a shared sense of class identity or interests. Different theories and classificatory schemes adopt different criteria for the identification of classes and class membership, one of the chief distinctions being between objective identification on the basis of attributes such as occupational status, income, education, etc., and subjective identification through the self-attribution of the class member.

Marxist theory defines classes in terms of their relations of ownership or non-ownership to the means of production, in terms of their employment or non-employment of the labour power of others, and in terms of the type of economic activity engaged in. Thus capitalist society contains two major classes: the bourgeoisie, the owners of capital or of the means of production; the proletariat, those who own no capital and live entirely by the wages of labour. The bourgeoisie is further divided into the three fractions, of industrial capitalists, financial capitalists, and large landowners. The proletariat is sometimes treated narrowly as the class of productive industrial manual workers, but it is often treated more extensively as the class of all wage and salary earners. Other class groupings include: the petty (or petite) bourgeoisie, owners of small businesses, shopkeepers, etc.; the lumpenproletariat, e.g. the unemployed, casual labourers, vagabonds; the middle class or classes, standing between proletariat and bourgeoisie, comprising white collar workers, professionals, servants, non-industrial workers, etc.; the peasantry; the landed aristocracy. The identification of these groups as separate classes is contentious, and many of them are commonly treated as strata or fractions of more broadly defined bourgeois and proletarian classes. Non-Marxist writers are inclined to use these broader groupings, and to refer to them as 'working class' and 'middle class'.

The usual point of this type of class analysis, whether or not it is explicitly Marxist, is to build explanatory theory using class categories, the relations between which correspond to the principal conflicts present in societies. A class so identified should then comprise a significant social force in its particular society, either through its members' possession of class-consciousness: some common perception of their class position, and some political organization through which they pursue their class interests (that is, in Marxian terms, the class is a 'class for itself' and not just a 'class in itself'); or, where such consciousness is absent, because the objective forces in society are manifested through class relations. This class analysis has been criticized for its concentration on factors which, particularly in advanced industrial societies, do not correspond to the interests underlying political activity, and which therefore cannot form the basis for collective action, a criticism which addresses the view of class as a self-conscious actor rather than class as an objective force.

Class typologies are also used in the analysis of political behaviour and its associated attributes. These typologies range from a simple threefold division into upper, middle and lower classes, to the more complex alphabetical categories used in market and opinion research, e.g. 'A' (upper-managerial, property owner, high income); 'B1' (middle-manage-rial, moderate income); 'B2' (clerical or administrative, low income); 'C' (white-collar skilled workers, moderate income); 'D1' (blue-collar skilled workers, moderate income); 'D2' (blue-collar unskilled workers, low income); 'E' (those on state pensions, social security, etc., very low income). See also: *aristocracy; capitalism; caste; elite; embourgeoisement; feudalism; interests; Marxism; pluralism; proletarianization; ruling class; socio-econ-omic status; status.*

Social contract See: *contract theory.*

Social democracy A term which originally denoted the broad aims of all socialist parties, but particularly those of the Marxist socialist parties in Europe during the late nineteenth and early twentieth centuries. After the rise of bolshevism and the 1917 revolution in Russia, the term came to be used for a type of reformist and non-Marxist socialism, advocated and widely practised in western Europe, consisting of a commitment to democratic politics, the administration of a basically capitalist economy, and the provision of relatively extensive welfare benefits. Thus social democracy comprises the mainstream beliefs of most of the socialist and labour parties of the western hemisphere, but the term is especially associated with the aims and practices of Scandinavian social democrat parties, and with the 'Godesberg Program' adopted by the West German SPD in 1959.

Social democracy, particularly in its rejection of Bolshevism and reinter-pretation of Marxism in the first few decades of the twentieth century, is sometimes referred to as 'revisionism'. (This term is, of course, also more widely applied to any modification or subversion of an orthodoxy.)

'Democratic socialism' is sometimes used to distinguish those doctrines which, while committed to democratic methods and institutions, retain a concern for socialism, by implication thought to be absent from current social democratic ideas. See also: *bolshevism; communism; democracy; Marxism; socialism.*

Socialism A doctrine or practice based on the belief that the means of production should be owned and controlled by the community; that production should be directed, at least in part, to the satisfaction of communal needs, rather than being determined solely by individual desires; that the distribution of rewards should be equal, or in accordance with some measure of work such as labour-time, or in accordance with need, but not simply a reflection of power, private property and market forces; and that individual fulfilment can only be realized when communal needs have been satisfied.

Until fairly recently, the clear moral commitment of most socialist thought has been coupled with the view that capitalist and market systems are inefficient and wasteful of both natural and human resources. If this were so, socialism would not impose costs in terms of the material well-being of the society as a whole. The experience of planned economies, however imperfectly socialist they may have been, has made this view difficult to sustain.

Despite the apparently inherent antagonism between socialism and systems of market exchange, attempts have been made to develop a form of socialism which combines collective ownership of the means of production with the allocation of resources and distribution of products through market mechanisms. Models of this type are often referred to as 'market socialism'.

Socialism has spawned many rival forms and movements. Utopian socialism, anarcho-syndicalism, guild socialism, Marxism, bolshevism, Trotskyism, revisionism, fabianism, and social democracy, have been among the most important.

The 'Socialist Internationals' were attempts to create a worldwide organization to coordinate and inform the actions of individual socialist groups. The First International, or International Workingmen's Association (1864-76), was riven by dispute between Marxists and anarchists, and collapsed following the transfer of its council to New York. The Second International, founded in 1889, was fused with the International Working Union of Socialist parties in 1923 to form the Labour and Socialist International, which, after the second world war, became the present Socialist International. The Third International (the Comintern), founded by Lenin in 1919 to promote world revolution, was soon effectively controlled by the Communist party of the Soviet Union. The Fourth International was founded by Trotsky in 1938 in an attempt to counter fascism and Stalinism. See also: *anarchism; anarcho-syndicalism; bolshevism; collecivism; communism; exploitation; fabianism; Marxism; social democracy; utopianism.*

Social structure The term 'social structures' usually implies reference to an analysis of social systems of the sort described in the entry for 'structure'. Mention of '*the* social structure' more often refers to a classification of individuals into various status positions, such as class membership, marital status, occupational positions, etc. See also: *classification; social class; status; structure.*

Society Abstractly, a set of structures and institutions ordering the relations between individuals; more concretely, a more or less continuous association of individuals whose interactions are governed by a distinct culture and institutional structure. Reference to a 'society' in political analysis most frequently refers to the population of a nation-state, considered in broader terms than those of the political relations comprising the state itself. But a 'society', as well as denoting a broader set of relations, need not coincide with the boundaries of a state. A society may exist without subjecting itself to state power (e.g. some tribal societies), and elements of a society may reside in different states. In this latter case it would be more usual to refer to such a group as a 'nation', or perhaps a 'culture', suggesting that shared political relations in a defined territory is a part of the usual connotation of 'society'.

The term 'civil society' is used to denote those relations which are a part neither purely of the private sphere of the family, nor purely of the public sphere of the state, particularly the relations within voluntary associations, including those of liberal economic institutions. The sphere of civil society is an area within which individual and group autonomy may flourish within a wide range of associations. As such, the term has recently been used in connection with the loosening of state control and the liberalizing of the economy in many of the countries of eastern Europe. Until recently, the most usual modern sense of the term (derived from the work of Hegel, Marx and Gramsci) has been critical rather than supportive of capitalist economic institutions and liberal democratic states. This critical usage suggests that civil society is one of the means by which liberal capitalist society is legitimated, presenting a sphere which is apparently free from state control but which is in reality strongly constrained by market relations and economic power, constraints themselves sustained by the state. See also: *capitalism; community; hegemony; legitimacy; liberalism; nation; state.*

Socio-economic status (SES) A designation of the relative status of a person within the social structure, based primarily on characteristics of income and occupation. It is used as a category dimension for the purposes of survey research, for example. It differs from social class, in that its basis is more restricted in terms of the factors which it includes, and in that such factors are objective, whereas social class may be ascribed because of subjective factors, such as self-identification with a class. A typical scheme of SES categories, employed by the Market Research Society in Britain, uses the following categories: 'A' (positions of high status and responsibility, such as a judge, a Member of Parliament or a bank manager); 'B' (other managerial and professional occupations, such as a teacher, a probation officer or a nursing sister); 'C1' (clerical and secretarial occupations, including also police constables, telephone operators and staff nurses); 'C2' (skilled manual workers, such as a bus driver, fireman or hairdresser); 'D' (other manual workers, such as a bus conductor or a chauffeur); and 'E' (those on state benefit). See also: *social class; status.*

Sovereignty The term has two distinct though related uses. 'Sovereignty' is a condition of political autonomy which a state enjoys when it is recognized by other states as the sole source of the legitimate exercise of power within its territory. The terms 'national sovereignty' and 'sovereign state' imply this meaning, as does the phrase 'disputed sovereignty' when it refers to competing claims, by two or more states, to jurisdiction over a particular piece of territory.

The term is also used to denote the ultimate power, of some person or institution within a political community, to make, interpret and enforce laws binding on all other members of that community. Both usages are derived from the concept of sovereignty developed, in the sixteenth and seventeenth centuries, as part of the ideology of the modern state. This concept, particularly associated with Jean Bodin and Thomas Hobbes, fuses together the ideas of, on the one hand, independent republics and monarchies, and on the other, the need for a single focus of allegiance, to form the notion of a supreme source of law within each polity.

The idea, particularly in the second sense, raises obvious difficulties. Sovereignty, as ultimate power, appears necessarily to be absolute, since its pronouncements cannot be legally challenged by any other person or institution. Those wishing to avoid this implication have attempted to ascribe sovereignty to basic constitutional rules, or to the state as a whole, allowing for each of these to contain limits on the form and content of rule.

The difficulty faced in dealing theoretically with sovereignty in a manner compatible with limited government is reflected in the characteristics of actual states. In states like the USA and Germany, the political authority of both federal and provincial units is limited; neither the constitution, nor the courts charged with regulating and interpreting the federal relationship, can be regarded as fully sovereign, since the former may be amended, and both lack the independent power to enforce decisions. In the UK, legal sovereignty is ascribed to 'the Queen in parliament', a phrase that does little to locate the whereabouts of sovereignty, but which indicates the absence of clearly established limits to parliamentary rule. The application of the concept of national sovereignty encounters similar difficulties where a state is bound by treaty to abide by decisions made outside its national political system, as in the case of the countries of the European Community. See also: *absolutism; authority; autonomy; constitution; law (b): stipulative law; power; rule of law; separation of powers; state; treaty.*

Special majority See: *majority.*

Standing orders The rules which govern procedure for some institution, such as a legislature, a party conference or a committee. Standing orders will probably specify among other things the conditions under which the deliberations of the institution validly can take place, the size of quorum necessary, methods of settling procedural disputes, terms of office and methods of election of office-holders, and ways of amending standing orders. See also: *constitution.*

Stalinism See: *bolshevism.*

State A term with the same roots as 'status' and 'estate', used from the twelfth century to refer to the high rank and legal standing of rulers and, by the fourteenth century, to the condition of the realm. During this period the term also started to develop what was to become its more particular modern meaning, through the expression '*status civitatum*', the condition of political autonomy enjoyed or aspired to by many Italian cities. The further development of the term parallels the emergence of a new form of political arrangement, the 'modern state', in western Europe.

The modern state may be defined as a set of institutions, separate from those of civil society, through which public policy and law are decided and executed: the state exercises sovereign power over its territory, successfully claiming compliance with its laws from those within that territory, and securing that compliance through its monopolistic control of legitimate force.

Although the political arrangements of all countries are now loosely referred to as 'states', many will meet these requirements very imperfectly. Perhaps no actual 'state' could be said to meet all the requirements. Legitimacy is not always recognized, and compliance incompletely obtained; the constraints of international politics and law may restrict the monopolistic control of legitimate force; the boundaries between public and private spheres may be hard to identify or ill-observed; and in a federal state there may be two sets of political authorities, each claiming compliance in its own area of competence.

The definitional requirements offered above are a mixture of the institutional, the functional, and the normative. Definitions which concentrate more exclusively on one or another of these elements will, of course, offer different sketches of the idea of the state, and will have different implications for the analysis of state activity. Functional definitions, for instance, couched in terms of the tasks performed by the state, will identify the state through aspects of all the institutions performing those tasks. This may blur some of the distinctions drawn above: that between public and private spheres; that between the modern state and earlier forms of political arrangements.

More specifically, different approaches to political analysis have been associated with distinctive views of the state, particularly of the modern liberal democratic state. The actual positions are complex, but in crude terms: pluralists tend to treat the state as an arena within which conflicts between competing group interests are resolved, or as a neutral umpire in the resolution of such conflicts (views which are often criticized for their inability to say anything specific about what the state is or does); 'orthodox' Marxism treats the state as an instrument of class power, wielded by or on behalf of the dominant class in society (a firm view of the function of the state, but less specific about the institutional detail of its performance); Marxist writing of the last few decades has tended to attribute more autonomy to the state, within the constraints imposed by the economic and social order; and in a somewhat similar manner, non-Marxist writers, sometimes called 'new-statists' or 'new-institutionalists', have treated the state as a specific organization with interests of its own, in a self-conscious attempt to fill the gap in pluralist analysis. See also: *anarchism; contract theory; federation; government (a): the institution; Marxism; nation; pluralism; polity; society; sovereignty.*

State capitalism A term sometimes applied to economic systems which exhibit many of the characteristics of capitalism but where the private ownership of the means of production is wholly or substantially supplanted by the state.

The term is used to describe either capitalist economies within which state intervention extends to its ownership and control of key industrial sectors or (usually pejoratively) nominally socialist economies where the state directs production, the major aim of production remains the creation and accumulation of a surplus, and the bureaucracy or ruling party occupies the position of an exploiting class.

It has been suggested that advanced capitalist economies reach a stage of state monopoly capitalism (sometimes called 'stamocap') where the state and the major corporations form a single bloc dominating society. See also: *anarcho-syndicalism; capitalism; corporatism (b): ideal type; interventionism; liberalism; Marxism; political economy; socialism.*

State socialism Originally used to denote a transitional period, preceding true socialism, during which strong central control would be necessary to transform the economy and dismantle the structures of capitalism. The term is now more usually applied to societies where production and distribution are controlled by a strong state apparatus professing socialist ideology. See also: *Marxism; socialism.*

Statism See: *interventionism.*

Status The position occupied by a member of a social group, such as the family, a community or a political party branch organization, defined by the positions which are occupied by other members of the group, and as limited by the norms, rules and values of the group. Status thus involves formal power relationships, privilege relationships, or relationships of responsibility and obligation.

A distinction is made for some analytic purposes between *achieved* status, the result of some type of competitive situation (e.g. the nominee of a political party for a presidential election, or the general secretary of a trade union), and *ascribed* status, acquired – at least potentially – at birth (e.g. a status in a family or tribe, membership of a caste or a ruling house). The various positions of status within a group may be stratified according to the amount of prestige associated with them by members of the group.

Status is regarded by many political sociologists as an important factor influencing many forms of political behaviour, including voting, political participation, attitudes towards authority, etc. See also: *hierarchy; socio-economic status.*

Straw poll See: *poll.*

Structural-functional analysis A method of analysis which examines a system in terms of the structures of which the system is composed, and the functions performed by those structures. A form of this analysis occupied an influential position in American and British political science in the 1950s, 1960s and early 1970s. The approach postulates that any political system has certain functions that must be performed if the system is to persist. The structures performing those functions are then identified and the manner of performance examined. Links are then established between the manner of performance of these requisite functions and the type of political culture present in the society. Prominent amongst the advantages claimed for such an approach are that it concentrates on the vital aspects of a system, and that it enables systematic comparisons to be made between systems through its identification of functions necessary to all political systems. Several problems are evident in the approach, notably the difficulties involved in formulating any defensible definitions of 'requisite function' and 'system persistence' or 'survival'.

Structural-functional analysis does not necessarily aim to produce functional explanation. To identify key structures and institutions through their performance of certain functions does not, for instance, commit the analyst to an account of their incidence purely in terms of their performance of functions. Nevertheless, the assumptions which identify and order the subject matter must imply some functional explanation of political systems at a basic level and structural-functional analysis is therefore accused of the same weaknesses and bias as functional explanation, these objections being linked to the particular definitional difficulties referred to above. Nor is structural-functional analysis necessarily a variant of *structuralism*. Many of those working within the approach outlined above were resolute in their commitment to individual behaviour as both the observational and explanatory base for the analysis of political systems.

Some Marxist analysis (of roughly the same period) is also described as structural-functional. Here the theoretical status given to structure is recognizably structuralist, and the explanations offered are often functional. See also: *behaviouralism; functional explanation; political culture; structuralism; structuration; structure*.

Structuralism The view that the social and political world should be understood in terms of the forces and relations underlying action and language, beyond immediate experience and therefore not directly observable. The role of human agency is further downgraded by the view that these 'deep structures' determine or constrain action and that they provide systematic explanation for the often irregular surface appearance of social activity. Structuralism is opposed to both methodological individualism and empiricism.

Attempts have been made to present structuralism as a unified method, appropriate to the analysis of all social phenomena. In fact significant variations are apparent in works both between and within different fields of enquiry. Structuralist analysis of language, for instance, bears little resemblance to structuralist analysis of non-linguistic aspects of politics. In political analysis the form of structuralism most often encountered is Marxist, rooting its approach in the forces and relations comprising a mode of production. See also: *determinism; empiricism; Marxism; reductionist theories; structural-functional analysis; structuration; structure*.

Structuration Structuralist political analysis treats structure as a determining or constraining factor, in opposition to human agency. Structural-functionalism treats structure as synonymous with the social system or pattern of social relationships. Analysts who wish to avoid these connotations, and who wish to use the term 'structure' to denote the collective rules and resources which enable individual action, sometimes refer to 'the process of structuration'. This process comprises the production and reproduction of social systems through individuals' interpretation and use of rules and resources in communication and action. The term is particularly associated with the work of Anthony Giddens. See also: *hermeneutics; norm; structural-functionalism; structuralism; structure*.

Structure The elements and their inter-relations together comprising some system, institution or practice. The structure of a political system might be described in terms of its institutions (legislature, political parties, interest groups, etc.), the relevant aspects of individuals who are 'occupants' of elements of the structure (legislators, party members, citizens, subjects, producers, consumers, etc.), and those practices defining and regulating the relevant aspects of institutions and individuals (law, authority, obligation, power, etc.). Each element in a structure may itself be accounted for in terms of its own structural elements, just as a structure may itself constitute an element of other structures.

Since some account of structure will be included in almost all forms of inquiry, reference to 'structure' does not always indicate that the account is properly 'structuralist'. Many pluralist writers, for instance, treat 'structure' as a synonym for 'institution', the former term being adopted to convey interest in the actual behaviour of individuals involved in institutional processes, rather than their formal position or office. Here structure is an aggregation of individual action and no reference to causal mechanisms beyond or beneath the level of observable individual action may be intended. See also: *pluralism; social structure; structural-functional analysis; structuralism; structuration*.

Subcommunity A social group which shares some more specific features than those possessed by the community as a whole. A community may therefore contain many different subcommunities, and an individual may belong to several subcommunities. In a territorially defined community like a town, there may be, for instance, several ethnic or religious subcommunities. Such subcommunities may be relevant political entities in a political system, by virtue of their common interests and opportunities for joint political action. See also: *community; political culture*.

Subgovernments A term used in policy analysis to denote those groups of political actors, including legislators, administrators, and representatives of interested organizations, that effectively make most of the routine decisions within some more or less specialized area of policy. The term is generally used to identify those actively involved in decisions and in regular cooperative contact with each other, rather than the broader group of individuals with some interest in the area, many of whom may be excluded from routine involvement.

'Subgovernments' is a term most commonly encountered in the American literature. British policy analysis tends to use the term 'policy communities' or 'policy networks' to denote a similar concept. See also: *decision-making analysis; incrementalism; policy analysis; policy network*.

Survey A detailed investigation of selected aspects of some 'population' (by which is meant a defined set of persons, groups, or impersonal items such as recurring events). Since, in many surveys, considerations of cost, time and other resources or the physical impossibility of dealing with every item within a population, rule out exhaustive investigations, sample surveys are often employed. Surveys analysis utilizes results of surveys to check or to formulate hypotheses, to classify cases, to create models, etc. See also: *panel study; sample*.

'Swing' The term used to denote the measure, in percentage terms, of relative transfer of support from one political party to another among the electorate of a single constituency, a group of constituencies, or the country as a whole. It is stated in terms of the 'swing' from one party to another, calculated by taking the percentage of the poll which one party has lost compared to the previous election, and adding to it the percentage share of the poll which the other party has gained since that election, then dividing the result by two to give the 'swing' to the second party. For example, in constituency X Party A may have seen its share of the poll since the previous election increase from 25% to 30%, and Party B has seen its share fall from 45% to 38%. The 'swing' from Party B to Party A is therefore 5 plus 7 = 12, divided by 2, i.e. 6%. If both of the parties have lost vote share (due to the existence of other parties in one or both elections) then the percentage loss of the first party is deducted from the percentage loss of the second party, and that result divided by two to give the 'swing'. Strict comparability of results is affected by the existence of third parties and variations in the percentage turnout of voters at the two elections under comparison. See also: *psephology*.

Syndicalism See: *anarcho-syndicalism*.

Systems analysis An approach to the analysis of political structures, institutions and processes, associated most particularly with the work of David Easton.

The Eastonian analysis of political systems (set out, for instance, in David Easton, *A Systems Analysis of Political Life*, New York, Wiley, 1965) focuses on the inputs of demands and support; the conversion processes by means of which the authorities (which in a modern state system will include the government, legislature, etc.) deal with those inputs; the outputs that result; the feedback mechanisms that adjust outputs to inputs; and the way the system persists in the face of stress arising from within the system or from its environment. Should stress reach critical ranges, and persist at such levels for some length of time, changes in the authorities (change of government in an election, for instance), in the regime (a revolution, for example), or in the political community (secession, for instance) may occur. Ultimately, stress may even bring about the destruction of the system itself.

The multiplicity of demands from the population of the community are aggregated into policy proposals ('issues') by, for example political parties, the mass media, or interest groups, and are dealt with by the system. 'Gatekeepers' of various types regulate the flow of demands, to avoid overloading the channels by which demands reach the attention of the authorities. Support for the authorities, for the regime and for the community itself is an important input, and should that support decline (e.g. through foreign subversion, a failure of legitimacy, a mismatching of outputs to demands) this would impose stress on the system. Constraints on the operation of the system exist, whether intra-system (lack of political resources, for instance, or failure of political communication) or extra-system (such as international intervention, economic or legal constraints), and it is an important function of the authorities to recognize, and then to adapt to, such changes.

The functional analysis of Gabriel Almond and his associates, although not normally classified as systems analysis, also posits the existence of a political system in which structures carry out requisite functions for the system and are involved in exchanges with the environment. Karl Deutsch, in his approaches to the study of political communication (e.g. in *The Nerves of Government*, New York, Free Press, 1963), focused on the channels by which communication occurs in the system, the feedback processes involved, and pathological states of communication structures and processes in terms of their effects on the political system.

The advantages offered by the systems approach to political analysis are: it permits consideration and comparison of non-state political systems, such as the international political system, a city, a political party branch organization, or a multinational commercial enterprise in its role as a political organization; it provides a universally applicable set of classifactory categories for the comparative analysis of diverse political units (modernized and developing polities, dictatorships and democracies, or unitary states and

and developing polities, dictatorships and democracies, or unitary states and federal states, for instance); and it draws attention to the processes of demand conversion, feedback, exchanges between the political system and its environment, and the methods by which political systems persist in the face of internal and external stress. However, the systems approach is criticized for the difficulties associated with the operationalization of some of its key concepts (such as 'system persistence', and 'stress') and with identifying the boundaries of what is, in the case of a political system, a heuristically defined system, rather than a physical system. See also: *feedback; gatekeepers; overload (b): communications overload; political system; structural-functional analysis.*

T

Tactical voting Tactical voting consists of making a choice of candidate or party in an election in order to try to ensure a more probable outcome than might be the case by selecting the preferred candidate or party. It is thus relevant to, for example, the British simple-majority system of election, but could also be used in STV systems of election (in terms of the ordering of preferences) and in list-based proportional representation systems where there is a minimum-percentage requirement for seat allocation (as in Germany). Examples would be: Labour and Liberal Democrat voters in a British constituency deciding (individually or through prior arrangement) to vote for the candidate of either party more likely to defeat the Conservative, rather than 'split' the anti-Conservative vote; or Free Democrat voters in Germany using their constituency vote for the major party with which the Free Democrats were in coalition, but giving the list vote to the Free Democrats. See also: *election; list system; single transferable vote system; voting.*

Technocracy The political system which would result from the replacement of politicians by technical experts. Technocracy as a form of rule is a utopian notion, which found favour in the USA in the economic depression prior to the second world war, and which is regarded as a possibly dangerous tendency in industrialized states today. It is based on assumptions that human well-being would be furthered by improving the efficiency of government, that such efficiency would result from an upgrading of the political role of experts from advisory to decisional, replacing the non-expert administrator or politician, and that as technical criteria would replace interests and ideologies in making political decisions, most controversies would be depoliticized.

Critics of these assumptions deny their validity on grounds of impossibility (e.g. many basic political controversies are disputes about ends, not means;

technical expertise tends to be compartmentalized, so there would still be a need for co-ordination of information and for overall 'judgement'), and they deny that the aims of those wanting technocracy are desirable, since, if politics is about the settlement of disputes about values, technical decisions should not be allowed to pre-empt the processes of debate and decision regarding values in a society. See also: *aristocracy; utopianism.*

Teleological explanation Any explanation relying for its explanatory force on some purpose or end-state of the phenomenon being explained, e.g. that political parties exist in order to pursue political power. Thus a subsequent intended effect rather than a preceding cause appears to provide the explanation of parties. In fact, a full description of the feedback mechanisms involved would show the teleological explanation to be part of a causal explanation. Apparently teleological explanations need careful consideration. Certain forms of organization may regularly bring about a certain effect yet that may be no part of the purpose of any individual involved. Effects may be unintended consequences of action and phrases like 'in order to' may be spurious and misleading. Explanations which appear teleological in form but which do not rely on human or divine purpose may be better classified separately as functional explanations, although some writers treat functional explanation as a type of teleological explanation. See also: *explanation; feedback; functional explanation; hermeneutics.*

Tendency statement A law-like statement, apparently in terms applicable to the actual world, but without any specific indication of conditions or mechanisms which may counteract the causes covered by the law. Thus the statement that proportional representation produces multi-party systems is a tendency statement rather than a law, since it lacks any indication of those other factors, possibly present in actual political systems, which also affect the number of parties in serious competition. Such statements appear to express, in theoretical form, real mechanisms and forces, but are not by themselves susceptible to empirical test.

'Tendency' is also used as a synonym for 'trend'. This usage is confusing since, as indicated above, tendencies may not manifest themselves in the regular movements that comprise trends.

Ideological factions within parties and movements are also referred to as tendencies, e.g. the Militant Tendency within the British Labour party in the 1970s and 1980s. See also: *law (a):scientific law; trend.*

Theocracy A form of government in which the ruler or rulers (who may also constitute a form of priesthood) claim to be acting in their political, as well as in their religious, role as direct agents of a deity, and in which religious laws are the direct source of political obligations. A theocracy is usually an absolutist form of government, on account of the imperatives of the religious laws upon which government is based. Examples of theocracies include the early Hebrew state, Calvin's rule in Geneva during the Reformation, Tibet under the Dalai Lama before the Chinese invasion, and, perhaps, Iran after the deposition of the Shah. See also: *absolutism.*

Theory An integrated set of laws or generalizations which is capable of providing systematic explanation of some area of knowledge or body of observations, or which may be used to predict events, or which prescribes conduct. This last category is a type of 'normative' theory. Political analysis is more centrally concerned with 'scientific' or 'empirical' theories, theories intended to explain and/or predict political events. Such theories are generally supposed to contain reference to entities and relations which are not themselves directly observable but which may be indirectly tested through observation. For instance, a theory containing reference to power resources and relations within a political system may be tested so long as it yields hypotheses concerning the actual outcome of conflicts between political actors.

One common, if rather simplistic, view of theory is called the 'layer-cake' account. The first layer is the body of empirical facts we gather by observation. Next, we make generalizations about these facts. Then we try to explain these generalizations by integrating them with propositions referring to unobservable entities, that is we construct a theory. This layering may continue, with higher level theories being constructed to explain the lower. These layers of theory are often labelled according to their range or level of generality: 'narrow-range' or 'partial' theories (e.g. concerning legislative behaviour in post-war British parliamentary politics); 'middle-range' theory (e.g. concerning legislative behaviour generally); 'general' theory (e.g. a theory of political action, or of the political system). Having constructed a theory we may use it to generate new hypotheses, the testing of which may lead us to modify or reject the theory.

The foregoing may suggest that political research is clearly separated into stages of observation, conceptualization, theory construction, operationalization, testing and application. This is seldom the case and this somewhat idealized scheme is often difficult to discern in the presentation of research. One reason for this is that the layer-cake account embodies a serious mistake. No observation can occur in the absence of criteria for selection. Some set of theories, assumptions and hypotheses must therefore be prior to the gathering of data.

The term 'theory' is also used in political science to denote any set of loosely related assumptions and concepts that is used in political analysis. 'Theories' of this kind are often said to be 'only of heuristic value'. By this is meant that the set of assumptions and concepts itself provides no substantive propositions about the world, but that it may stimulate some particular line of inquiry, suggest some particular approach to the subject, or otherwise assist in the quest for knowledge. See also: *concept; explanation; hypothesis; law (a): scientific law; normative theory; operationalization; political theory; realism (a): scientific realism.*

Third world A term used to indicate those countries of Asia, Africa and Latin America which do not belong either to the 'first world' (the European or Europeanized industrialized states) or the 'second world': the Soviet Union and, formerly, its communist satellite states and associated states of eastern Europe. 'Third world' states tend to be economically underdeveloped, to be former colonies or dependencies of western states, and frequently subject to autocratic rule. However, the 'third world' is a broad and rather imprecise category, since some states which are taken as belonging to this group are wealthy (e.g. some oil-producing states), some are democracies, and some are now so industrially advanced as no longer to qualify unequivocally as 'third world' states.

The term in the nineteen-fifties also carried connotations of non-alignment vis-à-vis the western and communist alliances, but this meaning has since been lost. See also: *political development*.

Totalitarianism Originally used by Mussolini to assert the supremacy of the fascist state over the individual, now an ideal type concept applied to a state attempting to exercise total control over all aspects of social existence within its territory. No distinction between the public and private, between the political and non-political, is countenanced.

The concept is almost always applied to modern states, being associated with the use of technologically advanced instruments of mass communication, organization, mobilization and control. It is usual to find totalitarianism identified with or explained by the coordinated pursuit of specific, often 'ideological', goals. Political power may be exercised chiefly through a single party, in symbiotic relationship to the state, which acts as symbol of the ideology and as the state's ideological vanguard. Since organizations other than the state would foster values and goals not necessarily in accord with those required by the ideology of the state, the state or the party must act as controller or sponsor of all permitted organizations. States most often thought to approximate to the ideal type include Nazi Germany, the USSR under Stalin, and China under Mao Zhe-Dong. See also: *absolutism; autocracy; corporatism (a): ideology; fascism; ideal type; ideology; mobilization; society*.

Treason A crime involving the attempt to overthrow the regime of a state by illegal means, by a citizen owing allegiance to that state. In some legal definitions of the crime, it is also held to include the attempted murder of the monarch, or aiding the enemy of the state in time of war. It is generally considered a capital crime in states which retain the death penalty. See also: *sedition*.

Treaty An agreement, or the formal record of an agreement, between two or more states, or between a grouping of states (such as a confederation) and other states. Treaties may also be made between provinces of a federal state (state treaties) or between a state and a church (e.g. a concordat between a state and the Catholic church). A treaty agreement discusses the future relationship of the signatory parties with each other, or, in some cases such as the non-proliferation treaty of 1970 (concerning nuclear technology), relations with states not party to the treaty. Treaties sometimes go under other names, such as agreements, pacts and conventions. They are major sources of international law. Among their purposes have been: the settlement of boundary disputes; formal recognition of an alliance; creation of multinational organizations; the terms and conditions of a peace settlement. The Geneva Convention on the Red Cross, 1864, the Treaty of Versailles, 1919, the Treaty of Rome establishing the EEC, 1957, and the treaties in 1990 between the Federal Republic of Germany and the German Democratic Republic preparing the way for German reunification, are examples. See also: *international relations; pact; protocol (b): treaty*.

Trend A more or less regular movement in some variable, or in the relation between variables, over a specific period of time, in a particular situation. Statements of trends differ from laws in that they refer to singular instances rather than to universal cases, and they require, rather than provide, explanation. See also: *explanation; law (a): scientific law; tendency statement.*

Trotskyism See: *bolshevism.*

Two-party system A party system where two, and only two, relevant parties (in Sartori's terminology) compete with each other for power. The USA is usually considered to be a paradigm case of two-party politics. However, if the indicator of a two-party system is taken to be the responsibility of no more than two parties, in alternation, forming governments, and doing so with no need of coalition, then the United Kingdom (and, at times, other Anglo-Saxon countries of the Commonwealth) may qualify as two-party systems, often as a consequence of using an electoral system which disadvantages third parties. See also: *multi-party system; party system.*

Typology The study of some general phenomenon (e.g. government, political culture) through its division into a set of classes or types; or a formal statement of the basic criteria by which phenomena are to be classified.

The term is fairly recent in its application to political and social enquiry. The process denoted is, however, as old as political enquiry itself. Examples include the classification of forms of government employed by Plato and Aristotle (monarchy, tyranny, aristocracy, oligarchy, etc.), Weber's typology of legitimate authority (charismatic, traditional, rational-legal), and Almond's typology of political culture (parochial, subject, participant). See also: *classification; ideal type.*

U

Underdog effect An increase in support for a candidate or party in an election, supposedly caused by communication of a prediction of the likely outcome of that election (e.g. by publication of opinion poll findings) indicating that the candidate or party was likely to lose the election, especially if such a loss would be unexpected, and that such an increase would not have occurred, or would have been smaller, had such a prediction not been communicated. See also: *bandwagon effect.*

Unicameral Used to refer to a legislature with only one chamber, such as the Knesset in Israel, the Hungarian parliament, the New Zealand House of Representatives, the legislature of the state of Nebraska (USA), and the Länder legislatures in Germany. Only a small number of democratic states have such single-chamber legislatures. See also: *bicameral.*

Unitary state A state in which sovereignty and the powers of government are concentrated in a central authority, and not shared with or divided among smaller geographical units, as in a federal state or a confederation. Unitary states will usually possess systems of local government, and may also have arrangements for regional devolution, but these are grants of authority by the state which may be amended or revoked by the state. The United Kingdom, France, Sweden and Israel are examples of unitary states. See also: *confederation; devolution; federation; sovereignty.*

Utilitarianism Fundamentally a moral doctrine, developed by Jeremy Bentham, modified by John Stuart Mill, and still occupying a central position in modern western thought, holding that happiness is the only intrinsically good thing and that all actions, particularly laws, should seek to promote the greatest happiness of the greatest number. Crucial to the doctrine's appeal is the suggestion that general agreement can be reached on the identification of happiness and the assessment of its different possible levels within a population.

Utilitarianism seeks to replace traditional standards of law and morality (e.g. theology, natural law) with the single, allegedly measurable standard of happiness or welfare. This standard is: liberal in its focus on the actual judgements and feelings of individuals and in offering a *prima facie* case for the state's non-interference in the private pursuit of pleasure; egalitarian in including all affected in its calculations; anti-conservative in its rejection of the intrinsic value of custom and tradition. Such tendencies may be countered by additions and modifications to the doctrine such as Mill's insistence on the differential value of 'higher' and 'lower' pleasures, Bentham's emphasis on the painful results of insecurity and discontinuity, and the recognition of situations where the free pursuit of pleasure by individuals may be collectively self-frustrating.

The term 'negative utilitarianism' is also used. This is the view that, morally, the alleviation of pain should be our main concern since any increase in pleasure must always be counted insignificant in comparison with suffering. Politically, we are enjoined to leave the pursuit of happiness to private decisions while seeking to adjust policy to reduce misery. See also: *public goods; liberalism; law (c): natural law; Pareto optimum; rational choice analysis; utility.*

Utility Pleasure enjoyed in the consumption of a commodity (goods, services, etc.), estimated by reference to the individual consumer's own scale of value or preference. Marginal utility is the increase in utility derived from the last unit purchased of a commodity. Utilities may be ordinally ranked or assigned cardinal values. Modern economists recognize that no absolute measure of utility is feasible and therefore avoid the use of cardinal utility, focusing instead on ordinal rankings of the marginal utilities of commodities. Since this is just a description of a person's preferences between alternatives many have found it useful, or have at least chosen, to talk of 'preference order' rather than 'utility'. See also: *game theory; rational choice analysis; utilitarianism; values.*

Utopianism A social philosophy or political theory based on speculation about the social and political arrangements of the perfect society. Such speculation may be outright prescription, in the sense that its aim is the full attainment of the ideal; or it may aim to provide an ideal standard by which existing institutions can be judged.

Some utopian writers offer specific, detailed plans for political and social reconstruction, e.g. Gerrard Winstanley's *Law of Freedom* (1652), James Harrington's *Oceana* (1656), Robert Owen's *A New View of Society* (1813-14). Others employ fictional constructions to explore more general social principles, both in explicitly philosophical works and in novels: Plato's *Republic* is usually cited as the earliest example; Thomas More's *Utopia* (1516) provides the label for the *genre*. Fictional constructions of highly imperfect and undesirable societies are sometimes called dystopias, Aldous Huxley's *Brave New World* (1932) and George Orwell's *Nineteen Eighty-Four* (1949) being noted examples.

Marx regarded early socialist thought, particularly that of Owen and Fourier, as utopian and unscientific. Such plans, he argued, limited themselves to blueprints for the future without regard for the forces preventing their realization. See also: *socialism*.

Valence issue See: *issues*.

Validation Assessment of the capacity of operational definitions, indicators, statistical techniques, and measurements, adequately to represent theorized entities and relations. 'Power', for instance, might be said to be exercised when '*A* gets *B* to do something that *B* would not otherwise have done'. The attribution of power to *A* solely on the evidence of *A*'s successful initiation of policy appears invalid since there are no grounds for the presumption that it is uniquely a *proposer* of policy who changes the behaviour of others. Initiation of policy is not a valid indicator of this concept of power and validity would be improved by the inclusion of some attempt to identify those whose support for policy was necessary and to confirm that some change in behaviour resulted from the policy.

Validity should not be confused with reliability. An indicator or measurement technique may be valid but unreliable if, for instance, the data to which it refers are inaccurate or if it may be applied differently by different individuals. In the absence of written records of policy discussion reliance on the recollections of participants may be an unreliable means of attributing 'power'. See also: *concept; operationalization; theory*.

Value judgement A term used in two related senses, sometimes distinguished as 'appraisive' and 'characterizing' value judgements: the former meaning is the more frequently intended.

Appraisive value judgements are statements expressing the worth of something according to some set of values or preferences. A statement such as 'Democracy is a good form of government', may refer to other criteria of worth which democracy is thought instrumental in satisfying (e.g. justice, liberty), or may simply express the view that democracy is intrinsically desirable, good in itself. The status of value judgements is disputed but they are often regarded as either reports of private sensations ('I feel good about democracy') or imperatives ('Promote democracy!'). Attitudes such as these underlie a commitment to 'value-freedom', the view that value judgements should not be allowed to influence the research process: political science aims to describe and explain the objective reality of the political world and the personal likes and dislikes of the individual investigator have no relevance. However, many would claim that this value-freedom is impossible since the very language we use to describe and explain the political world is shaped by consideration of value and hence is 'value-laden'. Most would agree that, at the very least, the selection of some problem or area of research must reflect a judgement of value and must therefore be 'value relevant'.

A characterizing value judgement is a decision to describe or classify which goes beyond the application of clearly established and publicly available criteria. Many of the concepts and categories used in political analysis involve the application of a number of different criteria. In deciding whether, for instance, to regard a political system as a democracy, it will be impossible to specify all the criteria in a manner sufficient to determine clear and unarguable classification of all actual cases. No matter how careful the process of operationalization, there will be cases where criteria can serve only as guidelines, considerations which may be used in different ways by different individuals. The ascription of the characteristic will be, in part, a matter of judgement.

What seems to unite these two usages, and the various alternative implications of each, is that no proper validation or verification of a value judgement can be made since its basis is either unspecified, incapable of adequate specification, arbitrary or non-existent. This may suggest that all value judgements are ultimately mysterious and immune from detailed investigation or critical examination. Such a conclusion should be avoided. Value judgements, in both senses, can and should be supported by intelligible reasons. See also: *essentially contested concepts; normative theory; operationalization; values.*

Values Objects desired or disliked by actors, e.g. security, democracy, equality, liberty; or the criteria applied in assessing the worth of such objects, selecting and rejecting goals or their means of attainment, etc. A set of values, in the latter sense, may be referred to as a 'value system': a more or less coherent range of criteria implicitly held or explicitly espoused by an individual or group.

Political analysis is concerned to identify values, their interrelationships, their association with political behaviour, and their relation to political structures. Being dispositional mental states, values cannot be directly observed but may be inferred from verbal and non-verbal behaviour. See also: *ideology; norm; value judgement.*

Variables Elements or characteristics which are capable of variation, either quantitatively (e.g. the age or income of individuals; the extent of popular support for a government; the level of industrialization in a society), or qualitatively (e.g. marital status or gender; the existence of a parliamentary opposition; the nature of the dominant mode of production). Elements which do not change state in the context under consideration are termed 'constants', e.g. in a study of the relation between revolution and international pressure in agrarian societies, agrarian society is a constant, revolution and international pressure are variables. In a wider study of this relation in both agrarian and industrial societies, agrarian society would be a variable. Variables may be classified as dependent or independent. These expressions have a number of different meanings. When change in one variable is associated with change in another they both may be said to be dependent (i.e. on each other). When no such association exists they each may be said to be independent. However, a pair of associated variables may be distinguished from one another by describing one as the dependent, the other as the independent variable. This implies *either* that changes in the independent variable cause changes in the dependent variable (and not vice versa) *or*, where no causation is implied, that changes in the dependent variable are being considered in relation to changes in the independent variable.

Where variables are associated, one may be said to be a 'function' of (and therefore to vary with) the other: government popularity might be, for instance, a function of some indicator of national economic performance. (This use of 'function' has no connection with functional explanation or analysis.)

Variables are also described as either 'endogenous' or 'exogenous'. The former are those variables comprising a theory or model. The latter are not exhaustively defined within the theoretical system and comprise the many and various conditions within which the system may be said to operate. See also: *operationalization.*

Verification The process of confirming the truth of a proposition through, for instance, observation or experiment. Difficulties in the ideas of truth and proof have led analysts to retreat from this ambitious expression to terms like 'corroboration'. Observation or experiment may corroborate a proposition in so far as the proposition survives (is not falsified by) a more or less severe test. We have grounds for the provisional acceptance of such survivors, but cannot properly claim to have confirmed or verified them, or even that they are probably true.

The term is also used to denote the process of checking the reliability of data, of techniques of data collection and measurement, the authenticity of documents, etc. See also: *experiment; falsificationism; scientific method; validation.*

Veto The exercise of an authoritative right of an institution or person to prevent a decision or action from acquiring the requisite legal assent for that decision or action to come into effect. A veto may be absolute, or qualified by being subject to overriding by some stated procedure. It may be a permanent veto, or a suspensive veto, i.e. valid for some stated maximum lapse of time.

The (now-redundant) absolute veto of the monarch, and the suspensive veto of the House of Lords, over British parliamentary legislation, the qualified veto of the US president (which can be overridden by two-thirds majorities in each of the chambers of Congress), the qualified veto of the Bundesrat over Bundestag legislative proposals in Germany, and the veto possessed by permanent members of the Security Council of the United Nations to prevent action by the UNO on other than procedural matters, are examples of veto power. See also: *veto group*.

Veto group Any group which has acquired a formal or informal status, such that it has the right to be consulted on matters which affect its interests together with the ability to prevent the promulgation of proposals that it considers harmful to those interests. Examples include: agrarian groups in the USA, the European Community and several European states; the military in certain Latin American republics; the Catholic Church in Italy and the Irish Republic; religious groups in Israel. The power of a veto group may result from the need of the government for political support from that group, the political culture and tradition of the society, or the strategic position of the group relating to scarce economic, social or political resources. See also: *pressure group; veto*.

Virtual representation See: *representation*.

Voice See: *exit*.

Voting A means of reaching a decision by parties to the decision selecting among competing and specified propositions (e.g. by referendum or by a division on a bill in the legislature), or of electing persons to fill specified offices by voters indicating their choices among the candidates for those offices. Generally, the proposition or candidate with the most votes wins, but qualified or absolute majorities may be required in particular cases.

The method of voting may be by show of hands, vocal or written indication, by mechanical methods (voting machines) or similar means, and votes may be cast openly or in secret. Generally each voter has an equal vote, but other distributions of voting power may be specified by voting rules (e.g. in the Council of Ministers in the EC). See also: *democracy; election; electoral system; majority; plebiscite; psephology; referendum; representation; tactical voting; veto*.

W

War A condition of armed conflict between political entities, usually, but not necessarily, territorial units such as states, but the term is not normally used (except in a metaphorical sense, as in 'gang wars' or 'trade wars') to refer to (except in a metaphorical sense, as in 'gang wars' or 'trade wars') to refer to conflicts between individuals or groups of a non-political type. Wars are initiated for the forcible achievement of goals, or the prevention of such achievement. Legal definition of a 'state of war' varies from society to society; it may be important in determining, for example, the commencement and termination of emergency powers given to the head of state or other institution of government. See also: *civil war; conflict approach.*

Welfare state A state which assumes governmental responsibility for ensuring the provision of basic economic and social necessities to its citizens through direct provision of certain goods and services, redistribution of incomes, and other means. There is dispute as to the precise scope of such welfare state provision; some include only cash payments to individuals and the availability of health provision, whilst others would include education, public housing or housing subsidies, and personal social services. Certainly there are vast differences in the provision of these welfare state benefits as between countries and within the same country over time (see P. Flora and A. J. Heidenheimer, eds., *The Development of Welfare States in Europe and America*, New Brunswick, Transaction Books, 1981).

Explanations for the establishment and growth of welfare states vary. Some rely on theories of responses to modernization (especially industrialization) which increase the demand for social provision no longer able to be met by other social institutions, such as the extended family. Others suggest that the growth of mass democracy has enabled voters to use electoral pressure and the influence of interest groups (such as trade unions) to stimulate the provision of welfare programmes, since the benefits from these outweigh, for large numbers of voters, any likely increases in taxation to pay for them. Marxist theories link the development of the welfare state to analyses of capitalist modes of production, arguing that the state must provide such services as a means of serving capitalist interests. Liberal justifications of the welfare state are based on the notion that society as a whole should be responsible for – and ultimately benefits from – the well-being of its members, and that the circumstances of poverty, unemployment, sickness and old age should not be regarded as marks of individual moral failure.

There are also disputes concerning the consequences of welfare state provision. Some argue that it is supportive of social harmony, political stability and economic growth. Others have criticized the unchecked extension of welfare spending by the state, on economic grounds (the burden of taxation, the disincentive effects of universal and generous benefits) and on moral grounds (the idea that the 'nanny state' displaces individual responsibility and choice). It has also been claimed that, politically, welfare state provision may tend to create a 'dependency clientele' with a political interest in maintaining and expanding welfare state benefits. Such critiques have been associated especially with the 'new right' in the USA and western Europe, and more particularly with the doctrines of 'Thatcherism' and 'Reaganism'. See also: *industrial society; liberalism; new right; socialism; social democracy.*

'Wets and Dries' Terms applied in British politics to Conservative Members of
Parliament (including ministers and peers), and, by extension, to party
activists, to refer to their general orientation to economic and social policy.
'Wets' tend to favour greater public spending and a more extended role for
the state in the provision of social services and in the economy than do 'dries',
who tend to emphasize the role of the market and the advantages of
privatization of state-owned enterprises and utilities. Broadly, 'wets' are
associated more with the paternalistic traditions of British conservatism and
the 'dries' with more modern radical and monetarist conservative ideas.

In relation to US politics between the two world wars, 'wets' and 'dries'
referred to those against and those in favour of prohibition of the production
and sale of alcoholic beverages. See also: *conservatism; privatization*.

X

Xenophobia Fear or hatred of strangers, specially foreigners, and of their
culture. Such fear may have political consequences, in the form of racialist
parties, malintegration of ethnic minorities, racial or ethnic discrimination,
etc. See also: *racism*.

Z

Zero-sum game See: *game theory*.

Zionism A Jewish movement, deriving from mainly late eighteenth- and
nineteenth-century ideas among European Jews, and acquiring a coherent
form especially in the writings and speeches of Theodor Herzl (1860-1904).
The word 'Zion' originally referred to Jerusalem and was also used to
indicate the Kingdom of Heaven. Zionism was based on a desire for the
re-establishment of a Jewish national state in Palestine, by means of the
migration of Jews from other countries. It also involved the revival of the
Jewish (Hebrew) language and a specifically Jewish culture. The ideas of the
Zionists, as today, were by no means acceptable to all Jews, nor was there in
the past (nor is there today) ideological agreement even within the
movement. The growth of European anti-semitism, the Balfour Declaration
(1917) and the refusal of Arabs in Palestine to compromise over questions of

Jewish immigration in the period of the British mandate all provided opportunities which the Zionists exploited to win support for their cause. Their ultimate triumph came with the proclamation of the state of Israel in 1948, and its immediate recognition by many of the major powers. However, Israel has been unable to obtain freedom from the need periodically to fight to retain its status and territory. Zionism has been incorporated into the Israeli 'Law of Return', which grants all Jews who emigrate to Israel automatic right of citizenship.